Fathering the Unthinkable

Brian Easlea

Fathering the Unthinkable

*Masculinity, Scientists
and the Nuclear Arms Race*

Pluto Press

First published in 1983 by Pluto Press Limited,
The Works, 105a Torriano Avenue, London NW5 2RX
and Pluto Press Australia Limited, PO Box 199, Leichhardt,
New South Wales 2040, Australia. Also Pluto Press,
27 South Main Street, Wolfeboro, New Hampshire 03894-2069 USA

Copyright © Brian Easlea 1983

7   6   5   4   3   2

90   89   88   87   86

Set by Grassroots, 101 Kilburn Square, London NW6
Printed in Great Britain by Cox & Wyman Ltd, Reading

British Library Cataloguing in Publication Data
Easlea, Brian
    Fathering the unthinkable
    1. Science — History   2. Atomic warfare — social aspects
    I. Title
    509 0125

ISBN 0 86104 391 X

Contents

That international politics is a 'world of men' is a central and probably consequential fact; one that may illuminate underlying sexual dynamics, and one that is important to the extent that males are more inclined than women to seek strength, power, activity, dominance, competitive achievement: such qualities make them more fearful of others and more predisposed to unleash violence. In truth I do not know whether hope is a realistic stance. Men may have the capacity to be rational, generous, and mutually cooperative, but as we face a world in which nuclear weapons and conventional armaments proliferate, it is sobering to know that the world in which they proliferate is a world of men.

Lloyd S. Etheredge, *A World of Men: The Private Sources of American Foreign Policy*, 1978

A world of science and great machines is still a world of men.

David Lilienthal, Chairman of the American Atomic Energy Commission (1946-50), quoted by Lloyd S. Etheredge

Human society today, as it was in the past, is patriarchal, that is, run by males. Today, as in the past, our societies unleash and justify behavior destructive in the extreme to our own and other species yet which is *not* considered 'mad' either by the ruling technocrats or the bulk of the citizenry that supports them.

Sally Sears, 'Women of Letters, Women and Madness: A Feminist View', 1979

Forcing [scientists] to jump through a series of political, moral and social hoops is utterly destructive of the creative process of doing science. It is dislocating; it is frustrating; it seems to have few relevant end-points — if any end-points at all. A real creative scientist needs to put on the blinkers and be undistracted by *anything*. Only those who are capable of total immersion in a problem and who can look at one situation in one hundred and fifty different ways can hope to come up with an imaginative, let alone a correct, solution. They have to close the door and hole up.

June Goodfield, *Playing God*, 1977

Yet a recurring reference [in the reminiscences] is to the lack of much thought about the social implications of the atomic bomb among Los Alamos scientists. Feynman's explanation is that, actively engaged in exciting technical tasks, people stopped thinking. The personal experiences of participants give no sufficient answers but evoke the question: What is a significant historical context for understanding the relative unmindfulness: the unique mood and circumstance of Los Alamos, or that of wartime generally, or individual psychology, or the general norm among scientists and engineers in modern Western society, or what?

Stephen Heims, Review of *Reminiscences of Los Alamos*, 1981

There is no harmonious scientific community interested only in the advancement of knowledge and its benefits for mankind. Yes, there is passionate commitment to driving forward their breath-taking discoveries; but there is also ambition, jealousy, lack of foresight, moral ambiguity and arrogance in these scientists, and there is absolutely no reason to assume that they are any better in these matters than we of a lesser breed.

Marie Jahoda, Review of *The DNA Story*, 1982

Introduction

The single most important issue facing humankind today is surely the nuclear arms race. Not only does the existence of this arms race prevent the solution of so many other problems confronting a divided humanity, in particular the eradication of the desperate poverty that still prevails throughout much of the world, but sooner or later a continuing arms race must end in world-wide nuclear holocaust and immeasurable catastrophe both for humanity and for much of the wild life with which we share, or rather with which we ought to share, this planet. The aim of this book is to focus on and investigate an important but, I believe, an insufficiently examined determinant of this insane race to total disaster, namely the overall 'masculine' nature of modern science and particularly of weapons science. Because I did not directly consider this particular determinant when I first published an analysis of the nuclear arms race in 1973, the reader may perhaps like to know at the outset why my views have in the meantime not so much changed as become qualitatively enlarged.

Having started adult life as a nuclear physicist, I decided to abandon this path when, working in Brazil in the middle 1960s, I could no longer make sufficient sense of the claim that nuclear weapons were necessary in order to defend Western civilisation against the aggressive and totalitarian intentions of the Soviet Union. Eventually, after moving into the 'Science and Society' area of studies, I came to the conclusion that of the several analyses of the arms race I had studied, Einstein's overall point of view appeared to me to have the most explanatory power. Based on the unpalatable but inescapable observation that while the regime in power in the Soviet Union was extremely unpleasant to its own citizens the United States was by far the more aggressive internationally, Einstein's strongly argued opinion was that the United States was heading for total disaster, taking the entire world in tow, and that only a democratic socialist society in the United States would be able to harness that country's immense resources for the benefit of both its own citizens and humankind in general. This is the crux of the argument put forward in my *Liberation and the Aims of Science*.[1] I was careful to illustrate the excitement and aesthetic appeal of science before going on to argue how science itself had become enmeshed in capitalist structures of production from the outset and increasingly so after Keynesian techniques had been applied in capitalist societies following the economically disastrous years of the 1930s and the start of the second world war. America's entry into the world war in December 1941 had, I claimed, saved the American economy and from that day on, I claimed and still claim, American capitalists, politicians and military never looked back. American society needs waste production, I believe, in order to function at near full employment and arms production is — or, rather, was — an 'ideal' form of such waste. However, the 'stabilising' impact of massive arms expenditure has in recent years been progressively undermined. Capitalist powers such as West Germany and Japan have taken advantage of America's militarily-maintained relative prosperity to develop and sell superior commodity goods while at the same time the manufacture of arms is becoming increasingly capital intensive. Unable any longer to help maintain near full employment, the American-initiated and maintained nuclear arms race has lost its last insane justification. Clearly, even were a nuclear Armageddon not to threaten on the horizon, the nuclear arms race would still constitute a searing indictment in a hungry world of, if not the intelligence, certainly the humanity of its principal protagonists. But the ever-closer approach of world-wide nuclear disaster makes the whole process quite insane. Believing all this I was therefore able to maintain through the early 1970s the optimistic opinion that the irrationality of the capitalist social and economic system would eventually be repudiated by the respective electorates, after which it would become possible to realise a world more commensurate with the fundamental humanity of men and women, a humanity from which, I believed, people have only reluctantly departed when goaded and provoked by unendurable oppression and deprivation.

However, it was in studying the many cruel persecutions of

people by people that I came to believe that economic causes were not *sufficient* to explain the intensity and brutality of many of these persecutions. In particular, aided by many feminist publications, my study of the relation of witch-hunting to the rise of science in the sixteenth and seventeenth centuries, discussed in *Witch-hunting, Magic and the New Philosophy*, convinced me that such non-economic factors as gender identity and sexual attitudes were also very relevant to an adequate understanding not only of the ferocity of the persecutions but also of their underlying causes. In my follow-up study, *Science and Sexual Oppression*, I reached the conclusion that, no matter how bizarre at first sight the research programme seemed, these 'male-female' factors must be included in any satisfactory explanation of the origins of the nuclear arms race and of the forces that so powerfully continue to sustain it. This, then, bizarre or otherwise, is the overall aim of the present book.

The argument of the book is that the nuclear arms race is in large part underwritten by masculine behaviour in the pursuit and application of scientific inquiry. Modern science is basically a masculine endeavour and in a world of competing nation states and blocs serves to fuel the fires of human conflict rather than to quench them. Broadly speaking, I argue that irrational male behaviour stems from men's oppression of women which in turn is a consequence of an unsatisfactory sexual division of labour between men and women in both the 'domestic' and 'public' domains, in particular in the domestic domain of childbirth, baby and infant care and in the public domain of control over nature. The connection between these two 'domains' will be made apparent in a brief discussion of preliterate societies and will form a principal underlying theme of the discussion of masculine science and the nuclear arms race. What, of course, makes masculine science particularly dangerous, as opposed to masculine prescientific magic and ritual, is that science truly 'works', that it really is efficacious, and therefore for the first time in history provides significant power over nature but provides it for men who are, to say the very least, humanly ill-equipped to make wise use of that power.

The book's structure is as follows. In Chapter 1, I sketch the position I adopt with respect to the causes underlying men's age-old oppression of women and the concomitant irrational behaviour of men in the public domain. I briefly look at prescientific societies in order to demonstrate male non-participation in the care of babies and infants and, together with this non-participation, pervasive male-female conflict and the irrationality of certain of the societies' *exclusively male* activities and rituals. It is this male irrationality, the book argues, which has been so very menacingly carried over into post-seventeenth-century scientific societies. For an analysis of the masculine nature of the 'new philosophy' and its potentially disastrous consequences, I use as a basis the most convincing feminist analysis of masculine science I know, Mary Wollstonecraft Godwin Shelley's *Frankenstein or The Modern Prometheus*. In *Frankenstein* we learn of the 'pure' research leading to the discovery of the secret of life, followed by the construction of the 'monster', its release into a harsh masculine world, with murder as the catastrophic public result. Analogously, Chapter 2 considers the 'pure' research in nuclear science leading to the discovery of the 'philosopher's stone', namely uranium fission, while Chapter 3 considers the secret making of the atomic bomb, its release into a world-at-war, with the destruction of Hiroshima and Nagasaki as catastrophic public consequences. In Chapter 4 I examine the making of the hydrogen bomb. Finally, in Chapter 5, I bring the analysis briefly 'up-to-date' and explore the implications of the book's argument for the movement against nuclear weapons and for the wide-ranging movement to realise a world considerably different from the present one.

Throughout this book it is, of course, clear that women have participated in masculine science in an important way. Nevertheless, it is also equally clear that the relatively few women in the physical sciences have had to participate on male terms. At Los Alamos, too, female scientists worked alongside male scientists but they were very much in the minority and all the principal scientists (as far as I know) were men. Hence my view of the Trinity test as an exclusively male ritual. It might be noted that during the first world war Marie Curie (together with her daughter Irène) and also Lise Meitner worked with X-ray apparatus in *caring for the wounded* while the Austrian and Jewish Lise Meitner, co-discoverer of uranium fission with Otto Frisch, refused to take part in the Manhattan Project although she was invited to do so and although she herself had had to flee Hitler's Third Reich in 1938 after the Nazi annexation of her homeland. The creation of nuclear weapons has been basically a male enterprise and one undertaken, as we shall see, in a paradigmatically masculine spirit.

Certainly I am aware of the fact that this whole book is open to the criticism that I place too great a significance on rhetoric and metaphor in the speech and writings of prominent scientists and spokesmen for science. Readers will make up their own minds on this matter. My view is that it is precisely through people's rhetoric and particularly metaphors that one can gain partial insight into motives and, more importantly, unconscious motivation. In her book *The Lay of the Land* Annette Kolodny makes the point that, for example, while the 'landscape' may be 'unthinkingly' spoken of as feminine, particularly through the use of metaphors, this does not mean that such language is without significance. As she explains, 'we may indeed have long ago ceased to self-consciously or attentively *think about* the feminine in the landscape, but that does not mean that we have ceased to *experience* it or to act in such a way that our behaviour apparently manifests such experience at its deepest level of motivation'.[2] In my view, to put it no more strongly, if the 'male-female relation' in modern society is unsatisfactory in an overall way and if science is basically a male enterprise that metaphorically views nature as female, then there is cause for concern on both counts, particularly as science is such a central feature of the modern world. However, a further and related criticism that can certainly be made against the present book is that it does not examine the metaphors used by scientists that do *not* imply a male sexual relationship to nature. My response to such criticism is that while a detailed examination of the many kinds of metaphors used by scientists would be very instructive, the fact that sexual and birth metaphors are commonly used should tell us something about the scientific endeavour and something that is important. Moreover, even if scientific men 'merely' and unthinkingly reflected a widespread use of aggressive sexual and birth metaphors in no way confined to scientific activity, then this would really only serve to underline the argument the book is trying to make. However, as far as I can see, modern science is unique in its repertoire of aggressive sexual and birth imagery. Our whole culture is basically masculine in character but modern science is its cutting edge. Finally, for an instructive analysis of the full range of images and metaphors that abound in our 'nuclear culture' readers are particularly referred to an excellent article by Paul Chilton on 'nukespeak' and also to his forthcoming book on the subject.[3]

To sum up, then, this book attempts to explore in a systematic way a point of view that is often hinted at but has not, to my knowledge, been elaborated and developed. In a television programme in June 1981 E.P. Thompson remarked with a wan smile that the real reason Trident was being purchased was because we are 'a post-imperial phallic system' and there is a need to show we can 'still get it up'. In early 1982 Dr John Gilbert, then chairman of Labour's backbench defence committee, referred critically to what he took to be the 'Trident virility symbol' (*The Guardian*, 26 February, p.1). For better or worse, this book takes such comments seriously and explores their implications. The reader is forewarned!

In two tumultuous years I have indeed been fortunate to have received the help of many friends, ranging from people who have helped daily to others who sent a cheering card from out of the blue. Although I won't make here a long list of all the people to whom I owe so much, above all I wish to express my gratitude to Dot Griffiths whose socialist commitment and work over the years has always been a continual source of inspiration to me and who in the past two years has personally helped me, and not only me, so very, very much. This book would never have been written, to say no more, had it not been for her seemingly inexhaustible human warmth and generosity. Other people have also helped so much in different ways, especially my mother who in particular has very kindly looked after my two cats for me; Maggie Hartley and Roger Hartley for so willingly helping out when only they were able to do so; Tom Whiston for the knack of being in the right place at the right time and for just being his kind and perceptive self; Haruko Leggett and Tony Leggett for all their very great kindness and support that never failed; and Anne Berg and Harry Rothman for turning up in Brighton (and Harry for a very opportune telephone call) just when *human* beings like them were most needed by me. I hope I haven't greatly exploited these much appreciated friends-in-need. Many other people helped so very much as well, especially Tony Wainwright who gave unstintingly of his time and helped enormously. All I can say here is thank you to all of them. To my dear friend Kimi I dedicate this book with its underlying hope that eventually there will come into being a generous and loving world.

Parts of this book have been given as talks in several universities and I should especially like to thank for their kind invitations Harry Rothman of the Technology Policy Unit, University of Aston, David Betts on behalf of the Physical Society, University of Sussex, Mary Maynard of the Sociology Department, University of York, and Charlie Owen of the Institute of Education, University of London. I profited greatly from the agreements and disagreements that emerged as a result of these talks, even if it appears to friendly critics that the contrary is the case. John Irvine was the first person to read the original draft and I should especially like to thank him not only for his very helpful suggestions but also for his constant encouragement and belief in the book. Mike Kidron, John Krige, Richard Kuper, Ian Miles and Tom Whiston also kindly read the typescript and I am most grateful to them for their useful comments. Paul Hoch, too, provided much-needed inspiration. Alas, I alone bear sole responsibility for this final version, particularly for whatever mistakes and misguided analyses still remain.

1. Compulsive Masculinity: 'Something at work in my soul, which I do not understand'

Until male 'identity' does not depend on men's proving themselves, their 'doing' will be a reaction to insecurity, not a creative exercise of their humanity.

> Nancy Chodorow, 'Being and Doing: A Cross-Cultural Examination of the Socialization of Males and Females'

Male science, male alchemy, is partially rooted in male uterus envy, in the desire to be able to create something miraculous out of male inventiveness. However, men in science have carried us all to the brink of total planetary, genetic, and human destruction. Repressed and unresolved uterus envy is a dangerous emotion... Men created civilization in the image of a perpetual erection: a pregnant phallus.

> Phyllis Chesler, *About Men*

From time immemorial, it appears, certainly for far too long, men have oppressed other men and have oppressed women. They have regularly made war on each other, raped and killed the enemy's women, and have prevented, on pain of severe punishment, their 'own' women from participating in certain of their own highly valued activities, so maintaining for themselves exclusively male activities. Certainly men have also done nice things to each other and to 'their' women in the course of history, but it is not the nice things with which this book is concerned. Its overall concern is with *problematic* male behaviour — and there is, unfortunately, a lot of it. Moreover, since the extent and brutality of such problematic behaviour have varied greatly both geographically and over time it is impossible to be satisfied with the pessimistic 'explanation' that men are 'by nature' part beast. We must therefore, and gladly, look elsewhere for explanations. The look presented below is necessarily brief since many specialist works are available on the causes underlying problematic male actions and I wish to reach as quickly as possible the central concern of this book, namely masculine science and the nuclear arms race. (Of course, we should not overlook that women as individuals have also done unpleasant things to each other and to men. Nevertheless, it is men who have organised collective violence on a massive scale and who have systematically oppressed women. Men, not women, have been and remain the problematic sex.)

Insecure masculinity

A preliminary reading of feminist and other literature suggests several different explanations of unwelcome male behaviour. The argument, however, which I find particularly compelling is that in any society in which a traditional sexual division of labour exists, that is, in just about all societies, a baby boy inevitably identifies first with his mother and then has to struggle to attain an unavoidably elusive 'masculine' identity defined negatively by the society's rigid denunciation of male participation in female work and especially of even a partial return by the male to anything resembling an infant's closeness to the mother.[1] This being the case, the male invariably comes to devalue typically female work and attitudes in order to protect himself against forbidden wishes and at the same time may well come to harbour a repressed hostility to his mother for denying him even temporary return to that once safe port of call, a hostility which he may well come to displace on to the female sex in general. Since the male is, of course, a male because he finds himself in possession of a penis instead of a clitoris, vagina, womb, and breasts, typically male activities will almost inevitably come to be associated with the 'power' of the penis. Since in addition the male may well, at either a conscious or unconscious level, resent being thus forced into elusive manhood through the absence of a womb, he may well come to envy women their reproductive capacity which, while denigrating at one level, he will at another level attempt to emulate or even surpass in the performance of certain of his masculine activities. From this point of view, then, a sexual division of labour invariably brings with it the seeds of hostility and conflict on the part of men towards women and then of reciprocated hostility and conflict on the part of women towards men.

To complicate matters yet further — and remember it is being suggested that all men are to some extent insecure in masculine identity status — it would seem that the insecure male becomes especially vulnerable in the act of 'love' itself. For should he fail to have an erection or otherwise prove 'inadequate' in his own eyes, and possibly in the eyes of his sexual partner as well, then he will suffer a potentially devastating blow to his masculine self-esteem. Moreover, one 'successful' act of sexual intercourse does not guarantee the success of the next. In addition there always exists for the insecure male the 'problem' of remaining masculine throughout the period of intercourse and especially after ejaculation, for the would-be masculine male must at all costs avoid resembling the behaviour of an infant in mother's arms. In that act, therefore, in which the insecure male wishes above all to confirm both to himself and his female partner an unassailable masculine status, he is vulnerable to failure and to the ridicule of a member of the sex he considers inferior. Little wonder, therefore, that tenderness is not always a feature of male 'lovemaking'. Moreover, the greater the extent to which such an insecure male is sexually attracted to women the greater is the threat their very existence poses to an always vulnerable masculine status. His attraction to all sexually enticing women will then be increasingly overlaid with hostility, and the sexual act of 'penetration' will not be a 'connecting' act between male and female but a demonstration of his masculine power — and woe betide him, and even more so the female partner, should his penis let him down. Perhaps he will divide all women into two classes: those 'pure' women who do not tempt him sexually and those 'impure' women who do and hence who constantly challenge and threaten his masculinity by their very existence. The insecure male is then in a quandary: if he rejects the sexual women's allure he denies his own masculinity, if he accepts their 'invitation' his masculinity is in jeopardy. Such a male cannot win and neither can the women he meets, 'pure' or 'impure'. It follows, then, that in a society characterised by a sexual division of labour, we see on the basis of the above hypotheses that there is considerable male motivation for sexual oppression of women, even on the assumption that individual women respond sympathetically to the predicament the sexual division of labour has generated in their males.[2]

Clearly in any one society there will be men with varying degrees of insecurity of masculine status, of repressed 'uterus envy', with a combination of repressed and unrepressed hostility towards women from insignificant to almost total. The fortunate creative man with a nearly-zero syndrome will be creative out of sheer intellectual pleasure or whatever; and he will not be a threat to women. Given, however, any one syndrome of extreme insecurity, envy and hostility a variety of 'acceptable' strategies may be adopted by the male in order to avoid a catastrophic end for himself or from bringing women he meets to a catastrophic end. But the possibility of failure remains. For example, the behaviour of Peter Sutcliffe, the so-called Yorkshire Ripper convicted in 1981 of killing 13 women during the years 1975-80, might be interpreted as the psychotic responses of a man to an almost total syndrome of insecurity, envy and hostility. At Sutcliffe's trial it was stated that his first victim had been a prostitute who had ridiculed him as 'fucking useless' for failure to obtain an erection and hence had ridiculed his masculinity. This ridicule apparently burst the dam and, 'seething with rage', Sutcliffe murdered her with a hammer from his car. From then on, Sutcliffe sought victims who were either prostitutes or appeared to him as equivalent to prostitutes 'by the way they walked'. That is to say, for no other reason than that they were women these human beings appeared to Sutcliffe to be threatening and on them he vented his psychotic anger with 'hard' not 'soft' instruments that would not let him down, his hammer and a sharpened screwdriver. Alternatively, it is possible that Sutcliffe's first victims were not prostitutes and that he simply chose to concentrate on prostitutes for a time because of their special vulnerability. Whatever his motives, his actions were ferocious in the extreme. Perhaps it is not irrelevant that the prostitute who was in Sutcliffe's company when he was arrested reported that she had been trying for some fifteen minutes to give Sutcliffe an erection but without success. If the 'Yorkshire Ripper' was, as once described, 'a pimple on the abscess', such a pimple surely manifests the almost unbelievable intensity of insecurity, envy and hatred that can lie partly repressed and partly unrepressed in an in dividual male mind while the abscess represents the greater or lesser extent of insecurity, envy and hostility that is to be found among nearly all men in masculine societies. Inevitably the male Eros in such societies can all too easily, and will all too often, manifest a destructive, even sadistic, aspect.[3]

Is it possible, though, for masculine men to cope with extreme insecurity, envy and hatred in a way that does not mean the physical annihilation of those female humans who are the mothers of 'their' children, who feed and care for them as adult males, who satisfy their sexual needs, and for whom they are capable of feeling genuine affection as sons, lovers, husbands and fathers? Clearly it is! Warfare kills enemy males, thereby releasing bottled-up hatred, it confirms masculine status to male colleagues, and it enables the warrior to rape — and often kill — enemy women, thereby affirming masculine status to himself, his male colleagues, and to the female victims as well, while the rape and killing of enemy women allows him to give effective vent to his accumulated feelings of hatred against women in general. While war, then, does enable men to affirm masculine status there are, nevertheless, several drawbacks from the male point of view. Masculine status has to be constantly reaffirmed; only heroic death in battle enables the beleaguered male to rest in peace with his masculine status forever secure. A second major difficulty with war as an exclusively male activity — and this applies also to hunting and killing animals — is that in so far as it resolves uterus envy it does so only by providing an activity that is exclusively male; it does not emulate or surpass the creativity of women but indeed negates it. On the other hand, exclusively male rituals that enable men to turn boys into adult males or that enable them to control aspects of nature demonstrate both to the male participants and to the women 'hiding away' that men, too, possess creative, magical capacities: while women can and do produce babies, only *men* can and do produce men out of boys, and only *men* can and do control nature — or communicate with the gods or whatever.

Prescientific 'masculine' societies

Since certain preliterate, prescientific societies display the male dilemma in a very transparent form — a dilemma that is basically carried over intact into modern societies — it will be instructive before turning to masculine science to comment briefly on male-female conflict in a few preliterate societies. The first two I choose are the Mbuti pygmies of the Zaire rain forest, often regarded as paradigmatically non-sexist, and then the Mundurucu of the Amazon rain forest, the males being only recently pacified head-hunters who remain ferociously 'sexist'.[4]

In Mbuti society a sexual division of labour exists: the mother has total control of her offspring for their first few years, breastfeeding her children until about the age of three. None of this activity, however, from giving birth to breastfeeding, prevents the mother from participating fully in her adult activities, one of which is her contribution to the hunting of wild game. A striking asymmetry, not to say inequality, therefore exists. While the woman can — and on occasion does — do everything the male can do, only she is able to give birth and breastfeed. Envy certainly exists on the part of the male, the anthropologist Colin Turnbull writes, and it is only partly compensated for by the belief that continued sexual activity during pregnancy — with the woman's permission — makes the baby strong and hurries along its successful birth. A further compensation appears to be necessary. At the age of about two an interesting ritual occurs when the breastfeeding child, who (we are told) 'naturally' prefers the mother's body to the father's, is passed by the mother to the father who presents the child with its first solid food. The 'male mother' has his uses after all but only by special permission of the suckling mother who, clearly, could equally well give her child both the solid food as well as milk from her breasts! The men, then, ap-pear to be 'second-class women' and, to make matters worse, any lack of sexual 'prowess' is often ridiculed by both children and youths. Something social, it seems, has therefore to be done to redress the biological imbalance and, as it turns out, the men have arranged one sure way of affirming their 'masculine' worth vis-à-vis women. They, and they alone apparently, are able to communicate with the forest and during their all-important ritual, the greater molimo, the men sing to the forest accompanied by the playing of a trumpet which the eyes of no child or woman may see (although men do say that in the past women controlled the molimo ritual until the men managed to steal it from them). The humans without wombs and breasts but with penises do therefore have their uses: their penises hurry babies along during gestation, they give children their first solid food, and they alone are able to and do communicate with the forest. What would the Mbuti women do without their menfolk! It would indeed be interesting to know what the Mbuti women think of the men's molimo ritual but since the anthropologist was male he necessarily stayed with the singing men during those nights of the ritual when the (awed?) women and children remained 'isolated' in their huts. In an article on 'Mbuti womanhood' Colin Turnbull remarks: 'As an adult I learned that adulthood is a time of conflict, primarily conflict between male and female.'[5]

In Mundurucu society the conflict between male and female is best represented as men's oppression of women together with women's resentment of male oppression and their reaction to it as best they can. Because the Mundurucu were studied by a male and female team, Yolanda and Robert Murphy, the views of both Mundurucu men and women were recorded and described in their fascinating book *Women of the Forest*. Mundurucu women, we learn from them, resent what they see as a perpetual cycle of pregnancy and childbirth, they practise contraception when they can, and they breastfeed their children until a new sibling comes along. The men profess no interest when childbirth occurs, quite unlike the women. Although extramarital intercourse is common, the husband can still be sure that the child is his since only the husband's repeated sexual access to the woman is, he claims, sufficient to provide the material from which the baby grows. In any case, the male enjoyed and retains special activities. Warfare is no longer practised but hunting remains an *exclusively male* practice by which male adulthood is affirmed. Virility is, however, another matter, although a related one. Here the adulthood of Mundurucu men is very much at the mercy of wives and sexual partners who often taunt their oppressors, it seems, for inadequate sexual endowments or prowess: a visiting male suitor had the size of his penis unfavourably commented on together with a chastening remark directed at nearby males that at least the visitor's penis showed more signs of life than the resident ones! The alligator's mouth is the men's not entirely endearing name for the vagina. The men, in addition, perform secret male rituals, characterised by the use of their sacred trumpet, the karökö tube, which no woman is allowed to see on pain of gang rape. As with the Mbuti, the Mundurucu males believe that women once owned the sacred trumpet, and moreover that great care must be taken to ensure that a counter-revolution does not take place. Indeed, in the opinion of the two anthropologists, the myth of the karökö is 'an allegory of man's birth from woman, his original dependence upon the woman as the supporting, nurturant and controlling agent in his life, and of the necessity to break the shackles and assert his authority and manhood'. Significantly the anthropologists note that the karökö tube suggests the presence of both male and female generative power. 'The long tubular shape of the karökö', explain Yolanda and Robert Murphy, 'is clearly a phallic symbol in the classic sense of the term.' Yet, as they point out, the karökö tubes are also hollow and 'in their cavities dwell the ancestral spirits, just as the real cavities of women contain the regenerative potential of the people and the clans'. For their part, however, the women are not particularly interested in the male rituals but are bitterly resentful of the fact that they are forced to do most of the work and subjected to gang rape should they disobey the male-imposed rules.[6]

Men in prescientific societies, it may be generally argued, attempt to affirm masculine and, for them therefore, dominant status through secret, exclusively male rituals. Quite often these rituals have a very direct 'pregnant phallus' aspect to them, the male participants thereby demonstrating that through their special phallic powers they, like women, are able to 'give birth'. Thus in the circumcision ritual of Ndembu boys of some seven or more years of age, the anthropologist V.W. Turner reports that the Ndembu regard circumcision as cleansing the boy from 'the dirt of childhood' and of making visible his manhood by removal of the prepuce, which they see as similar to the female labia. The male circumcisers also splash themselves with medicine made from a certain tree which, the anthropologist was informed, stands upright like a strong penis or the strong body of a man. At one point in the ritual the boys-to-be-reborn-as men must be held high by their fathers or must climb trees in order to avoid contact with the (female) earth; otherwise, the men-to-be regress to infancy. Although in Ndembu society the boys return after circumcision to their mothers, they return as 'men', the anthropologist informs, now privileged to sit in the men's shelter and to belong to the masculine 'politico-religious sphere'. While Turner cautions that the circumcision ritual has a multiplicity of aspects, sexual, social and religious, it can nevertheless, he believes be 'reduced to a change in the quality of being from a state of infantile filthiness to a state of clean maturity, ...[from] the indistinct and amorphous state of childhood... to be reborn into masculinity and personality'.[7]

Similarly a male anthropologist L.R. Hiatt has argued that Australian aboriginal men, unsure of the nature of their contribution to the creation of children and envious of the close physical and emotional bond between mother and son, assert through their rituals an 'ordained and pre-eminent supernatural contribution' to conception while forcing mother and son apart in the name of a 'spiritual imperative'. The success of the men's rituals, he suggests, one of which emphasises phallic power while the other ascribes female fecundity to themselves, depends on the men's ability to deceive themselves and through secrecy to mystify and intimidate the women. Not always successfully it would seem. One woman confided to a female anthropologist, Annette Hamilton, that the *Kunapipi* ceremony was 'man's rubbish', adding to this somewhat unflattering description of male ritual the explanation that 'men make secret ceremonies, women make babies'.[8]

And, indeed, in so far as male ritual through the ages and across continents has attempted to affirm phallic power and male fecundity and in doing so to put women in their proper and inferior place there have always been major drawbacks. Men just cannot give birth to children, they do not in compensation have control over nature — their rituals do not work — and their masculinity is always vulnerable to female ridicule, particularly if and when sexual penetration is attempted. Alas for the psychologically beleaguered male. From preliterate to highly literate society, the male dilemma remains basically the same. While the great Aristotle was anxious to argue that woman is a mutilated male both in reasoning power and in fecundity, merely supplying uninteresting matter for the male semen to act on, it nevertheless did not entirely escape Aristotle's attention that the formative power in the male semen regularly fails to completely overcome the recalcitrance of the female matter and so in general gives rise to as many female babies as male.[9] Attempts by men to ascribe to women mere container properties probably never seemed wholly convincing even to themselves, while attempts by men to command the natural world through their own special male brand of magic certainly never produced the sought-for effects: the rains just would not come or the frosts still came when they had no business to.

'The masculine birth of time'

So if, after this brief look at prescientific societies, we consider the situation in early modern Europe in the sixteenth and seventeenth centuries we see immediately a very interesting — and alarming — state of affairs indeed. People exist — mostly women — who can and do make the rains come and frosts as well but who do so only through invoking the aid of the Devil himself. As only to be expected, ruling-class men were making a determined effort to extirpate from Christendom these evil women whose insatiable, uncontrollable sexual appetite had, it was believed, made so many of them succumb to Satan's advances. The ferocity of this male endeavour to eliminate witches was quite extraordinary. 'One cannot begin to understand the European witch-hunt,' writes a historian of European witch-hunting, 'without recognising that it displayed a burst of misogyny without parallel in Western history.' At the same time as this ferocious male attack was taking place on perceived female wickedness, a concerted male attack was being launched on uncontrollable nature — a nature viewed, moreover, as essentially female by its would-be male conquerors. The principal problem confronting male philosophers was to find a Christian, i.e. a legitimate male way of subduing, controlling and commanding nature, a way that does not depend on communication with demons and that is truly efficacious, unlike the male-tried ways of the past. The well-born Francis Bacon claimed to have achieved success and called on his fellow men to inaugurate with him none other than, in his words, 'the truly masculine birth of time' and thus achieve 'the dominion of man over the universe'.[10]

Bacon's call to inaugurate 'the truly masculine birth of time' was a call for a purified natural magic that would really and truly work, unlike the magic espoused by Agrippa and Paracelsus who, according to Bacon, were interested mainly in personal glory and, most reprehensible of all, in doing the least possible work to achieve it. Throughout Bacon's writings all kinds of metaphors are used and a strong motivation of compassion for human suffering is often evident. But another incompatible motivation is also strongly present, namely a masculine one, and this is portrayed in terms of militaristic and aggressively sexual metaphors, particularly the metaphor of aggressive male conquest of female nature. Basically, the masculine Bacon calls on men to grow up, to put boyhood behind them, and with the use of his new method to prove their virility by collective and deep penetration into the secrets of female nature, to discover 'still laid up in the womb of nature many secrets of excellent use' that no man has reached before. Bacon's overriding purpose is not merely to *know* nature (which is the goal of insufficiently masculine philosophers) but to *gain power* over 'her'. Aristotle is ceaselessly derided for having adopted a passive attitude towards nature, expecting nature to unveil herself at a mere male request. 'I had not supposed, sons,' Bacon sarcastically writes, 'that we were on such familiar terms with nature that, in response to a casual and perfunctory salutation, she would condescend to unveil for us her mysteries and bestow on us her blessings.' What is true of Aristotle is true of Greek 'science' in general: 'The Natural Philosophy we have received from the Greeks,' Bacon tells his male readers, 'must rank only as the childhood of science. It has what is proper to boys. It is a great chatter-box and is too immature to breed.'[11] And so Bacon continues. Voyages to remote and hidden regions of nature can be successfully undertaken only by those following Bacon's experimental method. Only then can and will nature be conquered and subdued, made into a slave together with all her children, and, indeed, shaken to her very foundations. The call goes out to all those sons of knowledge who aspire to overcome nature in action and to penetrate deeper into nature than any men have done before to join together with him. Moreover, this prospective gang rape of nature is to unite men and make war between them unnecessary. 'Nor is mine a trumpet,' Bacon explains, 'which summons and excites men to... quarrel and fight with one another; but rather to make peace between themselves, and turning with united forces against the Nature of things, to storm and occupy her castles and strongholds, and extend the bounds of human empire, as far as God Almighty in his goodness may permit.' Elsewhere the reader is assured that God will not impose unduly severe limits on the extent of human control over nature. Indeed, as the chief priest in Solomon's House explains to the awed travellers, 'The end of our Foundation is the knowledge of Causes and secret motions of things, and the enlarging of the bounds of Human Empire, to the effecting of all things possible.' The effecting of all things possible! We shall be meeting on several occasions this succinct expression of the renewed spirit of Western civilisation. It remains now only to note that 'all things possible' will include natural magical effects that will look like veritable miracles to the uninitiated, the effects produced so vastly exceeding the apparently meagre causes. True, nature left to herself is niggardly in the production of such apparent miracles, Bacon agrees, 'but what she may do when her folds have been shaken out', the confident promise is made, 'time will show'.[12]

Bacon, then, that 'Patriark of Experimental Philosophy' (as he was called by one of his admirers, Henry Power), explicitly advocated among other things a masculine science — more properly a purified natural magic — which would consist of a united male attack on female nature, described in aggressive sexual metaphors, and which would give birth to products that would undeniably demonstrate successful male power and control over nature.[13] In the context of this Baconian vision, Evelyn Fox Keller writes, Bruno Bettelheim's conclusion appears inescapable: 'Only with phallic psychology did aggressive manipulation of nature by technological inventions become possible.'[14] Truth would be the means to technological power over nature for the experimental philosopher. It would be a truth that would consist of knowledge of nature's hidden 'forms', few in number but which explain and connect together nature's multiplicity of phenomena, a truth which would, according to Bacon, 'bring to light things never yet done'. It would be the kind of knowledge of nature, as Bacon never ceased to proclaim, that 'doth enfranchise the power of man unto the greatest liberty and possibility of works and effects'.[15] Clearly, such a power-bringing and power-enhancing science — for let us agree to call this natural magic science — would and did find a welcoming home in those industrialising capitalist societies which had not heeded Bacon's advocacy of peace among men but which were busy devising better and more efficient ways of killing enemy males. Equally clearly, men in such societies would not pursue Baconian knowledge of nature in unison but would, like the magicians of old so criticised by Bacon, vie with each other in their labours to unravel nature's secret forms. Masculine science in capitalist societies would not be an aggressive although co-operative male science — perhaps in any case a contradiction in terms — but an aggressive, hierarchical, competitive male science.

At this point, however, it is the masculine character of the proposed new science that I wish to emphasise as displayed by the constant use of aggressive sexual metaphors associated with such masculinity. It is as if a part of male anger against women — as manifest, for example, in the witchcraze — is displaced and deflected on to the natural world perceived as essentially female. Not surprisingly, during this period the metaphor of 'mother nature' is explicitly attacked and rejected, sexual penetration into 'mother nature' having forbidden overtones of mother-son incest. 'The constraints against penetration associated with the earth-mother image were transformed,' the historian of science Carolyn Merchant writes, 'into sanctions for denudation. After the Scientific Revolution *Natura* no longer complains that her garments of modesty are being torn by the wrongful thrusts of man.'[16] The 'mother nature' that kept would-be men tied to her 'apron strings' is killed off. In place of this mother nature masculine philosophers either conceived of nature as an alluring female, virgin, mysterious and challenging, or in their minds killed off nature entirely, writing of it as mere matter, lifeless, barren, unmysterious, above all unthreatening, but still female. It is worth pursuing in some detail this drastic remedy of once and for all disposing of mother nature by conceptually transforming 'her' into a lifeless, machine-like entity of mere matter in motion.

The man most closely associated with this remarkable conceptual transformation of nature is the French philosopher René Descartes. 'Know that by Nature,' Descartes declared, 'I do not understand some goddess or some other sort of imaginary power. I employ this word to signify matter itself.'[17] In place of a nature seen by Aristotelians as essentially organic and by natural magicians as full of occult secrets, Descartes declared the cosmos to consist only of unextended, immaterial (human) minds and an infinite universe of matter characterised only by the size, shape and velocity of its consti- tuent parts. I find this conception of nature to be truly astonishing and, moreover, aggressive in intent.[18] Matter is declared to be lifeless, mindless, barren, indeed devoid of any interesting properties at all. Metaphorically speaking, matter becomes grey in the extreme and life an infinitesimal speck in an infinite lifeless universe. Whether in addition Descartes believed animals to be mere lifeless automata is debatable but many of his followers certainly did and Descartes himself was interpreted as advancing that view. 'I recognise in you,' the English philosopher Henry More wrote to Descartes, 'not only subtle keenness but also, as it were, the sharp and cruel blade which in one blow, so to speak, dared to despoil of life and sense practically the whole race of animals, metamorphosing them into marble statues and machines.'[19] Truly with one gigantic intellectual blow Descartes had cognitively destroyed all non-human life in the cosmos; he and his followers had, in the relevant words of the historian of science R.S. Westfall, 'banished life itself from the universe'.[20] Such banishment was, I repeat, an aggressive act stagger- ing in its immensity. 'We shall become masters and possessors of nature,' Descartes declared in his famous, much-quoted phrase but it is often forgotten what an astonishing transformation Descartes had wrought on a nature once believed to be living.[21] Robert Boyle, the prestigious philosopher who introduced the expression, 'the mechanical philosophy', declared nature no longer to be 'a kind of goddess whose power may be little less than boundless' but instead a huge machine containing lesser machines. Female nature is a machine to be controlled by men. It is easy to see how machines came to 'acquire' a distinctly female character. 'I consider the frame of the world,' wrote Robert Boyle, 'as a great... pregnant automaton, that, like a woman with twins in her womb, or a ship furnished with pump, ordnance, etc. is such an engine, as comprises or consists of several lesser engines.'[22] While mind in this mechanical universe re- tained its distinctively male character, nature now became a sub- missive, mindless, female body or mere female machine over which the victorious male mind would eventually and perhaps not surpris- ingly win supreme mastery.

Mind is male and nature is female. Thus the purified natural magic advocated by Bacon was described in one of his gentler metaphors as a 'chaste and lawful marriage between Mind and Nature', the successful consummation of which would eventually giver rise to a compassionate 'race of Heroes or Supermen'.[23] Of course, it had to be recognised that not all men were blessed with God's supreme gift of a first-class mind. The majority of men had only their exteriors 'to justify their titles to rationality', wrote Henry Power, it being only 'by the favour of a metaphor we call them men, for at best they are but Descartes' Automata'.[24] According to Bacon it was regrettably true that the 'dry light' of reason 'parches and offends most men's soft and watery natures'.[25] Some men, in other words, had brains not much more capable of rational reasoning than women's brains. Because women can 'seldom reach any farther than to a sleight superficial smattering in any deep Science', a medical textbook stated, it was strongly recommended that those parents who wished to have intelligent children 'must endeavour they be born male'.[26] Even Margaret Cavendish, a philosopher herself, declared that it could not be expected that she wrote as wisely as men 'being of the effeminate sex, whose brains nature has mixed with the coldest and softest elements'.[27] Descartes's disciple, Nicolas Malebranche, agreed with the prevailing view that women's intellects were insufficiently powerful to penetrate to the core of things but added the reason that this was because their brain fibres were 'soft and delicate' unlike men's brain fibres which were characterised by admirable solidity.[28] All this meant that it was just and proper, as Aristotle had argued 2,000 years earlier, that the more rational of the two sexes, men, should rule over the less rational, women.

As we have seen, if women in early modern Europe were not noted for intellectual capacity, they were for their sexual voraciousness. The new philosophy can be seen as yet another exclusively male activity safe from the world of women, from their 'impurity', their sexuality and their fearsome powers. 'The terror of women, the belief that they work dark and mysterious deeds,' writes the historian of the Middle Ages Jeffrey Russell, 'is an ancient, almost universal phenomenon in men, and must thus be understood in terms of the history of the male unconscious.'[29] Certainly it was widely held that male spirituality and accomplishment could not easily coexist with a sexually active life. 'The act of procreation and the members employed therein are so repulsive,' wrote Leonardo da Vinci, 'that if it were not for the beauty of the faces and the adornments of the actors and the pent-up impulse, nature would lose the human species.' Happily, however, da Vinci confirmed, 'intellectual passion drives out sensuality'.[30] Similarly Albrecht Dürer strongly advised that the apprentice artist be kept away from women and on no account allowed to see one naked or touch her. 'Nothing weakens the understanding more than impurity,' warned Dürer.[31] The physician Thomas Browne wished that humans could procreate like trees 'without this twisted and vulgar way of union: it is the foolishest act a wise man commits in all his life'.[32] Descartes longed for and created in his mind a universe consisting only of pure rational mind in total control of mere matter while Newton recommended that the way to become chaste was to concentrate all one's energies on intellectual activity. Although the main task of women was held to be procreation, even here all creative powers were widely supposed to reside in masculine spirit and in the last analysis in the creative powers of God the Father. Women were intellectually and creatively redundant. Those philosophers who advanced the theory of *emboîtement* claimed that in the beginning God had created all forms of life that would ever exist, the ova of each female containing minutely small but perfectly formed offspring, whose ova in the case of females contained even smaller but still perfectly formed beings and so on. 'I would say,' wrote Malebranche, 'that the females of the first species were, perhaps, created with all those of the same species to which they have given birth and to which they will give birth until the end of time.'[33] However, even if ultimate paternity resided only with God the Father and even though women were still a biological necessity because of their unique 'container and nourishing' properties, the new philosophy could and would allow natural philosophers to demonstrate their masculine powers through virile mental penetration into the most deeply hidden secrets of nature and ultimately through their effective technological intervention in nature on a truly massive scale.

The expression, 'the secrets of nature', is significant. In the mid-seventeenth-century English translation of Giovanni della Porta's *Natural Magick* female genitalia are referred to explicitly as 'the Secrets', and the expression, 'penetration into the secrets of nature', accordingly takes on a strikingly virile character.[34] The new philosophy was a masculine one indeed. The reader will probably not be surprised to hear of one natural magician, Thomas Vaughan, boasting that he had all but broken nature's seal and exposed her naked to the world, only to be put in his place by a future member of the Royal Society, Henry More, who sadly found himself reading not of virile accomplishments but only of wet dreams.[35] The first Secretary of the Royal Society, Henry Oldenburg, himself announced that the aim of the Society was to erect a 'Masculine Philosophy' consisting of solid truths about nature. This nature was no longer 'mother nature' but rather the philosophers' mistress and, as such, explained Oldenburg, must be wooed with 'boldness and importunity' as 'the surest and most powerful way to win her'. In his *History of the Royal Society* Thomas Sprat agreed with Oldenburg: nature was a mistress 'that soonest yields to the forward and the bold'. Aristotle's approach had to be totally rejected, the Royal Society member Joseph Glanvill exhorted his fellow philosophers, explaining that 'if Aristotle had found Nature's face under covert of a veil, he hath not removed the old, but made her a new one'. What was required were deeds, not words. Deeds, after all, are masculine, words are feminine, announced Oldenburg, who added that the true sons of learning are those who, dissatisfied with well-known truths, strive to 'penetrate from Nature's antechamber to her inner closet'.[36] On Robert Boyle's death a fellow member of the Royal Society acknowledged in tribute to Boyle that whenever 'stubborn matter' had come under his friend's inquisition, Boyle had never failed to extract 'a confession of all that lay in her most intimate recesses'. (Mind is male and, we see again, matter is female.) Boyle himself had agreed with Seneca's view that 'I pay my acknowledgements to nature, when I behold her not on the outside, which is obvious to publick view, but am entered into her more secret recesses'. Sir Isaac Newton's teacher, Isaac Barrow, explained how the aim of the new philosophy was to 'search Nature out of her Concealments, and unfold her dark Mysteries', a feat later accomplished by his star pupil, at least to the satisfaction of one admirer, Edmond Halley, who wrote to Newton of the pride which the world would feel in recognising a man 'capable of penetrating so far into the abstrusest secrets of Nature'.[37] Thus was the new philosophy perceived by practitioner and admirer. In an instructive if not altogether lyrical poem we learn from one admirer about Samuel Wall's manly, although not aggressively sexual, exploits among plants:

> Coy Nature which Disdaines to bee embrac'd
> By ev'ry Love pretending Swaine,
> You have in all her dark recesses trac'd
> And did her by industrious courtship gaine.
> Through Trees, through Shrubs, you closely did pursue
> Until she knowledge of her she did grant
> For why? She would not hide her selfe from You
> No — not in th' smallest fibre of a Plant. [38]

An investigation into eighteenth-century science and medicine by Ludmilla Jordanova has revealed the same overall masculine orientation of the century's natural philosophers. Sexual metaphors abound which designate nature as a woman to be unveiled, unclothed and penetrated by masculine science. The image was eventually made explicit, Jordanova writes, in the statue in the Paris Medical Faculty of a young woman, her breasts bare, her head slightly bowed beneath the veil she is taking off, which bears the inscription 'Nature unveils herself before Science'. [39] At the beginning of the nineteenth century the impressive Sir Humphry Davy, future President of the Royal Society, explained how the man of science, motivated as always by the desire for glory, was achieving powers that could truly be called creative, powers that enabled him to *act* upon nature instead of merely seeking to *understand* her mysterious ways. In matters of physical science Davy was in agreement with Bacon, the Greeks were to the moderns but as children to men. Above all, Davy was impressed by 'the penetrating genius of Volta' whose discovery of the means of creating a continuous electric current was a key, he wrote, 'which promises to lay open some of the most mysterious recesses of nature'. The intimate details of female nature were at last being revealed to men of science. In his lifetime alone, Davy reported, this branch of knowledge had advanced in strength and power from a state of infantile helplessness to a state corresponding, if not to 'the full form and vigour of manhood', at least to the freshness and promise of youth. [40] Certainly the study of the electric current and of its effects was being taken up with an intensity comparable to that shown a century later in the investigation of the phenomenon of radioactivity, a phenomenon which promised to reveal even more intimate details of female nature than had the electric current. But that is the subject matter of Chapter 2. Before the man of science, Davy declared, there existed an unexplored country, a land of promise in philosophy, a land, as he remarked in a lecture concerning education in science for women, where intrepid men of science had not as yet 'penetrated into the interior fertile savannahs, nor to the grand mountain districts'. As to the chemistry involved in living systems, the prospect was even more exciting: 'The skirt only of the veil which conceals these mysterious and sublime processes has been lifted up,' Davy explained, 'and the grand view is as yet unknown.'[41]

These brief references to aspects of the sensibility of masculine science through the two centuries from Sir Francis Bacon to Sir Humphry Davy take me to the period of history in which, I believe, one of the most perceptive analyses of the implications of masculine science ever to be written was conceived and published by Mary Wollstonecraft Godwin Shelley. It is this novel, *Frankenstein or The Modern Prometheus*, on which I structure my analysis of masculine science and the nuclear arms race. Mary Shelley apparently believed that with the electric current all kinds of new and exciting possibilities opened up before mankind. In particular, electricity might provide the key to the mystery of life. There could be no discovery more designed to bring out the compulsive character of masculine science and Mary Shelley duly brings it out. Mercifully, the secret of life remains hidden (if only just) but the 'mysteries of the atom' do not and a résumé of *Frankenstein* will demonstrate the undiminished prescience revealed by Mary Shelley in this most famous of her 'Gothic' stories.[42]

Frankenstein or The Modern Prometheus

Although *Frankenstein* is a relatively short novel, I shall not give a complete account of the main events but simply highlight those aspects which are for me most relevant for an understanding of masculine science and which recapitulate in dramatic literary form the principal arguments of this chapter.

The novel opens with Captain Walton writing from some

northern region of Russia to his happily married sister, under whose 'gentle and feminine fosterage' Walton had passed a solitary youth. We learn from the letters that he is on a dangerous voyage of discovery to the North Pole, which, as he acknowledges, his sister has regarded from the outset with evil forebodings. Why, however, has the friendless Captain Walton declined the life of ease and luxury that could have been his? Because, he tells his sister, he seeks glory in the discoveries he hopes to make, such as the discovery of a land where snow and frost are banished, or, failing that, discovery of the secret of the magnet which would bring such inestimable benefit to mankind. But is the hope of glory a sufficient explanation of his passionate willingness to confront death? Apparently not, for Walton confides to his sister: 'There is something at work in my soul, which I do not understand', something that clearly hurries him out of, as he puts it, the common pathways of men to the wild sea and to the dangerous, icy polar regions.[43]

There, appropriately enough, surrounded by ice, the astonished Walton meets and takes on board the man towards whom he would develop such warm feelings of friendship, one Victor Frankenstein. Explaining to the recovered but taciturn Frankenstein his readiness to lose everything — fortune, every hope, his very life — in the pursuit of the knowledge available only at the North Pole, he provokes Frankenstein into telling him his own harrowing story of a passionate pursuit of knowledge that ended catastrophically in the destruction of all those people Frankenstein loved most dearly, his small brother William, the loyal Justine, his closest friend Clerval, his wife Elizabeth on their wedding night, and finally his father who could bear no more. The pursuit of knowledge had, for Frankenstein, ended with the annihilation of his own world. Frankenstein attempts to explain to Walton how this terrible tragedy had ensued.

Frankenstein's father on marrying had retired from his career and had devoted himself to helping his wife bring up their children, first Frankenstein himself, then an adopted daughter Elizabeth, then two more sons. The young Frankenstein, we learn, was not interested in the 'humanities' but rather in the secrets of heaven and earth, 'as always having been embued with a fervent longing to penetrate the secrets of nature'. First attracted to the works of Cornelius Agrippa despite his father's contempt for the writings of the notorious magician, Frankenstein longs for the glory that will attend discovery of the philosopher's stone and the elixir of life, particularly the latter since mere wealth is as nothing compared with discovery of the secret of life. Masculine science confronting female nature: the imagery was clear in Mary Shelley's description. 'The learned philosopher had partially unveiled the face of Nature,' Frankenstein tells Walton, 'but her immortal lineaments were still a wonder and a mystery. But,' as the young man then believed, 'here were men who had penetrated deeper and knew more.' Thanks, however, to the efforts of a modern man of science who had taken the trouble to explain to him the then known laws of electricity, the fifteen-year-old Frankenstein becomes disillusioned with the pretensions of Agrippa, Albertus Magnus and Paracelsus and resolves to abandon natural philosophy convinced that nothing truly significant will ever be known. This decision, he tells Walton, was due to the efforts of his guardian angel: 'her victory was announced by an unusual tranquillity and gladness of soul.' But the female angel's victory was only temporary.[44]

At the age of seventeen Frankenstein decides to study at the University of Ingolstadt but just before his departure — an ill omen indeed — his mother dies in nursing Elizabeth through the scarlet fever she had caught. Imploring the departing and now motherless Frankenstein to write often, Elizabeth, we read, has recovered sufficiently from her illness 'to bestow the last feminine attentions on her playmate and friend'. At Ingolstadt University Frankenstein's views are once again changed: while the magicians of old had, quite rightly Frankenstein believes, sought immortality and power, modern philosophers are quite wrongly content to seek after realities of but little worth. Not so, the natural philosopher M. Waldman tells him: 'The ancient teachers of this science,' Frankenstein was informed,

> promised impossibilities, and performed nothing. The modern masters promise very little; they know that metals cannot be transmuted and that the elixir of life is a chimera. But these philosophers, whose hands seem only made to dabble in dirt, and their eyes to pore over the microscope or crucible, have indeed performed miracles. They penetrate into the recesses of nature, and show how she works in her hiding places. They

ascend into the heavens... They have acquired new and almost unlimited powers; they can command the thunders of heaven, mimic the earthquake, and even mock the invisible world with its shadows.

The modern masters penetrate into the recesses of nature and show how she works in her hiding places! Now all Frankenstein's doubts concerning the worth of the new philosophy are resolved. 'So much has been done, exclaimed the soul of Frankenstein, — more, far more, will I achieve: treading in the steps already marked, I will pioneer a new way, explore unknown powers, and unfold to the world the deepest mysteries of creation.'[45]

And so Frankenstein devotes himself heart and soul to the pursuit of his chosen science. He does not visit Geneva for two years during which time he makes some minor discoveries which win him great esteem at his university. Then he sets himself the great task, to discover the principle of life. After days and nights of incredible labour and fatigue, Frankenstein tells Walton, he succeeded not only in discovering the nature of generation but also the process of being able to induce life into inanimate matter. 'After so much time spent in painful labour,' Frankenstein remembers, 'to arrive at once at the summit of my desires, was the most gratifying consummation of my toils.' What does Frankenstein then resolve to do? It is no less than to create a human being, a male of gigantic stature, more than full grown at birth we might say. How great would be the admiration of this motherless adult male and subsequent offspring for their male creator Frankenstein. For no father would be able to claim, Frankenstein reasoned, the gratitude of his child so completely as he would deserve theirs. And so Frankenstein continues his sexual penetration into female nature, a penetration whose end result would be the wombless birth of a gigantic adult male, fathered only by him with no human female aid whatever. 'With unrelaxed and breathless eagerness,' Frankenstein relates, 'I pursued nature to her hiding places... a resistless, and almost frantic impulse, urged me forward; I seemed to have lost all soul or sensation but for this one pursuit.' For two years Frankenstein worked in this obsessive way, visiting graveyards at dead of night, collecting what he needed for the creation of his gigantic male being. 'Often did my human nature turn with loathing from my occupation,' Walton is told; yet, urged on by an eagerness which perpetually increased, neglecting friends and family, even Elizabeth, paying no attention to the beautiful summer months, Frankenstein brought his work towards completion. 'I wished, as it were,' Frankenstein explained to Walton, 'to procrastinate all that related to my feelings of affection until the great object, which swallowed up every habit of my nature, should be completed.'[46]

And so it was. But Frankenstein's breathless pursuit of nature to her hiding places has resulted in the birth of something loathsome. As soon as the 'monster' stirs into life the would-be proud father cannot bear the sight of his motherless creation and rushes away from the monster's presence. That night he dreams he meets Elizabeth in the streets of Ingolstadt. But as he kisses her, her living features change into the corpse of his dead mother. Alas for Frankenstein. His 'unconscious', it would seem, relentlessly seeks to remind him of what he has done. He has been penetrating not a legitimate and willing female nature, as he might his Elizabeth, but, on the contrary, he has been incestuously violating the mother nature his seventeenth-century predecessors declared dead and buried. In panic he awakes from his nightmare to find the monstrous being attempting to touch him. Again the anguished father escapes, eluding any contact with his creation. The violence of Frankenstein's loveless penetration into 'mother nature' is now compounded by his total rejection of the unfortunate offspring.[47]

A serious mental collapse follows but Frankenstein is nursed back to health after the arrival of his friend Clerval. A letter from Elizabeth explains to him how, although her activities are trifling, her reward is to see only happy, kind faces around her. The recovering Frankenstein learns again to appreciate the beautiful aspects of nature and the cheerful faces of children. He learns also to read poetry in Persian, Arabic and Sanskrit. 'How different,' he tells Walton, 'from the manly and heroical poetry of Greece and Rome!' But then comes the shattering letter from his father: William has been murdered! After the trial and execution of the family's loyal servant, Justine, who had been falsely accused of William's murder, Frankenstein meets the creature whom he despairingly knew all along must have been William's murderer. And just as Frankenstein himself met Walton in a mountainous sea of ice, so in the vicinity of

Chamounix Frankenstein at last comes face to face with his own monstrous creation surrounded by ice and in a recess of a huge, bare perpendicular rock — a scene, we are told, 'terrifically desolate'.[48]

Easily evading his creator's attempts to destroy him, the monster eventually manages to tell his story to Frankenstein. It is a long one but the upshot of the story is that although the motherless creature longed to love and be loved, his hideous physical appearance generates only fear and loathing in the humans he meets, his attempts at communication and kindness provoking only violence in return. After laboriously teaching himself the wonderful science of letters and learning of the nature of his creation and of the whereabouts of Frankenstein's family through reading notebooks Frankenstein had left, the 'monster' travelled to Geneva and there murdered William in a fit of rage. He now implores Frankenstein to create for him a female companion and promises in return never again to cross the path of humans. Despite himself Frankenstein appreciates the justice of the monster's request, recognises that he does have a paternal responsibility after all, and that since he is not able to destroy his superior adversary he undertakes, to the monster's joy, to create for him a female companion.

After devoting several more months of profound study to the problem of composing a female — no light task this! — Frankenstein journeys to a remote island in the Orkneys, scarcely more than a barren piece of rock, where he plans to finish once and for all his ghastly endeavours. But whereas during his first experiment, as he tells Walton, a kind of enthusiastic frenzy had blinded him to the horror of the undertaking and had hurried him on to the creation of his hideous enemy, he is now continually sickened by what he is doing. Might not the female be ten thousand times more malignant than her mate? And what is the guarantee (does the thought pass through Frankenstein's mind?) that the male monster will not leave his female companion, just as he, Frankenstein, had left Elizabeth? As Frankenstein prepares argument upon argument to justify the treachery he is contemplating, he looks up to see the monster's face watching him through a window and perceives a face betraying the 'utmost extent of malice and treachery'. Having thus projected his own thoughts on to the monster, Frankenstein to the despair and rage of his first creation tears the nearly formed female to pieces.

Further tragedy inevitably ensues. The monster murders Clerval and Elizabeth and then leads the pursuing Frankenstein to the icy regions where he has met Walton, carefully leaving clues to his trail and even food in order to sustain as best as he can his ever-weakening pursuer.[49]

The novel ends dramatically. Walton's ship is stuck in mountains of ice, several of the seamen have already perished in the excessive cold, and the remainder insist to Walton that should the ship be freed he must instantly return southward. His mission to destroy the monster still unaccomplished, Frankenstein attempts in a heroic speech to prevail on Captain Walton's men to continue northward. It is apparent that there continues to burn in Frankenstein's soul the same mad intensity of desire to destroy his creation as that which made him create it in the first place! 'What do you demand of your captain?' exhorts Frankenstein.

> Are you then so easily turned from your design? Did you not call this a glorious expedition? And wherefore was it glorious?... Because danger and death surrounded it, and these you were to brave and overcome... You were hereafter to be hailed as the benefactors of your species... And now, behold, with the first imagination of danger... you shrink away, and are content to be handed down as men who had not strength enough to endure the cold and peril; and so, poor souls, they were chilly, and returned to their warm firesides. Why, that requires not this preparation... Oh! be men, or be more than men. Be steady to your purposes, and firm as a rock. This ice is not made of such stuff as your hearts may be... Do not return to your families with the stigma of disgrace marked on your brows. Return, as heroes who have fought and conquered...

All to no avail, the men insist on turning back, and Captain Walton gives in, his 'hopes blasted by cowardice'. The ice eventually begins to move, the ship survives the peril, and the route to the south becomes perfectly free of ice. A tumultuous shout of joy comes from the sailors. Frankenstein attempts to leave the ship to continue his pursuit of the monster but collapses on his deathbed. His last advice to Walton to 'seek happiness in tranquillity, and avoid ambition, even if it be only the apparently innocent one of distinguishing yourself in science and discoveries', still provokes a final lingering doubt in his mind, 'Yet why do I say this? I have myself been blasted in these hopes, yet another may succeed.' The monster subsequently appears on the ship and weeps over Frankenstein's body, explaining to Walton that he was powerless to resist the burning passion for vengeance: 'I knew that I was preparing for myself a deadly torture; but I was the slave, not the master, of an impulse, which I detested, yet could not disobey... The completion of my demoniacal design became an insatiable passion. And now it is ended.' As with Walton and with Walton's friend Frankenstein, there was in the monster's soul something at work which the monster himself did not fully understand. This 'race' between the two men — with the pursuing Frankenstein receiving help from the 'fleeing' monster when he threatened to fall too far behind — had consumed both male souls. Only when the race ends with Frankenstein's death is the monster heartbroken and, having no longer sufficient reason for living and consumed with grief, he promises to Captain Walton to put an end to his misconceived and wretched life in the icy depths surrounding the North Pole. Polluted by crimes and torn by remorse, rest is possible for him, he declares, only in death.[50]

Mary Shelley's indictment of masculine ambition

According to Mary Shelley, then, as I interpret her story, Walton, Frankenstein and the monster are all of a piece. Each professes noble intentions but Walton and Frankenstein were interested above all in personal glory, and Frankenstein in both personal power and glory. Walton's mad expedition brings death to several sailors before he is rescued by the actions of the surviving sailors from the total destruction of his own local world and of all life sailing on it. As for Frankenstein, he is attracted first to Agrippan magic by its claims to god-like powers. Like his seventeenth- and eighteenth-century predecessors, he uses sexual metaphors of penetration into female nature to describe scientific research, his ultimate aim being to penetrate — and to be the first to do so — the very womb of nature and there to discover the secret of life, and from thence to conceive and produce through masculine will and knowledge alone the ultimate expression of male power, a male 'child'. To be the first to do so will bring Frankenstein, he believes, eternal glory while the new creatures he has fathered will bless him as no fathers have ever been blessed before by 'their' offspring. Frankenstein's own quest for the secret of life and the making of his monster are likened by Mary Shelley to a prolonged all-consuming sexual intercourse leading to simultaneous orgasm and the birth of a fully grown, indeed gigantic, male which the proud Frankenstein has fathered with no help from any woman. But Frankenstein's scientific quest is not an erotic, playful, loving act, it is an aggressive sexual penetration of female nature without due regard, indeed without any regard, for the consequences of the action. While even in a human world such action would not be likely to produce beneficial results (although in a human world such action would in the first place be very improbable), in a masculine world the consequences are likely to be catastrophic. And so they prove to be. Motherless and because of Frankenstein's irresponsibility fatherless as well, the 'monster' is driven mad by solitude in a harsh masculine world and subsequently exacts a terrible relentless vengeance on his obsessive creator and on the creator's innocent intimates.

Masculine science, then, as Mary Shelley conceived it, is an obsessive quest not only for power over nature, described in metaphors of sexual penetration and phallic creativity, but also for public acclaim and glory. Its sensibility is likened to the texture of rock and ice, the spiritual home of both Walton and Frankenstein. Very pointedly, as Frankenstein temporarily drinks in the tranquillity of the charms of the Rhine valley, Clerval tells him that the spirit inhabiting and guarding the valley surely has a soul more in harmony with man than those to be found on glaciers and the inaccessible peaks of mountains. Yet it is Frankenstein, the man of science, who tells Walton's rebellious sailors to become as firm as rock and to make their hearts harder than ice! 'There is something at work in my soul, which I do not understand.' It is this something that drives ever onward the hapless Walton and Frankenstein. Having repressed the feminine inside themselves, they physically leave feminine company behind them as they embark on their respective mad missions, Walton from his sister who from the first viewed his expedition with evil forebodings and Frankenstein, following the death of his mother, from Elizabeth who in vain beseeched her betrothed to write often. Frankenstein was not to allow his motherless creation even the opportunity of beginning an intimate relationship with a female companion — a companionship which, the monster believed, would permit him to live in peaceful happiness. It is men's desperate flight from the feminine — both inside and outside themselves — that, Mary Shelley suggests, underlies most of the world's problems, the feminine representing for her intimate human contact and simple, domestic concerns. 'If the study to which you apply yourself,' Frankenstein moralises to Walton in the midst of his account of the monster's creation,

> has a tendency to weaken your affections, and to destroy your taste for those simple pleasures in which no alloy can possibly mix, then that study is certainly unlawful, that is to say, not befitting the human mind. If this rule were always observed; if no man allowed any pursuit whatsoever to interfere with the tranquillity of his domestic affections, Greece had not been enslaved; Caesar would have spared his country; America would have been discovered more gradually; and the empires of Mexico and Peru had not been destroyed.[51]

Yet the principal women in the lives of Mary Shelley's explorer and man of science, in particular Walton's sister and Elizabeth, are as one-sided as the two would-be male conquerors, both content to remain at home and seemingly indifferent to entering the masculine world outside their sanctuary. There is a tragic impasse, an abyss of incomprehension between man and woman. Men and women do not share domestic life together just as they do not share public life together. Thus the upbringing of both Walton and Frankenstein is deficient. Walton is apparently brought up only by his sister while Frankenstein, although brought up by both his mother and father, was born only after his father had ceased all public life in order to devote himself to domestic concerns. Again a tragic mistake, highlighted by the fact that when Frankenstein takes up the study of Agrippa his father merely scoffs at his activities, not taking the trouble to explain why Agrippa's writings are basically worthless. Needless to say, it appears that Frankenstein's mother has no comments to make at all, not even scoffing ones. Finally, Frankenstein's creation, the 'monster', has neither mother nor father to guide his

upbringing and deprived even of the possibility of female companionship the final result is wholesale destruction, the form severely
masculine activities usually take in 'this savagely fathered and un-
mothered world'.[52]

One hundred years, then, after the first publication of *Frankenstein*, men of science were well on their way to the discovery of the
age-old alchemical dream, the philosopher's stone. While Mary
Shelley could not have known that this would ever happen — had
not, after all, Frankenstein abandoned Agrippa and Paracelsus? —
what she did know was that any such discovery made by a predominantly masculine science in a predominantly masculine world
would and must lead inevitably to disaster, unless a human science
and a human world took their place before the final tragedy ensued.

A closing word of caution is necessary. When I write of
masculine science and masculine men of science I am writing about
an overall direction or tendency. Although few critics of science
could at present agree with Erwin Schrödinger's claim that 'the chief
and lofty aim of science' lies in the fact that 'it enhances the general
joy of living', there is, nevertheless, much that is human in science as
currently practised, much that is humanly admirable.[53] Within the
domain of science most familiar to me, physics, there is, I know,
much that is incredibly beautiful. Not only does physics provide
ways of successfully interacting with nature, which in a human
world can only be very much desired, but in physics it might well be
said that 'the way to Truth lies through the realm of the Beautiful'.[54]
Not all men of physics are, to say the least, concerned with power
over nature as an undeniable expression of masculine achievement or
of working their way up the physics and social hierarchies in order to
wield more power over their fellow human beings. Although C.S.
Lewis has very appropriately observed that 'what we call Man's
power over Nature turns out to be a power exercised by some men
over other men with Nature as its instrument', far from all men of
science actively seek such power.[55] The goals of truth, beauty and the
esteem of colleagues are some of the possible rewards motivating
pursuers of physical knowledge, quite apart from the sheer enjoy-
ment of 'puzzle solving', theoretical and experimental, and certainly
quite apart from any need to achieve and display power over nature
and other people. Moreover, within masculine men of science as

within masculine men in general there exists nearly always a human voice querying, questioning and attempting to circumscribe the more gross effects of masculine behaviour. Nevertheless, I believe that masculine tendencies in general predominate over human in at least a minority of highly important activities, including modern science, and that it is this insufficiently bridled reign of the masculine that is taking all of humanity and indeed the entire biosphere along the path to nuclear holocaust, just as Dr Frankenstein's unbridled masculine ambition eventually took him and all the people he loved to a miserable death.

Twin brother to the Paracelsian-Agrippan magician, Thomas Vaughan, Henry Vaughan recognised uneasily in the middle of the seventeenth century the masculine spirit of the new science. There was, brooded Vaughan in his poem 'Vanity of Spirit', an ominous force motivating the experimental philosopher:

> I summoned nature; pierced through all her store
> Broke up some seals, which none had touched before;
> Her womb, her bosom, and her head,
> Where all her secrets lay a-bed,
> I rifled quite; and having passed
> Through all the creatures, came at last
> To search myself, where I did find
> Traces and sounds of a strange kind.

The next four chapters will be directly concerned with these 'traces and sounds of a strange kind'. Strange indeed. For the mind of the modern scientist, summarises Evelyn Fox Keller appropriately, is 'a single entity, both phallus and womb' and the modern scientist's intimate kinship with Bacon 'continues to survive in his simultaneous appropriation and denial of the feminine'.[56]

2. The Discovery of the Philosopher's Stone: 'They penetrate into the recesses of nature, and show how she works in her hiding places'

The nuclear researches which had been pursued through the closing years of the nineteenth century and the first thirty eight of the twentieth could qualify as the purest of pure science — detached from foreseeable practicable application and concerned primarily with acquiring a deeper understanding of natural phenomena.

Margaret Gowing, *Britain and Atomic Energy, 1939-45*

Sometimes an accident that nobody could have predicted makes a particular toy grow monstrous. When Otto Hahn stumbled upon the discovery of nuclear fission in 1938 he had no inkling of nuclear weapons, no premonition that he was treading on dangerous ground.

Freeman J. Dyson, *Disturbing the Universe*

In the above passage from Margaret Gowing's absorbing history of the British contribution to the war-time making of the atomic bomb the claim is made that during the forty or so years from 1896 to 1938 the nuclear scientific protagonists were primarily concerned with, in Gowing's words, acquiring a deeper understanding of natural phenomena detached from foreseeable practicable application and that therefore the scientists' research can appropriately be considered as the purest of pure science. Relative to the post-fission years of nuclear science Gowing's description seems particularly apt. Nevertheless, in this chapter — preliminary to my analysis of the Manhattan Project — I want to present a rather more complex picture of these years of relative innocence from the one at first sight suggested by

Gowing's description and reinforced by Freeman Dyson's comments.[1] In particular I shall try to make plausible three claims, the first, that in investigating the radioactive properties of atomic nuclei the pioneering nuclear scientists were very much aware and in general welcomed the fact that their work was concerned with the possibility of releasing the awesome power locked in the nucleus and that such release would be likely to have momentous consequences for humanity; secondly, that sexual and birth metaphors were not uncommon in the rhetoric and informal prose of many of the scientists; and, thirdly, that these scientific pioneers were intensely competitive with each other, each hoping to outdo the other in the quest for personal glory and to that extent insufficiently concerned with the social consequences of their actions and achievements. Such a syndrome of attitudes would be, according to Mary Shelley, a certain recipe for disaster when the 'pure' scientists became applied or when their discoveries were released into a severely masculine world.

Before considering in turn these three claims I first illustrate that from the outset of the discovery of the phenomenon of radioactivity in 1896 to the announcement of nuclear fission in 1939 the scientific protagonists saw themselves as attempting to achieve and finally as having achieved an age-old dream: the discovery of the philosopher's stone. In a nutshell this is what they did. During the first four decades of the twentieth century the nuclear scientists discovered in 1902 the phenomenon of natural transmutation of atomic nuclei, then they managed in 1919 to transmute nuclei in the laboratory, then in 1934 they succeeded in transmuting nuclei into radioactive states, and finally in 1938-39 with the discovery of uranium fission there emerged the possibility of generating a chain reaction that could liberate the enormous internal energies of atomic nuclei on a massive scale.[2]

The philosopher's stone

Winding up his famous Romanes lecture of 1893 the renowned T.H. Huxley rejoiced in the claim that the successes of the new philosophy had given modern men of science 'a command over the course of non-human nature greater than that once attributed to the magicians'.[3] Just five years later in 1898, two years after the discovery of the mysterious blackening of a photographic plate near the presence of uranium-containing pitchblende, the president of the British Association for the Advancement of Science, Sir William Crookes, announced in his presidential address that the energy 'drawn upon naturally by uranium and other heavy atoms' only awaited what he called 'the magic wand of Science' for the marvels of the nineteenth century to be cast into the shade by those of the twentieth.[4] Indeed, in the very first years of the twentieth century the principal investigators of radioactivity saw themselves as taking the path that, in their eyes, had been so actively pursued by alchemists and natural magicians but which had been abandoned by the new philosophers as impossible; they were taking none other than the path leading to the discovery of the philosopher's stone and from thence to the elixir of life. Frederick Soddy recalls how in 1902, as he and Ernest Rutherford 'watched' thorium transmuting itself into an 'argon gas', he had called out to Rutherford in jubilation and ecstasy that they were watching transmutation and how Rutherford had replied, 'For Mike's sake, Soddy, don't call it *transmutation*. They'll have our heads off as alchemists. You know what they are.'[5]

The nuclear alchemists were aware of all kinds of implications of their work as we shall see. But one immediate implication, namely that the sun's life span was vastly greater than hitherto believed and hence that life would be able to continue on earth for eons of time more than had previously been thought possible, led Rutherford to correct the great Kelvin and led Soddy to point out that their joint discoveries recalled 'the strange medieval myth that the Philosopher's Stone, which had the power of transmuting metals, when discovered would prove also to be the elixir of life'. The artificial transmutation of elements would become possible, believed Soddy, but the final product would not be that element whose alchemical responses to 'philosophical' mercury had so delighted Isaac Newton. 'Energy, not gold,' wrote Soddy, 'will be the quest of the modern scientific alchemist.'[6] As research and discoveries continued, Charles Moureu, the chemist who had played a leading role in gas warfare in the first world war and a major propagandist for science, rejoiced in the belief that strange surprises awaited mankind, 'more astonishing than those attributed to the philosopher's stone and the elixir of life'.[7] This was a view shared by the French scientist Frédéric Joliot-Curie who, together with his wife Irène Curie, had produced the first laboratory-created radioactivity. Enthusing over dramatic discoveries in nuclear physics Joliot told his Sorbonne audience in an open lecture in 1935 that compared with the recently discovered neutron the philosopher's stone of the alchemists was but a 'childish fantasy'.[8] In 1937, the year of his death, Rutherford's book entitled *The New Alchemy* was published — no timidity now about the word alchemy! — while two years later, as physicists raced to establish the conditions necessary for a nuclear chain reaction, one of the leading contenders and a colleague of Joliot-Curie, Lew Kowarski, recalled his motivating conviction: 'To be the first to achieve the chain reaction was like achieving the philosopher's stone.' The glory following the first man-made nuclear chain reacton would, he was convinced, be far greater than a Nobel Prize.[9]

Common justice, if nothing else, requires me at this point to intercede on behalf of the age-old alchemical tradition and particularly the tradition as it was practised in Europe before the seventeenth century. For while interpretation of the alchemical tradition is, to say the least, difficult, it is clear that not all alchemical practice consisted only of the attempt to transform metals into gold; there was also an associated attempt to reach a state of heightened religious consciousness and awareness. While obviously these two goals of alchemy could become disconnected — and did become disconnected with the rise of modern science — true alchemists nevertheless clearly interpreted their activity to be as much spiritual as practical, believing it imperative that the techniques of alchemy should not be divulged to men spiritually unworthy to be entrusted with such powerful knowledge. After the rise of the explicitly 'masculine philosophy' in the seventeenth century and further disparagement and repression of the 'feminine', only the manipulative aspect of alchemy remained of what had once been a more holistic endeavour. The role of the true alchemist as man-midwife to 'mother nature' had been replaced by the goal of the masculine philosopher to be master and possessor of brute (female) matter. In his sympathetic account of alchemical practice, F. Sherwood Taylor, the then Director of the Science Museum in London, has not inappropriately written: 'The material aim of the alchemists, the transmutation of metals, has now been realised by science, and the alchemical vessel is the uranium pile. Its success has had precisely the result that the alchemists feared and guarded against.'[10]

Before turning directly, however, to examine the three-fold syndrome of power over nature, pregnant phallus metaphors, and personal glory characteristic of those four decades of masculine 'alchemical' physics, we can gain an insight into the problems that faced women attempting to compete in such a masculine race by noting the experiences of the first woman to establish herself in the physical sciences, the twice Nobel Prize winner Marie Curie, née Maria Sklodowska, the woman who predicted the existence of, identified and isolated that most formidable of elements, radium.

'It is with women that we have to struggle'

We learn from one of Marie's biographers, Robert Reid, that as a student in Paris in the early 1890s Marie Sklodowska was more than prepared to make the personal sacrifices necessary to achieve success in her chosen discipline. Reid relates that the student Sklodowska began to live an almost unrelievedly solitary existence and that by the end of her second year she had severed almost every one of the personal relationships that might have distracted her from study. 'All my mind,' she wrote, 'was centred on my studies.'[11] But after passing her exams Marie Sklodowska allowed herself to be courted by the 36-year-old bachelor Pierre Curie who told her that he had so far remained a bachelor because he did not believe he would ever meet a woman who could be a companion to him, 'who could live his dream with him'. And what a masculine dream it was! For while Pierre longed for an equal female companion in the male sphere of physics, he did not see himself as an equal male companion in the female sphere of child care and the home. Neither did Marie Sklowodska, it would appear, expect him to be, accepting for herself as 'natural' the double role of physicist and wife and mother, and quoting with approval some extracts from a diary the young Pierre had kept. At the tender age of twenty Marie's future husband had written, 'We must eat, drink, sleep, be idle, love, touch the sweetest things of life and yet not succumb to them', and two years later he had expressed the guiding conviction of his masculine philosophy:

Women, much more than men, love life for life's sake. Women of genius are rare. And when, pushed by some mystic love, we wish to enter into a life opposed to nature, when we give all our thoughts to some work which removes us from those immediately about us, it is with women that we have to struggle, and the struggle is nearly always an unequal one. For in the name of life and nature they seek to lead us back.

The flight from the feminine. It is almost as if Mary Shelley had read Pierre's diary and had written *Frankenstein* as a grim warning. As for Marie, she wrote after Pierre's death that her husband had, in renouncing the pleasures of life, resolutely subordinated his thoughts and desires to this 'anti-natural' dream, 'adapting himself to it and identifying himself with it more and more completely. Believing only in the pacific might of science and of reason, he lived for the search of truth.'[12]

The Curies' first child, Irène, born in 1897, was looked after during the day by a woman servant and by Pierre's father. This enabled Marie to spend long periods of time with Pierre in their 'miserable shed' of a laboratory, described by her twenty years later as the best and happiest years of their life together. She found it impossible, she wrote, to express 'the joy of the untroubled quietness of this atmosphere of research and the excitement of actual progress with the confident hope of still better results'. How enthusiastically, too, would Pierre Curie express his pleasure at the eventual isolation of radium and at its mysterious blue glow. 'This is the light of the future,' he would proclaim to the embarrassment of his wife. But by the end of 1902 both Pierre and Marie were tired, Marie working without zest and sleep-walking at night. Their condition so worried the young physicist Georges Sagnac that in April 1903 he wrote a long letter to Pierre, chiding him for not properly looking after either himself or Marie, for attempting to live too intellectual a life, and in particular for neglecting his small daughter. 'Don't you love Irène?' he asked Pierre. 'It seems to me that I wouldn't prefer the idea of reading a paper by Rutherford, to getting what my body needs, and of looking at such an agreeable little girl. Give her a kiss from me. If she were a bit older she would think like me and she would tell you all this. Think of her a little.'[13]

To such criticism of their hectic life, the couple replied that they did take holidays in the summer. However, according to their second daughter, Eve, Pierre would become restless after two or three days passed in the same place, gently telling Marie that they had been doing nothing for a long time. Such difficulties notwithstanding, on 25 June 1903 the pregnant Marie became the first female Doctor of Physical Science at the University of Paris, a satisfaction, however, abruptly ended with the miscarriage of a baby girl followed by Marie's bitter self-reproach at the way she had, she believed, pushed herself beyond breaking point. Although the joint award of the Nobel Prize to her and Pierre (and also to Becquerel) in December of that year eased the couple's financial situation, it conspicuously failed to bring them greater happiness. Concerned about the relative slowness of their present work, we read that Pierre tried to accelerate their rate of progress. Tired in both body and mind it seems that Marie was unable to respond to her own satisfaction and as a result accused herself of intellectual impotence and 'stupidity'.[14] However, the birth at the end of 1904 of their second daughter brought both enforced rest and also pleasure to Marie who subsequently began to regain her appetite for work. But Pierre, his body consumed by radium's penetrating rays, became increasingly ill and desperate. Although during a temporary recovery in June 1905 he managed to go to Stockholm to make a very overdue Nobel Prize acceptance speech, the end of his address betrayed a now anxious physicist. 'It is possible to conceive,' he warned his Stockholm audience, 'that in criminal hands radium might prove very dangerous, and the question therefore arises whether it be to the advantage of humanity to know the secrets of nature, whether we be sufficiently mature to profit by them, or whether that knowledge may not prove harmful.' But Pierre professed optimism: 'I am among those who believe with Nobel,' he concluded his address, 'that humanity will obtain more good than evil from future discoveries.'[15]

The following year, Robert Reid relates, saw Pierre Curie's sickness at its worst. Depressed and permanently tired, even disenchanted with the investigation of radioactivity, Pierre gained temporary relief by spending Easter in the Chevreuse Valley with his wife and two small daughters. 'Those were two sweet days under a mild sun,' remembered Marie Curie, 'and Pierre Curie felt the weight of weariness lighten in a healing repose near to those who were dear to him. He amused himself in the meadows with his little girls, and talked with me of their present and their future.'[16] Reid writes that although other couples might well not have survived the stress the Curies' marriage surmounted, nevertheless the strain on Pierre's health was clear to all their intimate friends. Shortly after Easter the exhausted Pierre Curie stepped accidentally under a horse-drawn carriage, one of the wheels passed over his head, and Marie Curie was left grief stricken to the point of nervous collapse. Radioactivity, Pierre Curie's light of the future, had claimed its first victim and radium had shown itself a basely ungrateful element.

It is surely an irony of history that the principal protagonist in the discovery and isolation of radium was a woman and another irony that she married a man who had so explicitly expressed his fear of woman's subversive influence on all-out masculine endeavour. Perhaps, however, Pierre Curie's apprehension was somewhat misplaced. For wives who accept the value of masculine endeavour in science without being scientists themselves, who provide back-up typing support for their husbands and a place of rest for their husbands at the end of each competitive day, can perhaps contribute more to their husbands' progress and careers than wives who strive to undertake the double role of scientist and comrade in arms while at the same time being mother and keeper of the home. Such 'loyal' wives presumably help to maintain more effectively the mad momentum of masculine endeavour than those wives who seek to participate directly in the scientific quest as did Marie Curie.[17] We read, for example, that nearly all Ernest Rutherford's papers and letters were typed by his wife — homekeeper and mother of a daughter — and that during a period of frenetic activity undertaken by the young and then unknown Niels Bohr successive drafts of his world-famous papers were dictated to his wife — homekeeper and future mother.[18] The masculine Pierre Curie, on the other hand, seeking both a masculine *and* feminine female companion, i.e. a complete human being, was not prepared to marry unless to a woman who would work alongside him and he alongside her each day in the laboratory. It is also a tribute to the sincerity of his conviction that this remarkable man never tried in any way to claim for himself professional credit properly belonging to his wife. Nevertheless, the fact remains that Marie Curie had to struggle on both fronts, the masculine and the feminine, while her husband had basically, it would seem, to struggle only on one front, the masculine. However, again ironically — it is as if Mary Shelley were writing the sequel to *Frankenstein* — Marie Curie was partially saved by the desire she felt for children. For Reid writes that she was never so creative as when she was pregnant or suckling one of her babies.[19] On the other hand, Marie Curie could not be, and was not, so spiritually consumed by science as her obsessive husband. She was both the mother of two daughters and the mother of radium, as she proudly told one of her students, and while the help she received in the home enabled her to work daily in the laboratory for long periods of time, the needs of two small girls prevented her from becoming totally absorbed by the world of radium. Moreover, whatever the reason it appears that the unfortunate and honourable Pierre Curie was more seriously affected by the rays emitted from radium than his wife, who was certainly seriously enough affected. His hands were both very badly cracked and raw when he gave an address to the Royal Institution in London in June 1903, he had had difficulty in dressing himself for the occasion, violent pains in various parts of his body constantly made his life a misery and severe trembling in his legs often confined him reluctantly to bed. All due, he explained, to rheumatism. Writing to a friend in September 1905, Pierre Curie complained that he had had several new attacks of rheumatism which the slightest fatigue would bring on. Would he ever, he wondered, be able to work seriously again in the laboratory in the state he was then in? Pierre Curie — struck down by the substance he and his wife had created together — was never to know the answer to that question. It was an ill omen indeed when Curie, not a year after his hesitant declaration that the discovery of radium boded well for humanity, stepped off the pavement, apparently so thoughtlessly, to his instant death.

The prediction, discovery and production of radium were some of the essential steps along the multifaceted path to the discovery of nuclear fission, the path labelled so unproblematically by Margaret Gowing as 'the purest of pure science'. In the three sections that follow I focus on the very pronounced masculine aspect of these four decades of nuclear science and I analyse them in terms of Mary

Shelley's three-fold syndrome of the masculine scientist's fascination with power over nature and history-making breakthroughs, his use of pregnant phallus metaphors, and his desire and quest for priority and glory. Were I to be writing with a more comprehensive purpose in mind, I would include a section entitled 'Beauty and Truth in the New Physics' and I would have great pleasure in writing it.[20] But my purpose is, regrettably, not to focus on 'truth' and 'beauty' in twentieth-century science, even less on 'playful eroticism', but on the fundamentally aggressive and threatening aspects of the new and awesome physics.

History-making power over nature

'I know of no more enthralling adventure,' Ernest Rutherford stated towards the end of his life, 'than this voyage of discovery into the almost unexplored world of the atomic nucleus.' The founding father of the masculine philosophy had declared that the voyage of discovery so ardently advocated by him would, if undertaken, ultimately rock nature to her foundations. Self-aware heirs of Bacon or not, it was immediately apparent to the two co-discoverers of atomic transmutation of the literally explosive significance of their work. In 1903 Frederick Soddy suggested to readers of *The Contemporary Review* that the planet was a storehouse stuffed with inconceivably powerful explosives and that perhaps only a suitable detonator was necessary to cause the earth to revert to chaos. This was apparently also Rutherford's private view for we read of the physicist W.C.D. Whetham making a request to Rutherford in 1903 for permission to quote Rutherford's 'playful suggestion' that if only the proper detonator could be found ' a wave of atomic disintegration' might be generated in matter 'which would make this old world vanish in smoke' and Whetham went on to refer to Rutherford's joke that 'some fool in a laboratory might blow up the universe unawares'! Rutherford himself put the matter rather more circumspectly and optimistically in his book entitled *Radioactivity*, published the following year in 1904. 'If it were ever found possible,' he wrote, 'to control at will the rate of disintegration of the radio-elements, an enormous amount of energy could be obtained from a small quantity of matter.'[21] Soddy, however, publicly pursued the more directly menacing implications of their joint research, in 1904 informing the School of Military Engineering in Chatham that it was quite possible that all heavy matter possessed quantities of energy comparable to that possessed by radium and that, if so, then the man who managed to put his hand on the appropriate lever 'would possess a weapon by which he could destroy the earth if he chose'.[22] The possibilities opening up before mankind along the path being pioneered by the new alchemists were staggering in Soddy's opinion. In his book *The Interpretation of Radium* published in 1909 Soddy predicted how a mankind that could transmute matter would have no need to earn its bread by the sweat of its brow, that on the contrary such a race of men would be able to transform a desert continent, thaw out the frozen poles (quite outdoing the ambitions of Mary Shelley's explorer Captain Walton!), and indeed would be able to turn the entire earth into 'one smiling Garden of Eden'. Such a knowledgeable humanity might also be able to use its atomic power in order to explore the outer realms of space. But caution was necessary. For a single mistake, Soddy warned, might mean not the smiling Garden of Eden but extremely disastrous consequences for mankind, perhaps a return to conditions of the Stone Age or even worse.[23]

Greatly impressed by Soddy's writings for the general public H.G. Wells wrote his famous and influential science-fiction novel *The World Set Free* in the spring of 1913; he explicitly dedicated it to Soddy's *The Interpretation of Radium*. Three months after its publication Europe was at war and Wells's readers would appreciate only too well the novel's dramatic and sombre opening message. We learn how Wells's nuclear physicist, already 'possessed by a savage appetite to understanding' at the age of only fifteen, builds on the pioneering work of Rutherford and Soddy in particular and, to his own delight yet also consternation, manages to induce radioactivity in an element in the watershed year of 1933 (the year before it was actually induced by Irène Curie, daughter of Marie and Pierre, and her husband Frédéric Joliot-Curie). In Wells's prescient words, the inducer of artificial radioactivity 'knew that he had opened a way for mankind, however narrow and dark it might still be, to worlds of limitless power'. Wrestling with his conscience as to whether he had the right to disturb so dramatically and irreversibly the ordinary everyday existence of human beings, Holsten decided that he had:

> He reassured himself against the invasion of this disconcerting idea that he was something strange and inhuman, a loose wanderer from the flock returning with evil gifts from his sustained unnatural excursions amidst the darknesses and phosphorescences beneath the fair surfaces of life. Man had not been always thus; the instincts and desires of the little home, the little plot, was not all his nature; also he was an adventurer, an experimenter, an unresting curiosity, an insatiable desire. For a few thousand generations indeed he had tilled the earth and followed the seasons, saying his prayers, grinding his corn and trampling the October winepress, yet not for so long but that he was still full of restless stirrings...[24]

Convincing himself uneasily that perhaps the gift of atomic power would mean only yet more soft glow and colour and feasting to human existence, that in any case it was not for him to worry about unforeseeable consequences, and that even were he to burn all his papers some other man of science would undoubtedly make the same discovery within a couple of decades, Holsten took the fateful decision to publish. For the next twenty years, according to Wells, minor developmental difficulties prevented any striking practical applications of the discovery but three years later, in 1956, the most striking of all practical demonstrations occurred when a world war took place with the use of atomic bombs. Wells's description of an atomic explosion as experienced by a survivor, a dim broken human thing with only moments to live, is graphic:

> The sound struck her like a blow. She crouched together against the masonry and looked up... There was nothing else in the world but a crimson-purple glare and sound, deafening, all-embracing, continuing sound... She had an impression of a great ball of crimson-purple fire like a maddened living thing... that seemed to be attacking the earth furiously, that seemed to be burrowing into it like a blazing rabbit...[25]

The four years of non-atomic European warfare in which scientists of both sides were mobilised for military purposes horrified both Soddy and Rutherford. In a series of open lectures at Aberdeen which he delivered throughout the war years and which was afterwards published as a book, Soddy asked his listeners and readers to try to imagine what the present war would have been like, ghastly enough as it was, if atomic explosives had already been discovered instead of remaining only a horrible future reality. Should imagination be defective, Soddy informed them that by the use of such nuclear explosives any part of the world, or the whole of it if necessary, could be depopulated with an efficiency that would leave nothing to be desired. From then on Soddy 'dragged his scientific feet' believing it more important to try to discover the underlying causes of human folly and in particular of warfare than to make further progress in the arts of physics and hence of warfare as well.[26]

Rutherford, like Soddy, was also alarmed and in 1916 declared how fortunate it was that at the present time no method of releasing atomic energy had been found, adding that he remained very hopeful that 'we should not discover it until Man was living at peace with his neighbours'. Despite such an eminently sensible opinion Rutherford nevertheless continued his nuclear researches after the end of the war — which in any case he had never entirely abandoned — and continued them with all the zest for which he was justly famous. Perhaps he reasoned as Wells's Holsten had reasoned, that if he were not the one to make the next significant breakthrough then within twenty years it would only be someone else! It was, however, the impressive Rutherford who announced to the world in July 1919 that he had achieved the first laboratory transmutation of an element, changing nitrogen into oxygen by bombardment with alpha-particles. It could not have been an entirely tranquil Soddy who wrote personally to Rutherford to congratulate him on these 'brilliant results' which had so emphatically marked the next step 'towards the solution of the problem of artificial transmutation'.[27]

In the postwar years scientists continued to be aware of the awesome possibilities that their work heralded for humanity. The well-being of the human race or its suicide was the stark message of Sir Arthur Eddington in his 1920 presidential address to the British Association.[28] The biologist J.B.S. Haldane recalled in a talk at Cambridge in 1923 how during the war years which he had passed in India he and two other Europeans had strayed from a dance to look at a new star in the heavens and the three of them had wondered if they might not possibly be watching, if not the result of a stellar collision, then either the last judgement on some inhabited world or a too successful attempt in the induction of radioactivity on the part of some of its inhabitants — whether indeed they might not be witnessing 'the detonation of a world on which too many people came out to look at the stars when they should have been dancing'! Was mankind going to release from 'the womb of matter', Haldane wondered, a Demogorgon which at any moment might hurl him into the bottomless void?[29] Charles Moureu, the chemist referred to earlier, expressed considerable optimism concerning the future prospects of the great quest for ever-increasing power over nature. Science, Moureu promised in his book *Chemistry and the War* would eventually level mountains, subjugate the seas and bend the forces of the atmosphere to its will. A mere kilogram of uranium would be sufficient to produce the energy now supplied by the burning of 500 tons of coal. Entirely new atoms would be created, he enthused. During the early 1930s Ernest Rutherford took the precaution of having a quiet word in the ear of Sir Maurice Hankey, the then Secretary of both the Cabinet and the Committee of Imperial Defence. Taking his distinguished and influential companion to one side at a Royal Society banquet, Rutherford confided to Hankey that he 'had a strong hunch that nuclear energy might one day have a decisive effect on war' and urged the future Lord Hankey 'to keep an eye on it' — advice that Hankey never forgot. This, however, was not the view that Rutherford stated publicly. In the year of Hitler's accession to power in Germany the Director of the Cavendish Laboratory expressed, to say the least, strong scepticism, that nuclear transmutations would ever have commercial or military significance. Why, then, were experiments on transmutation of such interest in the scientific world? 'It is not that the experimenter is searching for a new source of power or the production of rare and costly elements by new methods,' Rutherford insisted. 'The real reason,' he declared, 'lies deeper and is bound up with the urge and fascination of a search into one of the deepest secrets of Nature.'[30]

Frédéric Joliot-Curie, on the other hand, begged leave to differ with the reassuring view that radioactive atomic nuclei could never be made to explode on a large scale. Celebrating in 1935 the award of a Nobel Prize for the discovery of induced radioactivity the French scientist assured his Sorbonne audience that with the ever-increasing pace of scientific research there could be no doubt that future researchers would discover how to bring about transmutations of an explosive character, with one transmutation provoking many others as in chemical chain reactions. As to the question whether such a researcher would be bold or foolhardy enough to try the experiment were he to discover the right process, Joliot informed a Moscow audience in 1936 that he thought the researcher would. The reason given? 'The researcher is curious and loves adventure,' the scientist Frédéric Joliot declared. (Twenty incredible and devastating years later Joliot had not changed his opinion. Enthusiastically looking forward to space travel Joliot asked rhetorically, 'Are we not forever driven forward by our insatiable curiosity and our thirst for adventure?')[31]

In England, however, Sir Arthur Eddington followed Rutherford in expressing public doubt that the new scientific Prometheus, no matter how much he loved adventure, would be able to ignite on earth the fire that perpetually burns in the heavens. Yet the possibility existed and could not be ignored. And that possibility, he argued in 1935 in his *New Pathways in Science*, seemed to him not so much a hope as a threat. In America, Eddington observed, crops were being burnt in order to raise the price of food. It therefore seemed impossible to deny, he concluded, that for a society in which abundance spelt disaster, that was only able to save its members from starvation by creating scarcity, in which unlimited energy meant unlimited power for war and destruction, an ominous nuclear cloud was looming in the distance 'though at present it be no bigger than a man's hand'. Although Frederick Soddy did not altogether share the view of his socialist fellow scientists that capitalism was the principal cause of the world's massive misuse of scientific knowledge, he did agree to write the foreword to their 1935 collection of critical essays, *The Frustration of Science*. Denouncing the universities and learned societies for evading their responsibilities in having no ambition higher than being the hired servants of the rich and powerful, he called on them to carry out that task for which they were supported in their release from routine occupations, namely — and this was H.G. Wells's battle cry — to 'speak the truth though the heavens fall'. Matters were coming to a head. The following year Rutherford himself publicly expressed the view that the release of nuclear energy might be closer than had seemed possible to him only a few years earlier. 'The recent discovery of the neutron,' he now explained, 'and the proof of its extraordinary effectiveness in producing transformations at very low velocities opens up new possibilities, if only a method could be found of producing slow neutrons in quantity with little expenditure of energy.'[32]

By this time the Hungarian-born Leo Szilard, who was to play such an important role in the Manhattan Project in the United States, had already been three years in England. After spending seven years as a (non-nuclear) physicist at the University of Berlin, he had in 1932 read and been very impressed with H.G. Wells's *The World Set Free* and in the same year had met Wells's publisher in German, Otto Mandl. Szilard recalls how Mandl had earnestly tried to convince him that the only way of preventing humanity from destroying itself in a series of recurring wars would be through the inauguration of space travel. Since men, Otto Mandl claimed, could never be satisfied with a happy idyllic life but needed to be heroic, to fight and to confront danger, only a hazardous enterprise aimed at leaving the earth would make war unnecessary on it. If this were so, reasoned the somewhat bemused Szilard, then only the future release of nuclear energy would provide danger-seeking mankind with the necessary energy for making its departure from the earth and solar system. Escaping from Hitler's Germany in 1933 and reading in London that year a report of Rutherford's notorious speech to the British Association in which the prestigious physicist had publicly stated that no commercial exploitation of nuclear energy would ever be possible — 'meerest moonshine' is the famous expression found in *Nature*'s report — Szilard first hit upon the idea of a nuclear chain reaction and then became convinced of its feasibility after learning of the work of Joliot-Curie and Irène Curie. His previous plans to abandon physics for biology were now discarded. 'Physics became too exciting for me to leave it,' wrote Szilard. Exciting and, perhaps one should add, dangerous! Certainly it was very fortunate for the world, Szilard later suggested, that he completely failed to get the financial backing he so badly needed. For while determined to try to keep his proposed experiments secret, Szilard came to doubt that this would have been possible in prewar England and, had it not been, then

Hitler's already mobilised Germany would have been in a far better position to drive such research onwards towards the creation of war-winning nuclear weapons. In any case, it was a very concerned Leo Szilard who wrote to Rutherford in May 1936, about the possible need to keep secret any work bearing upon the feasibility of nuclear chain reactions.[33]

Elsewhere in Europe, particularly in Berlin, Rome and Paris, the 'pure' investigation of artificial radioactivity and of the means of inducing it was proceeding at a gruelling rate. The discovery of the philosopher's stone lay just around the corner. After Enrico Fermi and his team had bombarded uranium with neutrons and tentatively suggested the creation of a new element (of atomic number 93) the nuclear chemist Ida Noddack cautioned as early as 1934 that reactions of a hitherto unknown kind could be occurring such as the disintegration of the uranium nucleus into several fragments. Ignoring such a possibility — and to be fair to them Noddack failed to follow up her original suggestion — nuclear scientists puzzled for a further five years over the nature of the radioactive elements produced by such neutron bombardment of uranium. When in early 1939 Otto Frisch and Lise Meitner, drawing upon the experimental results of Otto Hahn and Fritz Strassmann, confidently announced that neutron bombardment of uranium is able to produce a reaction whereby the uranium nucleus splits into two approximately equal parts accompanied by the liberation of enormous quantities of energy, it became apparent to nuclear researchers that the 'detonator' first joked about by Rutherford in 1903 had in principle been found provided only that a sufficient number of neutrons is released during each 'fission' process.[34] After publishing their papers in March and April 1939 announcing an average number of between three to four neutrons released with each uranium fission, the jubilant Paris team of Joliot-Curie, Kowarski and von Halban proclaimed an exciting and challenging future. 'We were talking about our changing the face of the world map,' Kowarski recalled, 'diverting the Mediterranean into the Sahara, things like that.' Francis Perrin recalled that the group forecast centralised atomic power stations: 'It was,' he declared, 'altogether the atmosphere of a Jules Verne novel.'[35]

If, however, the interests of the Paris team were directed towards the peaceful industrial application of nuclear energy, such praise-worthy attitudes were far from shared by some of their German counterparts. Indeed, on 24 April 1939, just two days after the publication of the Paris group's letter to *Nature*, Ernest Rutherford's former Cambridge researcher Paul Hartek together with his assistant Wilhelm Groth wrote to the Nazi War Office in Berlin describing how the newest developments in nuclear physics had made possible, in their opinion, an explosive many orders of magnitude more powerful than any hitherto used. The Nazi War Office was informed that that country which first made use of such a weapon would enjoy 'an unsurpassable advantage over the others'. It is therefore not surprising that at the start of the world war Germany alone of the future belligerents had a military office exclusively devoted to the study of the military applications of uranium fission which by that time had been declared a strict state secret. An article by a Siemens physicist submitted to the military authorities for clearance shortly after the start of war was totally suppressed: the discovery of fission 'by German researchers' had made possible, the author argued, as had Hartek and Groth before him, the production of a uranium bomb powerful enough to 'blast the ruins of a giant city up into the stratosphere'. 'What terrific powers of annihilation an air force would have,' the military censor read, 'if it could fight an enemy with bombs like these!'[36]

The purest of pure science? It would appear that during the four decades of 'pure' research from 1896 to 1938 the embryonic nuclear scientists knew very well that they were playing with fire, that moreover the play both fascinated and alarmed them, and that at least some of them rejoiced in the thought that the peaceful uses of atomic energy promised to make mankind, through their scientific mediation, the undisputed lords and masters of nature. The privilege of realising the explicit goal of the masculine philosophy announced by Francis Bacon some three centuries earlier would be theirs and theirs alone. Unfortunately, however, as so clearly seen by Frederick Soddy and others, there could be no chance at all that in a competitive, warring world the advent of nuclear energy would bring anything other than potential and perhaps actual disaster to humanity. Only in a *co-operative* Baconian world would there be a chance that nuclear energy might serve to make the world a more pleasant, a more human place to live in. But even so the chance would be a small one. As Mary Shelley had dramatically predicted over a century earlier, a masculine science with its obsessive pursuit of history-making power over nature, reinforced by an aggressive attitude towards nature viewed as female, fuelled by an ever-increasing urgency of its practitioners to be the first to achieve scientific paternity, a pursuit characterised by the total or near total exclusion of affective ties that distract from the task at hand, compounded by insufficient regard or concern for the consequences of the ensuing achievements — such a science would be likely to bring disaster even in a world where men waged war only on nature, not on each other. But the world in the first four decades of the twentieth century was never remotely such a 'harmonious' one. It was, however, certainly a masculine one.

The pregnant phallus

In her famous book, *The Second Sex*, Simone de Beauvoir makes the argument that male accomplishments in the field of science and technology can and do serve to bestow a virile status on the respective male achievers and thereby underwrite a claim to masculinity. Since masculinity is, however, most directly affirmed in the successful penetration of a female partner, willing or unwilling, and her resulting pregnancy, it is relevant to inquire to what extent the new alchemists displayed an aggressive attitude towards nature, viewing it metaphorically as essentially female, as very much a virgin territory to be penetrated, mastered and rendered fertile by its male conquerors.[37]

Clearly, as Simone de Beauvoir has asserted, and as Mary Shelley knew, a predominant male image of nature has always been that of a mysterious, female entity, enticing, confronting, resisting and challenging the male. The four decades of pre-fission nuclear physics between 1896 and 1938 were no exception. In 1898, the year of the isolation of radium, the ageing Sir William Crookes represented nature as female in several different ways, none of which presumably provoked a second thought in any of his British Association audience. New sources of energy were necessary for the continued well-being of the 'great Caucasian race' and of civilisation in general; this much was indisputable. 'We must develop and guide Nature's latent energies, we must utilise her inmost workshops,' therefore declared Crookes. His concluding sentences expressed two different, indeed conflicting, attitudes adopted by masculine men of science towards female nature, the attitude of merely lifting, one by one, her successive veils while looking in awe at the increasingly resplendent view contrasted with an attitude conveying a more manly, aggressive, penetrating approach to the mysteries of nature: 'In old Egyptian days,' Crookes proclaimed,

> a well-known inscription was carved over the portal of the temple of Isis: 'I am whatever hath been, is, or ever will be; and my veil no man hath yet lifted.' Not thus do modern seekers confront Nature — the word that stands for the baffling mysteries of the universe. Steadily, unflinchingly, we strive to pierce the inmost heart of Nature, from what she is to reconstruct what she has been, and to prophesy what she yet shall be. Veil after veil we have lifted, and her face grows more beautiful, august, and wonderful, with every barrier that is withdrawn.[38]

By common consent one of the greatest experimental physicists of all time was Ernest Rutherford, recipient of the Nobel Prize in 1908, knighted in 1914, raised to the peerage in 1931, and honoured after his death with the title of 'father of atomic physics'. It is fascinating to observe how Rutherford himself saw and expressed his relation to the world of atomic nuclei and also how that relation was described by his associates and contemporaries. So great, after all, was to become Rutherford's reputation that in his Rutherford Memorial Lecture of 1939 Sir Henry Tizard declared that to less privileged men of science it seemed that Rutherford had managed to achieve a very special relationship with nature, in Tizard's words, 'we got to regard Rutherford as someone to whom Nature had imparted her secrets in a mysterious way'.[39]

First and foremost, the fledgeling Ernest Rutherford comes across, not surprisingly, as an ambitious young male. Arriving at the Cavendish Laboratory in 1895 he confided the following year to his fiancée Mary Newton, who was still in New Zealand: 'I have some very big ideas which I hope to try and these, if successful, would be the making of me.' Next month he wrote to his fiancée that after successfully presenting a paper to the University Physical Society he was told by his professor's wife, 'Mrs J.J. [Thomson]', that while he had been expounding the most difficult parts of his paper she had been wondering how the young man was faring romantically. 'Truly the ways of women,' Rutherford joked to Mary Newton, 'are not for men to understand.' When in 1898, two years later, the 27-year-old Rutherford received news that he was to replace the distinguished professor of physics at McGill University in Canada, Mary Newton was informed: 'Your acute mind will at once gauge my importance if they place me in his shoes when the beard of manhood is faint upon my cheeks.' There is nothing untoward here. Rutherford simply comes across in his letters as a pleasant, straightforward, very ambitious young man. However, in Rutherford's case his very considerable ambition was matched by a very considerable ability indeed.[40]

Rutherford's life-long attitude to nature is epitomised by the word 'attack'. His opening sentence of a 1933 review article on transmutation is indeed typical of Rutherford's blunt style and strikingly conveys a central feature of the physicist's relationship to nature. 'Many of the laboratories of the world,' the article begins, 'are now being equipped for an attack on the atomic nucleus.' Typical also is the good-humoured boast made in a letter to Niels Bohr: 'My work on the atom goes on in fine style. Several atoms succumb each week.'[41] An aggressive attitude without doubt, but an aggressive attitude against female atoms? This was certainly the way Rutherford's activity was perceived by one of his contemporaries, the distinguished astrophysicist G.E. Hale, who in June 1914 congratulated the great physicist on his manly approach: 'The rush of your advance is overpowering and I do not wonder that Nature has retreated from trench to trench and from height to height, until she is now capitulating in her inmost citadel.'[42] Rutherford, the undisputed and respected head of the various laboratories he presided over in his life, was later affectionately nicknamed Papa by his 'boys', as Rutherford liked to call his students, the 'boys' who under his leadership were forcing the 'coy' elements into 'yielding up their secrets'.[43] That Rutherford's approach was thoroughly manly seems to have been appreciated by his researchers. One of them recalls how that most brilliant of Rutherford's students, H.G.J. Moseley, suggested to him why an experimental arrangement they had chosen had a serious disadvantage: 'Rutherford will think it very effeminate of us to use a null method when we might measure the deflection instead'![44] In 1926 Rutherford's former student Niels Bohr eulogised the great Rutherford in the following striking manner:

> Surrounded by a crowd of enthusiastic young men, working under his guidance and inspiration, and followed by great expectation of scientists all over the world, he is in the middle of a vigorous campaign to deprive the atoms of their secrets by all the means at the disposal of modern science.[45]

Only fleetingly, however, do images of a female nature appear in the writings of Rutherford that I have read although they do appear in the letters and talks of colleagues. Giving an account of a dinner arranged to celebrate his 1904 award of a Rumford medal Rutherford described to his wife a 'humorous and capital speech' in which the speaker apparently 'drew a harrowing picture of the state of mind of radium — a shy shrinking thing which had been dragged into the glare of publicity and all its secrets laid bare and instanced it as an example of scientific oppression'. Radium was here no doubt presented in fine after-dinner form as the chaste virgin unveiled by an 'oppressive' science. The following year in 1905 Rutherford's friend, the chemist Bertram B. Boltwood, jovially presented to him the alternative masculine version of the typical female in drawing an unfavourable comparison between thorium and radium: 'I am beginning to believe,' wrote Boltwood, 'that thorium may be the mother of that most abominable family of rare-earth elements, and if I can lay the crime at her door I shall make efforts to have her apprehended as an immoral person guilty of lascivious carriage. In point of respectability your radium family will be a Sunday school compared with the thorium children, whose (chemical) behaviour is simply outrageous. It is absolutely demoralising to have anything to do with them.' Nature is here regarded as female, whether chaste or unchaste, and, as Soddy explicitly confirmed, the discovery of radioactivity meant that scientists 'had penetrated one of Nature's innermost secrets'.[46]

The question arises, however, as to whether 'pure' experimental physicists can justifiably be called fathers of their discoveries in so far as they do not create theories as do theoretical physicists, but rather discover 'real' features of the physical world which enjoyed an existence prior to their discovery. Justifiably or not, Rutherford was to gain this coveted appellation. As is well known, in 1911 Rutherford was led to propose the famous solar system model of the atom after observing the very rare but dramatic back-reflection of an alpha-particle from a metal plate. 'It was quite the most incredible event that has ever happened to me in my life,' declared Rutherford in the last public lecture of his life.[47] His student C.G. Darwin to whom Rutherford had confided his theory had no doubt that the major masculine feat of all had been achieved: 'I count it as one of the great occurrences of my life,' he wrote following the death of Rutherford, 'that I was actually present half-an-hour after the nucleus was born.' Future atomic physicists also had no doubts about the propriety of conferring paternity rights on Rutherford: 'The title of father of the atomic theory is given to Rutherford,' acknowledged Max Born in his classic text on atomic physics, 'to him we owe our concrete, quantitative ideas on atomic structure.'[48] When, however, the paternity rights conferred on Rutherford were widened to embrace all of atomic physics, Rutherford's co-discoverer of the transmutation of elements, Frederick Soddy, was to complain bitterly to his biographer of what he saw as a gross injustice, asking her in particular to note the last wounding sentence of an obituary on Rutherford by the physicist Sir Oliver Lodge: 'It may be future generations will speak of Rutherford,' Lodge had declared to Soddy's anger, 'as the father of the new atomic chemistry and physics.' It is this often bitter competition between scientists for recognition of priority or rather paternity which is the subject matter of the next section.[49]

Certainly Rutherford's contribution to atomic physics was very great and, it is sometimes claimed, unique. For if Rutherford had not fathered atomic physics, how might the nucleus have come to be born, if at all? Thus in the words of one of Rutherford's many admirers, what would have happened to atomic physics if Rutherford had not won his scholarship to Cambridge from New Zealand or had early on abandoned physics — let us say because of his realisation that his work could contribute one day 'to this old world going up in smoke'? In a 'partial portrait' of Lord Rutherford, delivered in 1950 by the scientist A.S. Russell, the answer was unambiguously given that the loss would have been irremediable. After describing the 'puritan qualities of heart' that Rutherford showed to nature 'when he was brooding over her secrets', Russell declared himself convinced that 'the more fundamental the science the greater is the need of the big advances which only great men can make'. Where the great man does not do his work, Russell affirmed, 'the darkness remains permanently unpierced'. 'By probing the atom to its very depth, he not only revealed great truth and beauty,' Russell eulogised Rutherford; 'he showed us by example what one man can do when he makes the most of his great gifts.' (Interestingly, in his Madame Curie Memorial Lecture of 1935 Russell declared that Marie Curie's creative period had been from 1896 to 1903 and that by 1911 her attitude had become 'protective and maternal rather than creative' and that she was now 'constantly returning to the old work to meet criticism of it, to keep, so to speak, its honour bright'. Not so Ernest Rutherford.)[50]

There is no doubt that Rutherford clearly enjoyed his physics and the infectious zeal and enthusiasm with which he so successfully attacked and penetrated 'the formidable defences of the nucleus' communicated itself to his many admiring co-researchers and students. Their uninhibited praise of Rutherford is very moving. Yet when a principal colleague and biographer A.S. Eve declares that Rutherford's activities can be accurately likened to the description of Percy Bysshe Shelley given by the poet Francis Thompson, namely that 'He stands in the lap of patient Nature, and twines her loosened tresses after a hundred wilful fashions, to see how she will look nicest in his song', we may feel that understandable admiration has perhaps got the better of judgement. Rutherford's favourite song as he toured his laboratories was 'Onward Christian soldiers, marching as to war' — recognisable, we are assured, only by the words! — and his physics was conceived by him in true Baconian spirit as an army's attack on the remaining unpenetrated defences of nature led by his very great person. And as we have seen earlier, Rutherford knew very well from the very outset of his work on radioactivity that the stakes for mankind were possibly very high indeed.[51] If Rutherford was himself personally interested only in penetrating the secrets of nature, there were others who had far more worldly interests.

Finally, it seems entirely appropriate that what Niels Bohr said so admiringly of Ernest Rutherford has repeatedly been said, equally admiringly, of him and of the physics institute in Copenhagen that he headed from 1921 onwards. The Nobel laureate physicist, Victor F. Weisskopf, who had spent a rewarding two years at Bohr's Institute (and who afterwards worked at Los Alamos together with so many of Europe's top non-Aryan scientists), has described how Bohr generated among his visiting colleagues and younger physicists 'a spirit of attack, a spirit of freedom from conventional bonds and a spirit of joy that can hardly be described'. Admitting that the physicists of the Institute manifested 'a certain contempt for the rest of the world', Weisskopf nevertheless felt that this was more than compensated for by the truly international nature of the Institute. Francis Bacon would have felt vindicated. 'The international community of men around Bohr,' Weisskopf affirms, 'was held together at that time by his personality and by a common urge to penetrate into the secrets of nature.' Their work was mainly theoretical and it was hugely successful: 'The intellectual eye of man,' Weisskopf writes with understandable pride, 'was opened on the inner workings of Nature that were a secret up to this point.' Years later, one of the most brilliant members of that international community of physicists, Werner Heisenberg, recalled the anguish of that compulsive quest to understand the secrets of the atom: 'I remember discussions with Bohr which went through many hours till very late at night and ended almost in despair; and when at the end of the discussion I went alone for a walk in the neighbouring park I repeated again and again the question: Can nature possibly be as absurd as it seemed to us in these atomic experiments?' If Heisenberg was to solve to his own satisfaction the riddle of atomic phenomena, others were to dissent, including the great Einstein — and to dissent in anguish. The question arises once again, does such impassioned, compulsive investigation into the secrets of the atom legitimately evoke the description, 'the purest of pure science'? Many years later, long after the second world war, Heisenberg would attempt to recall his first impassioned defence of quantum mechanics against Einstein's life-long objections, a defence that suggests the aesthetic purity of his science. 'If Nature leads us to mathematical forms of great simplicity and beauty,' he remonstrates with Einstein, 'we cannot help thinking that they are "true", that they reveal a genuine feature of nature... You may object that by speaking of simplicity and beauty I am introducing aesthetic criteria of truth, and I frankly admit that I am strongly attracted by the simplicity and beauty of the mathematical schemes with which nature presents us.' In physics, it may indeed be the case that the way to Truth lies through the realm of the Beautiful. There is nothing in these sentiments by Heisenberg to suggest a motive of desire for power over nature reinforced with pregnant phallus imagery. But it nevertheless remains the case that a very effective way to power over the 'inanimate' world does lie through the discoveries of physicists. Moreover, once again we see that the physicists then engaged in the development of the new domains of quantum mechanics and nuclear theory, apparently working in areas so remote from the concerns of humanity, knew very well that their ideas were anything but that. 'We were very well aware of the fact,' Weisskopf confirms, '— and this I would like to emphasise — that these ideas were of very deep significance for the world, right from the beginning.'[52]

Certainly, of very profound significance for the world was the achievement in 1934 by Frédéric Joliot-Curie and Irène Curie of laboratory-induced radioactivity. Once again a woman was at the centre of the search for the philosopher's stone — a woman of science and a mother. Nearly ten years earlier in March 1925 Irène Curie, daughter of Marie Curie, had told a woman journalist at her doctoral examination that she considered science to be the primordial interest of her life and that family obligations were only possible for a woman of science on condition that they were accepted as additional burdens. Some two years later, however, she was to give birth to a daughter Hèlène and in March 1932 to a son Pierre, confiding to a close woman friend, 'I recognised that if I did not have any children, I could not console myself by the fact that I had not made that remarkable experiment whilst I was still capable of it.' Devoted as she was to her work in the laboratory, we are told that it was she who regularly had to persuade her reluctant husband to leave the laboratory for lunch or to go home at night.[53] The newly invented Wilson cloud chamber was an apparatus specially beloved by Frédéric and in describing it (he had made an improved version for himself in 1931) he would say and ask, 'In this chamber an infinitely tiny particle reveals its own trajectory, in a succession of drops of condensation. Is it not the most beautiful phenomenon in the world?' And we are assured by a scientist colleague and biographer of Frédéric Joliot-Curie that if the pregnant Irène was present she would reply, 'Yes, my dear, it would be the most beautiful phenomenon in the world, if there were not that of childbirth'![54] Just nine months after the birth of their son, Irène and Frédéric jointly discovered, investigated and announced to the world the phenomenon of artificial radioactivity. But in Maurice Goldsmith's biography of Frédéric Joliot-Curie we read, somehow appropriately, that 'the original final observation was made by him alone working with his Wilson chamber'. Alone at the time of the final confirmation of the phenomenon, Joliot expressed his uninhibited joy at the achievement and 'thought of the consequences which might follow from the discovery'.[55]

At Berkeley in the United States the results of Joliot and Curie were immediately tested and corroborated by Ernest Lawrence and his team in their Radiation Laboratory. A new centre of nuclear physics and chemistry, in addition to those in Paris, Berlin, Cambridge and Rome, was in the process of reaching maturity. It had been to Berkeley that J. Robert Oppenheimer came in 1929 after his years of study in Europe, to meet and develop there a close friendship with the prestigious and pioneering 'atom-smasher', Ernest Lawrence. We read from one of the Berkeley graduates, the future Nobel laureate Willard F. Libby, how the 'strong men' in the University of California, especially Wendell Latimer, had welcomed, kept and supported Ernest Lawrence 'in his bold attack on the atomic innards' which was in due course to arm the United States, according to Libby, with the personnel and know-how required for both military and peaceful applications of atomic energy. Latimer, however, did considerably more than just welcome Lawrence. In the early 1930s he was mainly responsible for initiating a seminar on nuclear chemistry which was chaired by Libby himself who described the experience of being one of the 'Latimer boys' as a 'rough, tough life, but a great one'. As to the development of nuclear chemistry in California we learn from the colourful Libby that 'Berkeley radiochemistry was conceived first as a glint in the Chief's eye, and then after about a nine-year pregnancy, came full born in the golden years of the thirties'. That Berkeley seminar in developing the discipline of nuclear chemistry was to help pave the way in the early 1940s for the identification and separation of the man-made element, plutonium, the fissile element whose creation in a uranium pile the work of Joliot and Curie had made possible and which so tragically, was to be the explosive constituent of the bomb dropped on Nagasaki.[56]

The word 'fission' had been introduced by Lise Meitner and Otto Frisch in their short but momentous paper to *Nature* (which although posted on or shortly after 16 January 1939 was not published by *Nature*, much to Frisch's annoyance, until 11 February).[57] In Copenhagen Otto Frisch had consulted an American biologist about the terminology used in biology to describe cellular division and had decided to adopt the word 'fission' to describe the splitting of the uranium nucleus after absorption of a neutron. It would seem a most inappropriate choice. Cellular division is a complex process whereby one cell gives rise to two 'daughter' cells, each cell genetically identical to the 'parent' cell, and which occurs in an ordered process that leads to the creation of highly complex, differentiated living beings following the initial fusion of female and male germ cells. But when after absorption of a neutron the uranium nucleus splits into two approximately equal parts the two resulting nuclei are quite different from the 'parent'. It would therefore appear to be a process far removed from whatever process is responsible for the growth and development of living beings. Yet, as we shall see in the next chapter, the Los Alamos physicists chose to interpret their development of the fission process in terms of a successful penetration into fertilisation of female nature followed by the successful birth of the desired products.

It was, after all, the philosopher's stone being discovered, not the secret of life, despite the 'pregnant phallus' metaphors to be found in the writings of the physicists. Nevertheless we might note that during the 1930s the Bohr Institute was playing its part in generating the sequence of events that would help lead to the discovery in 1953 of the structure of the gene. In 1932, that *annus mirabilis* of nuclear physics, Niels Bohr had had the temerity to deliver in Copenhagen a stimulating address on the nature of life; its theme was that life's ultimate secret was essentially and inevitably safe from the analytical methods of science.[58] Provoked and challenged by Bohr's thesis, a young and ambitious German-born physicist, Max Delbrück, accordingly left Copenhagen to become Lise Meitner's assistant in Berlin, correctly reasoning that the proximity of the capital's scientific institutes would greatly facilitate his quest to gain a mastery of biology. In 1937 this renegade physicist, armed with a manuscript entitled 'Riddle of Life', journeyed as a Rockefeller Fellow to the United States and there in his new homeland helped found an important school of 'molecular biology', one of whose graduate students, James D. Watson, was to be a co-discoverer of the 'double helix'. We should indeed bear in mind as we examine some of the consequences of the discovery of the philosopher's stone that the quest to discover 'the secret of life', Frankenstein's dream, is more than under way.

Two years after Max Delbrück's journey to the United States, the man who had indirectly sent off the fledgeling physicist on a life-long mission to unravel life's ultimate secret, himself travelled to the United States. But Niels Bohr was armed during this January voyage not with a manuscript posing the problem 'Riddle of Life' but with the momentous secret confided to him in Copenhagen by a trusting Otto Frisch, the discovery, no less, of the philosopher's stone. Having given Frisch his word that he would let nothing slip in the United States about the process of 'uranium fission' until Meitner and Frisch's letter to *Nature* had been published (recall that horrible four-week delay!), Bohr spoke of the momentous secret only to a physicist companion, Leon Rosenfeld, while on the sea journey to America but somehow or other forgot to tell his suitably impressed companion of his promise to Frisch. Thus after a 'well-meaning but imprudent' Rosenfeld had immediately announced the discovery of fission at a meeting of American physicists and set a 'fantastic race' in progress, both Bohr and Rosenfeld subsequently had a very difficult task in establishing the priority of Meitner and Frisch in the announcement of nuclear fission.[59] A new and fantastic race had indeed been set in motion and no one knew for sure where it might lead. But wherever it led, one feature of the preceding race remained very clear, namely that its leading participants had done everything possible to outstrip fellow competitors and to ensure peer and public recognition of the priority of their own very considerable achievements.

Priority, publication and glory

In this section I wish to underline the above remark that it was scarcely in a spirit of co-operation with each other that physicists planned and carried out their attacks on the atomic nucleus but rather in a spirit of intense, competitive rivalry — rivalry for fame, rivalry for the funding that successful achievement helps to attract, and rivalry for the institutional power over other human beings that accompanies the control of resources. The demands of such rivalry allowed little time for physicists to reflect on the wider human significance of their work but rather dictated that the maximum possible working time be spent in attempting to outdistance rivals and so establish a commanding lead in the race to be the first to make that historic breakthrough and to communicate it in print to rivals, colleagues, and the world. The historian of science Spencer R. Weart has summed up this aspect of the matter admirably: 'The point of science is to discover things, and it means little to be the second to make a discovery; by universal agreement among scientists the first to publish is the first and often the only one to get credit, so in a fast-moving field much can depend on speed of publication.' Accordingly, as noted by Derek de Solla Price, many scientific journals with weekly publication were started in the period of hectic activity following the discovery of radioactivity. Providing facilities for rapid publication these journals enabled scientists to quickly establish their claims to priority and hence their claims to further resources and greater institutional power. A few dramatic examples will serve to highlight the frenetic pace of the new physics, as individuals and small groups sought to make and communicate all-important breakthroughs ahead of rivals.[60]

When in late February 1896 Sir George Stokes received a letter from a London professor of physics, Silvanus P. Thompson, informing him of Thompson's discovery of the photographic activity of uranium salts, Stokes wrote to him, 'You will, I presume, publish it without delay, especially as so many are now working at the X-rays,' adding an implicit warning not to communicate the discovery to Lord Kelvin before publication owing to the unfortunate fact that Kelvin's enthusiasm sometimes outstripped his discretion. Less than a week later, however, Stokes wrote to Thompson, 'I fear you have already been anticipated.' Indeed, according to Marie Curie's biographer, Robert Reid, had Becquerel not announced his discovery to the Paris Academy of Sciences on the very next day after he made it, credit for the discovery of radioactivity would have gone to Thompson together with the coveted Nobel Prize. The Academy, meeting every Monday, conveniently guaranteed the publication of any paper presented to it within ten days. Marie Curie, after her discovery that thorium emits rays as does radium, chose this same rapid means of publication as had Becquerel. Nevertheless, Curie's paper, which was read for her on 12 April 1898 (as she was not yet a member of the Academy), turned out to be too late by two months. Despite this disappointment, however, her paper did contain the unique observations that the uranium ore called pitchblende was more photographically active than uranium itself, and that this phenomenon clearly suggested the existence of an element immensely more radioactive than uranium. It was for this latter insight, we recall, and her subsequent identification and isolation of polonium and radium that she, together with Pierre Curie and Becquerel, was awarded the Nobel Prize in 1903.[61]

The young and ambitious Ernest Rutherford also knew that he was competing in a race. Two years after arriving at McGill University he wrote to his mother: 'I am now busy writing up papers for publication and doing fresh work. I have to keep going,' he explained to her, 'as there are always people on my track. I have to publish my present work as rapidly as possible in order to keep in the race.' Part of Rutherford's publishing programme included a book on radioactivity as did, however, the publishing programme of Rutherford's co-worker, Frederick Soddy, an intention the latter announced after arriving in England in 1903 and which more than suggested the possibility of his establishing precedence over the 'senior' collaborator. Rutherford's biographer, A.S. Eve, relates that Rutherford felt so strongly on the matter that he wrote Soddy a 'firm letter', after which it was finally agreed that Soddy's proposed book should not appear until one or two months after the publication of Rutherford's. Despite this guarantee of priority over Soddy, Eve comments that Rutherford's book was still 'pressed forward with all possible speed' in order to forestall several other authors, both in England and elsewhere, who were writing on the new, exciting and undoubtedly epoch-making topic of radioactivity.[62] Rutherford's career, however, was already assured. In 1907 he accepted the Chair of Physics at the University of Manchester and in 1919 the then Sir Ernest Rutherford became the powerful Director of the prestigious Cavendish Laboratory at Cambridge.

Ernest Rutherford was not the only would-be leader of men who at one time continually felt and feared the breath of rivals down his neck. Niels Bohr, assiduously working in Copenhagen on the papers on atomic structure that were to make him world-famous, conveyed in an anxious letter to Rutherford at the beginning of November 1912 the difficulties he was having in completing his work. Despite Rutherford's reassuring reply that there was no need to hurry as no other physicist seemed to be taking Bohr's approach, Bohr nevertheless became increasingly impatient, writing on 5 February 1913 to a physics colleague in Uppsala: 'I am afraid I must hurry, if it is to be new when it comes; the question is such a burning one.' And hurry Bohr did, the first of his epoch-making papers appearing just five months later in the July issue of the *Philosophical Magazine*. Only three years later Bohr was appointed to the newly established position of Professor of Theoretical Physics at the University of Copenhagen and five years later he became the first Director of the also newly established Institute for Theoretical Physics. As his Danish colleague, J. Rud Nielson, remarked half a century later, Bohr at that time was an incessant worker and was always in a hurry, 'serenity and pipe smoking came much later'![63]

Bohr's work, however, was concerned with the nature and behaviour of the electrons orbiting the atomic nucleus, not with the nucleus itself. It was not until the discovery of the neutron in 1932 that new theoretical and practical approaches to determining the structure of nuclei became possible. Again the work proceeded at a frenetic rate, as frenetic as had been the pace of events associated with the discovery of the neutron itself.

On 28 December 1931, not three months away from giving birth to her second child, Irène Curie had reported to the Paris Academy of Sciences the detection of what she believed to be very penetrating rays, similar in nature to X-rays. Three weeks later in a joint paper with her husband she gave a further account of these remarkable rays. In Cambridge, however, it took James Chadwick from the time he read Irène Curie's first paper in early January only six weeks to initiate and complete experiments that clearly indicated the existence not of very penetrating rays of the type claimed by the Curies but of a particle having approximately the same mass as a proton but no electric charge. By 17 February 1932 Chadwick had written a short report and ten days later *Nature* had published it. It was therefore singularly unfortunate that on 22 February Irène Curie and Frédéric Joliot-Curie postulated to the Paris Academy a new kind of interaction between the atomic nucleus and the rays they believed they had discovered, to which they gave the symbol $\mathcal{J}$. The work of the Curies had not only been very quickly taken up in the Cambridge laboratory by Chadwick but the glory of the 'correct' interpretation — the discovery of the neutron — was Chadwick's alone.[64] It was a bitter Joliot-Curie who, after informing a friend in Moscow of the good news of the safe birth of their son three weeks earlier and the good health of Irène, went on to complain:

> We have been working very hard during the last few months and I was very tired... We had to speed up the pace of our experiments, for it is annoying to be overtaken by other laboratories which immediately take up one's experiments. In Paris this was done straight away by M. Maurice de Broglie with Thibaud and two other colleagues. In Cambridge, Chadwick did not wait long to do so either.[65]

The Curies' feverish activity continued. Once Irène had recovered sufficiently after the birth of Pierre, the couple spent two weeks on the Jungfraujoch in Switzerland studying the effects of cosmic rays on the atomic nucleus. Once again they were in a position to make a major breakthrough but once again they missed out, this time on the experimental discovery of the 'positron'. The next major breakthrough, however, and one long awaited in the world of nuclear physics, belonged only to the Curies — the induction of 'artificial radioactivity'. On Friday 15 January 1934 a friend and colleague, Pierre Biquard, received an excited telephone call which promptly brought him to the Curies' laboratory to witness for himself the creation of radioactive phosphorous by the bombardment of aluminium with alpha-particles. Sweet was the couple's long-sought success. According to S.R. Weart, 'Joliot began to run and jump about the basement room with childlike joy. The discovery was beautiful, significant, and entirely their own. "With the neutron we were too late. With the positron we were too late," he told his assistant Wolfgang Gentner. "Now we are in time." ' The following Monday, Jean Perrin presented the epoch-making discovery to the Paris Academy of Sciences.[66]

In Rome the publication of the Curies' results in the *Comptes rendus* of January 1934 immediately gave Fermi the idea of attempting to induce artificial radioactivity by bombarding nuclei not with alpha-particles but with neutrons. Although negative results were obtained with hydrogen, beryllium, boron, carbon, nitrogen, and oxygen positive results were obtained with fluorine and needless to say produced a very prompt letter to the *Ricerca Scientifica* on 25 March 1934. Thereafter, Fermi's group consisting of himself, Amaldi, D'Agostino, Rasetti and Segrè pushed their work as hard as they could, publishing several letters in the *Ricerca Scientifica* between March and July 1934. When that summer a paper describing the group's neutron work was personally delivered by Amaldi and Segrè to Lord Rutherford for publication by the Royal Society, Segrè happily remembers how Rutherford replied to his query concerning the possibility of rapid publication with the remark, 'What do you think I was president of the Royal Society for?'! The day of 22 October 1934 turned out to be memorable indeed for the Rome group. In the morning the group discovered the remarkable result that neutrons passed through a paraffin filter become extraordinarily effective in inducing radioactivity; in the afternoon Fermi produced an explanation of the 'miraculous effects' of the paraffin filter; by dinner time the hypothesis of the effectiveness of 'slow' or 'thermal' neutrons was confirmed; and after dinner the group met to write a short paper describing their results. These were the results, we recall, which had suggested to Rutherford that an effective path to liberating the energies of the radioactive nuclei might indeed be found. During this creative period the Rome group had, to be sure, already begun the fateful neutron bombardment of uranium, thorium and other heavy metals.[67]

Following the lead of Fermi's team in Rome, the Curies in Paris and Otto Hahn, Lise Meitner and Fritz Strassmann in Berlin also bombarded uranium and thorium with neutrons. Competition was

intense. Hahn, believing that the work of the Berlin group was insufficiently recognised in Paris, wrote to Rutherford both chiding him
for insufficient citation of their work and telling him that the Berlin
group had been 'a little angry with Mme Irène Curie for not having
cited us properly... We regret this very much, for a scientific echo
has never been as necessary to us as just now.' The final round of the
struggle between the Paris and Berlin teams went, however, decisively
to Berlin although by this time the Berlin team had lost Lise Meitner
(who had prudently fled Hitler's Germany to Sweden following the
Nazi annexation of her native Austria). The burning question confronting the investigators was the nature of the radioactive elements
produced by the bombardment of uranium with neutrons. What
were they? Towards the end of December 1938 the two remaining
investigators in Berlin, Hahn and Strassmann, were reluctantly forced
to a conclusion which unambiguously implied that nuclei of
uranium burst asunder under neutron bombardment. This implication, as we have seen, was momentous and the two radiochemists
knew it. Writing their report throughout the day of 22 December
they telephoned Hahn's close friend and editor of the German scientific periodical *Naturwissenschaften* who, arriving at the Kaiser-
Wilhelm Institute that same evening, arranged for Hahn's and
Strassmann's paper to replace a run-of-the-mill paper in the issue of
Naturwissenschaften then in proof and also for the inserted paper to
bear that day's date, 22 December 1938. Published on 6 January
1939 the paper arrived in Joliot's office some ten days later (just as
Bohr and Rosenfeld were arriving in the United States bursting to
tell the secret of uranium fission). 'The news,' writes Weart, 'struck
the Paris physicists like a thunderclap. Irène Curie was exasperated
to find how close she had come to the truth without actually seizing
it.' One of Joliot's co-researchers, Hans Halban, relates how Joliot
first locked himself in his office for a few days refusing to talk to
anyone, and only then made a report on Hahn's and Strassmann's
results to himself and Irène Curie. The all-important question remaining, namely the determination of the average number of
neutrons emitted in each 'fission' of the uranium nucleus, was the
missing vital ingredient which the Paris team of Joliot, Kowarski and
Halban was determined to be the first to tell the world. Leo Szilard,
however, now in the United States, was preoccupied with matters of

a very different nature than winning a priority race.[68]

Learning, like Joliot, of Hahn's and Strassmann's results sometime in January (and noting the furore in the United States following Rosenfeld's disclosure) Szilard wrote to Joliot in early February suggesting the possible need for secrecy. The cat was not yet out of the bag, thought Szilard, but its tail certainly was and more would follow unless action was taken. After confirming by the middle of March the ominous result that neutrons were definitely liberated in each fission process, Szilard accordingly sent off on 16 March a paper to the *Physical Review* accompanied by an explanatory letter to the editor requesting non-publication until further notice. Before this sequence of events had happened, Enrico Fermi, distressed and concerned about the anti-semitic campaign undertaken by Italian fascists in the summer of 1938, had decided to emigrate to the United States with his Jewish wife, Laura, receiving en route in Stockholm that December the coveted Nobel Prize for his pioneering work on uranium. After arriving in the United States in the first days of January Fermi quickly and independently reached the same results as had Szilard and after some arm twisting by his Hungarian colleague he and his collaborators agreed to adopt the same delayed publication strategy as pursued by Szilard. In Paris, however, Joliot's team had been working frantically between twelve to fourteen hours in the laboratory each day with every intention of immediately publishing their results. Indeed, as soon as the team had obtained its first publishable results, a letter to *Nature* was quickly written which Lew Kowarski then took himself to Le Bourget airport, one hour's train ride from Paris, in order to supervise personally its entry into the London mailbag! As Kowarski later recalled, 'We knew that the whole scientific world was boiling over these things.' On 18 March, just ten days after Kowarski's journey to Le Bourget airport, the whole scientific world was able to read in *Nature* the Paris team's letter dramatically entitled 'Liberation of Neutrons in the Nuclear Explosion of Uranium'. Far more than the cat's tail was now out of the bag and it was a very dismayed Szilard who first cabled Joliot requesting him to agree not to publish any further results, then the next day sent a follow-up letter together with a copy of his own communication to the *Physical Review* which had still not been published at Szilard's request. Joliot's negative response to

Szilard's cable, followed by a letter two weeks later on 19 April containing his regrets that he had been unable to cite Szilard's paper in his second communication to *Nature*, gave the still reluctant Szilard little choice but to agree to the publication of the two sets of American results. Looking back on this strange race a co-worker in Enrico Fermi's team, Herbert Anderson, recalls that the Paris group's subsequent publication in *Nature*, describing essentially the same experiment as their own, 'appeared a week or two earlier than ours in the *Physical Review*'. 'However rapidly our work went in those first few months,' commented Anderson, 'the French group managed to publish something along the same lines a week or so ahead of us.'[69]

As already noted, the sequence of events which Szilard had hoped to delay, perhaps even prevent, occurred very rapidly indeed. In 1933, the year of the Nazi triumph in Germany, Rutherford had proclaimed the impossibility of finding a detonator. Less than six years later a detonator had in principle, although certainly not yet in practice, been found and publicly announced. Within only a few days of the publication of the Joliot team's communication in the 22 April issue of *Nature*, two letters had gone to Nazi Ministries from German physicists about the possibility of constructing nuclear weapons. A week later, at a secret Berlin meeting on 29 April, the head of the research department of the Nazi Ministry of Education would be strongly criticising Otto Hahn for having published his discovery for the whole world to read.[70] Before long the secret meeting in Berlin would be followed by others of a similar nature in Britain and America and, in time, all results relevant to uranium fission declared state secrets. After the imposition of secrecy, publication of results would take a form unchallengeable in its assertion of priority — namely an atomic explosion.

The community of nuclear scientists

Three centuries earlier, we recall, Francis Bacon had called on men to cease making war on each other and to join forces in a determined masculine wooing, not to say gang rape, of nature. Not even scientists, however, let alone all men, have heeded Bacon's appeal. In particular, although the internationality of science has always been a much acclaimed feature of the new philosophy, the world-wide 'community' of nuclear scientists was certainly rather a long way from constituting a happy band of brothers even before the discovery of uranium fission. Indeed, in the very middle of this period of 'the purest of pure science', as nuclear scientists strove to tap nature's awesome reservoirs of energy, scientist went to war with scientist. During this war Rutherford worked on methods to detect submarines; the brilliant Harry Moseley was killed in Gallipoli; Hans Geiger, Rutherford's Manchester assistant and later a personal friend, fought in the German trenches while Otto Hahn, Rutherford's former student at McGill University and a close personal friend, worked throughout the war on the new science of gas warfare under the authority of the famous chemist and Nobel laureate Fritz Haber.[71] In view of the principal reason usually given for the atomic bombing of Hiroshima and Nagasaki, namely that it quickly brought the war to an end and hence saved millions of lives, it is salutary to pause over Hahn's own justification and account of his wartime activities, the Hahn whose interned colleagues feared he would kill himself the night he heard of the destruction of Hiroshima.

Initially opposed to the use of poison gas on the grounds that it violated the Hague Convention, Hahn states that he wholeheartedly threw himself into the work after being convinced by Haber's arguments that the French had, although not very efficiently, already used gas-filled bullets and that, most important of all, the use of gas was a way of saving countless lives since it meant that the war could be brought more quickly to a victorious end for Germany. Following one of his gas attacks on the Eastern front, however, Hahn recalls how profoundly ashamed, perturbed and personally guilty he felt after witnessing at first hand the pitiable condition of its Russian victims. Nevertheless, as a result of continuous work with such highly toxic substances, Hahn explains that his mind eventually became so numbed that he no longer had any scruples about the whole thing; so much so that although by early 1918 it was clear to both Haber and Hahn that victory for Germany was out of the question — the hope of winning the war quickly and so saving countless lives being only a dim memory — the gas warfare continued unabated. 'Still, we continued our efforts,' Hahn writes, 'and set up quite a number of more or less successful gas attacks.'[72] Thus, some three years and ten million deaths *after* the use of gas was justified in order to shorten the war and thereby save lives, Hahn and his colleagues were *still* using gas — and in a hopeless cause! Although at the end of the war Rutherford felt able to renew his friendship with Hahn and Geiger, even in 1933, fifteen years later, Rutherford refused on principle to befriend or even to meet the disgraced Fritz Haber, then temporarily in Cambridge following his dignified resignation in protest against Hitler's racist policies.[73] Ironically, it was the scientists driven out of Nazi Germany and fascist Italy, who were either Jewish or had Jewish wives, who were to play such a predominant role in the British and American wartime atomic weapons projects.

In the last six years of this period of relative innocence for physicists, times were very difficult indeed for German-Jewish scientists. Certainly they were very greatly helped by fellow scientists outside Nazi Germany but the fact remains that they were given very little public support inside the Reich. Although, for example, the physics and chemistry departments of the Universities of Berlin and Göttingen were very seriously depleted by Hitler's initial purge, yet at neither of these prestigious universities nor for that matter elsewhere did any non-Jewish scientist see fit to protest publicly. If anything, quite the contrary. When, for example, the Jewish physicist and Nobel laureate James Franck, who like Haber and Hahn had been active in gas warfare during the first world war, resigned from Göttingen in protest at the treatment of his Jewish colleagues he was bitterly attacked by many 'Aryan' scientists for supposedly playing into the hands of foreign propagandists.[74] Whatever their reservations about the Nazi regime, whatever the depth of their revulsion at its conduct, it is Joseph Haberer's conclusion in his study of 'Aryan' scientists that they always showed themselves ready to serve the Nazi state when called upon to do so.[75] International ties proved weak indeed for most of these Aryan scientists. From Rutherford's laboratory in Cambridge Paul Hartek left to fill the post in Hamburg rendered vacant by the departure of the Jewish physicist Otto Stern (who like Haber, Hahn and Franck had also been an active participant in the German gas warfare of the first world war). It was, moreover, this ex-researcher from Cambridge who was to be one of the principal driving forces behind the German atomic bomb project.[76] As for the international band of physicists united during the 1920s and 1930s under Niels Bohr's leadership in Copenhagen, it was Bohr's 'favourite', the renowned Werner Heisenberg, who was to become the leading theoretical light in the Nazi atomic weapons project, apparently prepared to see such devastating weapons supplied to the Nazi government for no other reason than that the government consisted of patriotic 'Aryan' Germans. In any case, from April 1939 onwards, the era of 'the purest of pure science' had definitely come to an end. From then on the international community of scientists was divided into two mutually hostile camps.

How, then, shall we sum up the *peaceful* activities of the nuclear scientists during the age of relative innocence prior to 1939? What were they striving for? Clearly they often enjoyed their science immensely. Hans Bethe remembers the 1930s as 'a very happy period', Robert Wilson remembers the decade as 'a joyous, marvellous time' (both these scientists we shall be meeting in the next chapter).[77] The nuclear pioneers relished the fact that they and they alone were daily bringing closer to reality the age-old dream of the philosopher's stone; and they were more than prepared to utilise aggressive energies in battle with nature and in both friendly and not so friendly competition with each other. Far from in general being a delightfully erotic play with nature giving sensuous pleasure, even joy, to all participants alike, the exuberant if obsessive activities of many of the scientists can best be likened to competitive charges against enemy defences, all glory to him first 'over the top' and first to penetrate the opponent's defences. Above all, the nuclear researchers knew that their work sooner or later would undoubtedly have momentous, although, they hoped, beneficial, consequences for mankind and they knew also that their names would be indelibly attached to such consequences. In his impressive analysis of the French atomic energy project, S.R. Weart has attempted to analyse the motives underlying the science of his three principal protagonists, Joliot, Halban and Kowarski, and needless to say he found their motives 'complex': 'they yearned for respect as scientists, they took pleasure in discovering the ways of nature, they hoped to improve humanity's lot, and of course they harboured personal ambitions.' But while, like most people, they struggled to rise, Weart's opinion is that the scientists' chief ambition went far beyond their careers. 'They meant to set in motion forces that would transform society for all time to come,' he declares, 'and they did.' Of course, as history has duly recorded and as Weart points out, once the scientists had succeeded in setting such epoch-making events in motion, they found they no longer occupied the driving seat.[78] They had been performing masculine science in a masculine world. They had initiated and were the standard-bearers of what Rutherford proudly called in 1923 the heroic age of physical science. Their masculine achievements were immense and impressive. At the end of the day, however, when their labour had reached the glorious and exciting stage of confinement, they reluctantly or otherwise came to the conclusion that the masculine world in which they lived and worked, divided as always against itself, now required from them that they direct their research into producing the most frightful weapon ever known to humankind.[79]

3. Alamogordo, Hiroshima and Nagasaki: 'Almost full grown at birth'

Is not the tremendous strength in men of the impulse to creative work in every field precisely due to their feelings of playing a relatively small part in the creation of living beings, which constantly impels them to an overcompensation in achievement?

Karen Horney, 'The Flight from Womanhood'

Here we have the key to the whole mystery... In serving the species, the human male also remodels the face of the earth, he creates new instruments, he invents, he shapes the future... [Woman's] misfortune is to have been biologically destined for the repetition of Life, when even in her own view Life does not carry within itself its reasons for being, reasons that are more important than life itself.

For it is not in giving life but in risking life that man is raised above the animal; that is why superiority has been accorded in humanity not to the sex that brings forth but to that which kills.

Simone de Beauvoir, *The Second Sex*

In a masculine world human beings are all too often forced into the unbearable position of having to decide between evil courses of action and of choosing what appears to be the least monstrous path. In 1939 the discovery of uranium fission and the possibility of the manufacture of nuclear weapons inescapably presented anti-Nazi scientists with the necessity of making such an unenviable choice between evils. Believing that Nazi Germany had the scientific and industrial potential for making such weapons, British and American scientists — and particularly those physicists who had fled the Third

Reich and knew at first hand of its horrors — were forced to the conclusion that they had little alternative but to try to bring into being a crash programme to create and produce atomic bombs, if race there was to be. The far more *unacceptable* evil was to allow Hitler undisputed monopoly of such devastating weapons. The humanly acceptable strategy must presumably have been to undertake a combined Allied attempt to design and manufacture atomic bombs as quickly as possible and after the war was won (without having to use the new weapons) to do everything possible to ensure continued co-operation between the Allies and to use nuclear energy, if possible, to help supply the energy needs of a world at peace. Whatever the motivation and objectives of leading participants, the reality turned out to be very different.

Work continued on the design and construction of atomic weapons after it was clear that Germany had failed in its atomic bomb project; moreover, work on the atomic bomb was intensified after VE Day in May 1945; the American and British governments failed to notify the Soviet Union of the existence of the Manhattan Project; three months after VE Day two atomic bombs were used against Japan (a country never in a position to produce such weapons); a nuclear arms race developed between the United States and the Soviet Union; Russia exploded its first atomic weapon in August 1949 whereupon both countries proceeded in a race to make hydrogen (thermonuclear) fusion bombs, some 1,000 times more powerful than the atomic (nuclear) fission bombs exploded over Hiroshima and Nagasaki. From 1950 onwards the arms race has inexorably accelerated, a state of affairs that Victor Weisskopf denounced in 1978 as the 'apotheosis of irrationality and antilogic, the triumph of craziness' — an indictment with which no doubt many would agree.[1]

In this chapter I limit my inquiry to attempting to answer two much discussed questions, namely why did the Los Alamos scientists *intensify* their efforts to make the atomic bomb *after* Nazi Germany had surrendered to the Allied armies and why, subsequently, were atomic bombs dropped on Japan? The answers necessarily involve not only the state of world politics at the time but the (interdependent) motivation of the principal participants: scientists, politicians and military.

The Fathering of the Monster:
The Manhattan Project

Many prominent physicists in the postwar years have not surprisingly spoken of their fear of atomic weapons in the possession of the Nazi government as being one of the principal reasons, or indeed the principal reason, why they attempted to initiate the Manhattan Project and then worked within it with such dedication. As is well known, in August 1939 Albert Einstein agreed to sign the now famous letter drafted by the émigré physicist Leo Szilard which warned President Roosevelt of the possibility of the construction of atomic weapons and — the sting in the tale — of related German interest in supplies of uranium ore. Subsequently Szilard was a prime mover in the American project to construct nuclear weapons. Undoubtedly nearly all scientists who worked on the Manhattan Project, no matter what their country of origin, were motivated to a greater or lesser extent by their fear of Nazi Germany. Thus the Austrian émigré physicist, Victor Weisskopf, writes how 'the fear that Hitler would make the bomb had much to do with' his decision to join the Manhattan Project.[2] Weisskopf even suggested to Oppenheimer in October 1942 that an attempt be made to kidnap Heisenberg and volunteered to go himself on such a hazardous mission, the German-born Hans Bethe, another future Los Alamos physicist, agreeing with him that the risk was worthwhile. The entirely justified apprehension then felt by such émigré scientists concerning Nazi Germany's nuclear potential is only too clear and was widely shared by both British and American scientists. Thus the American-born physicist, Richard Feynman, explains that the 'original reason for joining the project was that the Germans were a danger'. And so with many, many others.[3]

The Frankenstein effect

Well and good. However, so much more mysterious becomes the fact that the Los Alamos scientists *intensified* their efforts *after* the surrender of Nazi Germany. Feynman himself poses the central problem and riddle: 'What I did immorally was not to remember the reason why I was doing it. So when the reason changed, which was that Germany was defeated, not a single thought came to my mind that it meant I should reconsider why I was continuing to do this. I simply didn't think.' Another physicist, Bernard Feld, states that 'there was a mesmeric quality about the bomb'. Recalling how he had rejoiced at the end of the war in Europe, he also recalls the intensified efforts to complete the atomic bomb: 'Nobody stopped and said, "We are not at war with the Germans any longer, do we have to stop and think?" We were caught up in this activity, which was all consuming. Nobody worked less than 15, 16, 17 hours a day. There was nothing else in your life but this passion to get it done. We went through to the desert and exploded it — and ecstatic that it had worked.' 'I still don't understand the psychology,' he told an interviewer thirty years later. Weisskopf also poses the same fundamental problem, although less explicitly than Feynman and Feld. After once again explaining that the danger of the bomb falling into the hands of an 'irresponsible dictator' was one of the more important factors keeping the Los Alamos scientists at work, Weisskopf continued: 'After Hitler's defeat, it turned out this danger was in fact not so great; still, the work and the spirit continued until the task was accomplished — until, in the desert at Alamogordo, for the first time a nuclear fire was kindled by man.'[4]

On Weisskopf's five-letter word 'still' hangs a story of considerable length. For example, it might even appear that the menace of Hitler was simply a convenient excuse whereby the Los Alamos physicists could guarantee themselves the necessary resources for lighting their Promethean fire and, after that, abundant resources for the postwar development of such a successful activity as physics. Indeed, the surrender of Nazi Germany could even be viewed as having posed a threat to the satisfactory completion of the physicists' Promethean task. Emilio Segrè would, however, dispute such a view. For when news of Germany's surrender reached those Los Alamos scientists who were then in the desert at Alamogordo testing a firing device, the reaction of several European physicists was, according to Segrè, that 'Our efforts have come too late.' Hitler was for many of them, Segrè writes, evil incarnate and the principal reason for making the bomb; they therefore had second thoughts about completing the bomb 'now that it could not be used against him'. Nevertheless, Segrè agrees, work not only continued at Los Alamos but 'the efforts to assemble the atomic weapon were redoubled during the late spring and early summer'.[5] Certainly, according to Oppenheimer, there did occur a change in tempo at Los Alamos after VE Day and the direction of that change was not downward but 'upward'. There was no period of time, Oppenheimer emphasised, 'where we worked harder at the speedup than in the period after the German surrender and the actual combat use of the bomb'.[6]

The Los Alamos scientists, then, had set out to make an atomic bomb and had done so magnificently. They had, to be sure, little choice — even if some of them welcomed this fact — but to attempt to set out to make an atomic bomb as quickly as possible as a guarantee that such a weapon would not be used by Nazi Germany against America or its wartime allies. But the much analysed end result was that between 100,000 and 200,000 Japanese people were killed in a few seconds at Hiroshima and Nagasaki, and a desperate arms race between the United States and the Soviet Union had started. Perhaps it is therefore very understandable that Oppenheimer should tell President Truman in 1946, much to the President's annoyance, that he, Oppenheimer, had blood on his hands and would write in 1948 that 'the physicists have known sin and that this is a knowledge which they cannot lose'.[7] A principal component of that sin, I would suggest, is the momentum the project gained in the minds of leading male scientists and the desire they experienced, perhaps against their better judgement, to see the bomb through to completion and even to use. We have observed the central characteristics of such insane momentum in the behaviour of Dr Frankenstein and to a lesser but still significant extent in the actions of nuclear scientists during the half century preceding the discovery of uranium fission. These characteristics, we might bear in mind, consist, in brief, of the powerful urge to participate in huge history-making conquests over nature, explained and adorned with the frequent use of pregnant phallus metaphors, and reinforced by the obsessive desire to win fame and glory in passing the finishing line ahead of all rivals. In this chapter we shall see not only that many of the male protagonists of the Manhattan Project displayed such characteristics to a striking extent but that, like their fictional counterparts Captain Walton and Dr Frankenstein before them, they were seemingly determined to be drawn evermore inexorably into the kind of tragic situation described by Mary Shelley.

History-making power over nature

In September 1942 Major Leslie Groves of the United States Army was appointed Military Commander of the Manhattan Project and promoted to Lieutenant General. Twenty years later, at the end of his personal account of the Project, General Groves relates how as a boy living with his father at a number of the Army posts that had sprung up during the Indian wars in the Western United States he had heard at first hand the stories of the old soldiers and scouts who had devoted their lives to 'winning the West' and had become dismayed at the thought that there was nothing left for him to do. Yet after the successful testing of the world's first atomic bomb at Alamogordo on 16 July 1945, the General understood how none of the participants would ever succumb to such doubts again: 'We know now,' he declared, 'that when man is willing to make the effort he is capable of accomplishing virtually anything.' The feat of General Groves and his team had all but relegated the winning of the West to the rank of a mere historical episode; the Manhattan Project, Groves informs readers in the preface to his memoirs, must be recognised as 'the greatest scientific and technical achievement of all time'.[8] This was also the view expressed during the war to Senator Truman by Groves's civilian superior, the American Secretary of War, Henry Stimson. When Truman in his then capacity as Chairman of a Senate Committee investigating the national defence programme requested information from Stimson concerning the top secret and mysterious (Manhattan) project, he recalls Stimson informing him, 'I can't tell you what it is but it is the greatest project in the history of the world.'[9]

Now whatever their horror at the nature of the weapon that they initially believed ethical and political considerations allowed them no choice but to make, those scientists employed on the Manhattan Project also knew and relished the fact that making the bomb would be a fantastic challenge to their scientific and technological expertise and they also knew and relished the fact that they would be making history — the world after the atomic bomb would be qualitatively different from the world before the atomic bomb. This was a feature of the Manhattan Project appreciated not only by its protagonists. In internment by the British following Germany's surrender, the physicist Max von Laue told his German colleagues on 6 August 1945, after hearing of the destruction of Hiroshima: 'When I was a boy I wanted to do physics and watch the world make history. Well, I have done physics and I have seen the world make history. I will be able to say that to my dying day.'[10] From among many published examples of scientific fervour within the Manhattan Project I quote from a representative few to give the flavour of the history-making awareness of leading participants.

In his book *Atomic Quest* the American physicist and Nobel laureate Arthur Compton, who had been placed in charge of the Chicago Metallurgical Laboratory which was to produce the world's first uranium reactor and hence initiate the production of plutonium, reported a near rebellion 'among our men' when in June 1942 he told them that industrial production of a full-scale reactor would have to be taken out of their hands. His men's point of view, he confesses, was very understandable — for 'here was perhaps the greatest technological gift of science to mankind that would be made in all history' and the physicist pioneers of the Metallurgical Laboratory not unreasonably 'wished to present it to the world as a completed achievement'. Indeed, in the opinion of one member of Compton's team, Edward Creutz, the Chicago physicists were engaged in what appeared to him to be 'undeniably the most far-reaching and significant project in the history of man', a project that could well be, the physicist thought, 'the determining factor in the continued existence of civilisation itself'.[11] Disappointed as they were, these physicists did, however, enjoy the satisfaction of achieving the world's first chain reaction when, in the words of Compton, 'on 2 December 1942 in the city of Chicago, USA, man first liberated and controlled the power within the atom'. How well Compton remembers that historic moment and particularly the behaviour of the reactor team's leader, Enrico Fermi. In that 'moment of great achievement', Compton recalls, the face of Fermi was not elated but 'swarthy, alert, and in full control of his experimental crew as is the captain of a ship engaged in critical action'. Certainly Captain Fermi's voyage had truly achieved its history-making objective: not only had Fermi's crew supported him all the way, unlike Captain Walton's faint-hearted sailors, but the land they had reached, once so hidden and remote, was truly to become the gateway to the immense continent of nuclear power and energy. 'The Italian navigator has just landed in the new world' was Compton's coded and triumphant telephone message to the Chairman of the S-1 (Atomic Bomb) Committee. Even more vividly, however, than the Italian navigator's face Compton remembers the face of the Du Pont representative and future president, Crawford Greenewalt: 'His eyes were aglow. He had seen a miracle.' To the few human beings who knew of this miraculous event, Compton dramatically explains, 'it was a turning point in history, the birth of a new era'.[12]

That historic birth was to be the prelude to an industrial follow-up on a huge scale, a follow-up scarcely less dramatic than the birth process itself. Thus, writing of the Oak Ridge 'calutron' designed to separate the rare isotope of uranium (U-235) from natural uranium, Compton vividly describes the 'spirit of adventure' that is necessarily associated with the establishment of a new industrial operation: 'the hope of success,' he tells us, 'the fear of failure, the challenge of great new possibilities, the life-stuff of intense effort, hard-working days and sleepless nights.' Even though, Compton writes, the ultimate objective of the Oak Ridge plant was known only to a few men, he stresses that its thousands of workers nevertheless still enjoyed 'a sense of sharing in the making of history'. And a little further on in his book he emphasises what a 'thrilling experience' it had been for him to share in the 'development of the great [plutonium] production plant at Hanford'.[13]

While Hanford and Oak Ridge were designed to provide the necessary fissile ingredients for nuclear weapons (plutonium and uranium-235 respectively), the challenge of making the bomb itself was assigned to the staff of the newly created laboratory at Los Alamos under the scientific directorship of J. Robert Oppenheimer. Appointed by Groves (despite the General's knowledge of his left-wing views during the 1930s and his still remaining connections with communist sympathisers), the influence and prestige of Oppenheimer were important factors in the decisions of leading physicists to work at Los Alamos. There were, of course, many other reasons. In addition to the entirely justified and widespread fear of the Nazis, it is clear that the scientific challenge of designing and constructing the bomb was also a powerful motivating force in the minds of many of the future stars of Los Alamos. Thus, when in April

1942 Arthur Compton first offered him the task of co-ordinating activities on the bomb's design and construction, Oppenheimer declared that he 'felt sufficiently informed and challenged by the problem to be glad to accept'.[14] When in turn Oppenheimer invited Hans Bethe to join him at Los Alamos, Bethe agreed, in part because although he apparently considered radar more militarily important than atomic energy, he considered the latter more scientifically challenging. As for Enrico Fermi, who joined Los Alamos after his experimental triumph at Chicago, his friend Emilio Segrè could write: 'I sometimes thought Fermi believed that when the noise and excitement of the hour had long been forgotten, only physics would last and assert its perennial value.'[15] Indeed, in the opinion of Isidor Rabi, winner of the Nobel Prize in 1944, the Manhattan Project was no less than 'the culmination of three centuries of physics'. What a challenge, then, to bring the Project to successful fruition! 'Fermi,' as Segrè explains, 'completely immersed himself in the task.'[16] For younger scientists, however, not only was making the bomb a great scientific challenge but it also gave them a unique opportunity of knowing and working with world-famous physicists. The then young and unknown Richard Feynman, who worked under Hans Bethe, recalls how he met 'very great men' at Los Alamos, that it was 'one of the greatest experiences' of his life to have met all those 'wonderful physicists', singling out for special mention 'the great mathematician', John von Neumann, and remarking that even to the 'big shot guys' Niels Bohr was a 'great god'.[17]

Immediately after the war the Director of Los Alamos, Robert Oppenheimer, conveniently enumerated what he saw as the various motives that had induced scientists to come to the remote weapons laboratory. Certainly, he affirmed, there was the initial fear of Nazi Germany's nuclear potential; there was also straightforward curiosity and a sense of adventure; there was the desire to make the bomb, if it was possible to do so, in order that the world might know of its awesome destructive power and hence strengthen, he hoped, a future postwar resolve to abolish war for ever; there was the belief that if the bomb was going to be developed anywhere the chance of disaster was smallest if the bomb was developed in the United States. But these were not the rock-bottom reasons why the bomb was made. 'When you come right down to it,' Oppenheimer explained, the reason that we did this job is because it was an organic necessity. If you are a scientist you cannot stop such a thing. If you are a scientist you believe that it is good to find out how the world works; that it is good to find out what the realities are; that it is good to turn over to mankind at large the greatest possible power to control the world and to deal with it according to its lights and values.[18]

(Turn over to mankind at large! Perhaps it is not irrelevant to bear in mind that Oppenheimer and the Los Alamos physicists turned over the bomb to a handful of very economically privileged and powerful white male Americans.) Nearly ten years after the war Oppenheimer would once again explain his success in recruiting scientists to the unpleasant isolation of a pioneer settlement in the New Mexico desert by repeatedly stressing the undeniable challenge of Los Alamos: 'Almost everyone realised that this was a great undertaking. Almost everyone knew if it were completed successfully and rapidly enough, it might determine the outcome of the war. Almost everyone knew that it was an unparalleled opportunity to bring to bear the basic knowledge and art of science for the benefit of his country. Almost everyone knew that this job, if it were achieved, would be part of history.'[19]

History was indeed made and the world irrevocably altered when some two years and three months after Kitty and Robert Oppenheimer had arrived at Los Alamos and some two months after the defeat of Germany a plutonium bomb was detonated on 16 July 1945 at Alamogordo in the New Mexico desert. The events that followed exceeded the wildest expectations of the assembled physicists. Emilio Segrè, watching the nuclear explosion, wrote afterwards that although he knew it was not possible (disregarding error!) he nevertheless thought for a moment that the explosion might set fire to the atmosphere and thus destroy the earth's entire biosphere. 'Even though the purpose was grim and terrifying,' Segrè wrote, '[the Alamogordo test] was one of the greatest physics experiments of all time.' Recalling the satisfaction and pride the physicists felt in their work, Segrè enthusiastically declared that their feat would stand 'as a great monument of human endeavour for a long time to come'.[20] The physicists, however, were not the only ones impressed with the power of the bomb they had made. As soon as possible after the test explosion General Groves had sent a triumphal cable to Henry Stimson who, as a member of the American delegation to the Potsdam conference, was anxiously awaiting news of the test. 'For the first time in history there was a nuclear explosion,' Groves exultantly informed Stimson. 'And what an explosion!' In the words of Groves's deputy, General Farrell, the Los Alamos scientists had unleashed forces 'heretofore reserved to The Almighty'.[21] While the Nazi atomic bomb project had, it turned out, been all but a non-starter — according to the Los Alamos scientist Joseph O. Hirschfelder, 'the sheer magic of large-scale atomic energy was too fantastic for Hitler to comprehend' — the scientists and engineers gathered together in Los Alamos had, in the opinion of Hirschfelder, produced more than mere magic. 'In a period of two and a half years,' Hirschfelder glowingly records, 'they produced the miracle — an atomic bomb which creates temperatures of the order of 5,000,000° Centigrade... and pressures of the order of 20,000,000 atmospheres... while unleashing the tremendous energy stored in the atomic nuclei.'[22]

Such, then, was the apocalyptic nature of the bomb that had been personally witnessed by the Los Alamos scientists, originally so concerned that Nazi Germany might be ahead of the United States, but who intensified the momentum of their work until, and even after, the bomb was tested in the New Mexico desert more than two months after the surrender of Germany. It seems reasonably clear, however, that a principal reason why the physicists pushed so vigorously ahead to the Alamogordo climax of their work resulted from their knowledge that a successful atomic explosion would represent a major landmark in history and the physicists undoubtedly did not wish to be denied establishing this historic landmark by the surrender of Nazi Germany. One might appreciate this a little more clearly by recalling one of the reasons advanced by Isidor Rabi against the complete militarisation of the Los Alamos laboratory, namely that Los Alamos represented 'the culmination of three centuries of physics'. Nearly three centuries earlier there had existed in Europe an expectation that the *annus mirabilis* of 1666 would mark the return of Christ to the earth in the Second Coming. As it happened, the decade of the 1660s did see the establishment of the Royal Society of London and the Paris Academy of Sciences with their message of ever-deepening penetration into the secrets of nature for the benefit of mankind. At the beginning of the twentieth century it even seemed that men of science might be able to achieve the impossible through discovery of the philosopher's stone. By the early 1940s that hope had become a certainty. For the very first time on earth metals could and would be transmuted with the release of enormous quantities of energy. It seems only too plausible that by early 1945 the enormity of what the Los Alamos scientists were doing had taken precedence over the political reason why they were doing it and the surrender of Germany was neither here nor there — perhaps perceived rather as a threat to the continuation of their project. As Hirschfelder tells us, the Los Alamos scientists eventually produced not mere (successful) magic but a *miracle*. According to Rabi, 'Los Alamos just simply rose to the occasion and worked miracles, absolute miracles.'[23] Could Christ Himself have done better? (Indeed, how vividly Bacon's confidence comes to mind that the natural magic he advocated would eventually produce 'miracles', the effects generated so overwhelmingly exceeding the 'slight' causes — in the case of Trinity the stupendous effects being produced by the 'mere' implosion of a small hollow ball of metal.) Before I examine further the total dedication of the Los Alamos physicists to their apocalyptic task and the grim consequences that resulted, I want to demonstrate what I think is the surprising pervasiveness of sexual and birth metaphors in the writings of some of the scientists and their associates — a further indication, perhaps, that together with very worldly considerations and ambitions a powerful subterranean motivation was at least in part determining the actions of principal 'actors' at Los Alamos.

The pregnant phallus

In what one might take to be the austerely asexual world of theoretical and experimental physics practised at Los Alamos, it is surely remarkable how both sexual and birth metaphors frequently make an appearance in the writings, memoirs and reminiscences of participants. I give below, as an example, some direct and allusive sexual imagery used by or about two of the principal protagonists at Los Alamos. More examples will follow in due course.

Despite the 'tremendous intellectual power' manifested by

Oppenheimer — 'intellectual sex appeal' is the phrase used by an admiring colleague — Oppenheimer at the age of nearly forty had not displayed sufficient creative power to warrant the award of the coveted Nobel Prize. 'He was a dilettante,' explained one of his graduate students, David Bohm. 'He just would not... get stuck in. He'd got the ability, certainly, but he hadn't got the staying power.' Oppenheimer, however, was to refute this adverse assessment of what appears to be his masculinity, at least with respect to the quality of his scientific directorship of Los Alamos. He had, after all, been recommended by Ernest Lawrence as combining 'solid common sense' with 'penetrating insight' into the theoretical aspects of the whole bomb programme. After having made fun of the title of 'Co-ordinator of Rapid Rupture' bestowed on an unfortunate Gregory Breit (who had been charged with overall responsibility for the atomic bomb's design) Oppenheimer himself donned this 'wonderful title' before accepting scientific responsibility for the embryonic laboratory at Los Alamos.[24] Progress was rapid. By July 1943 the new laboratory — described proudly by Arthur Compton as 'a child of our Metallurgical Project' — had already achieved 'full vigour and independence'.[25] In his widely read history of the atomic scientists, Robert Jungk reports how carefree was the attitude of the laboratory's physicists at the start of their project, illustrated, in Jungk's view, by the 'thoroughly naughty' limerick with which, he claims, Edward Teller greeted his colleagues in a seminar describing the 'intimate' mechanism of the bomb whereby a 'subcritical' projectile of uranium-235 is fired sufficiently quickly into a receptacle of similar uranium in order to produce the most violent explosion ever known on earth.[26] Male scientific penetration into the secrets of female nature was to produce, it would seem, an undeniable demonstration of the virility of Los Alamos physicists in the 'birth', as we shall see, of a 'baby boy' of unprecedented vigour.[27]

Lest it be thought that considerations of manly status were out of place at Los Alamos, the writings of the Harvard professor of chemistry, George Kistiakowsky, suggest otherwise. Contrary to the experience of most, Kistiakowsky had managed to establish the happy state of affairs of amicable relations with General Groves which he ascribed to Groves's appreciation of the 'really hard, tough and dirty work' that Kistiakowsky performed in the manufacture of high chemical explosives. Because of his association with what many considered to be such 'very dangerous' work, General Groves accepted Kistiakowsky as, in the chemist's words, 'a sort of kindred spirit', as altogether 'more manly than the effete physicists'.[28] If, however, as Simone de Beauvoir suggests, it is not in giving life but in risking life that men acquire superior masculine status, then some of the physicists were also undeniable contenders for such honours. In the Metallurgical Laboratory at Chicago a 'suicide squad' had anxiously waited on a platform above the uranium reactor, ready to throw buckets of cadmium solution over the pile should the chain reaction get out of control. There can be no doubt that measuring the critical masses of plutonium and the more readily fissile isotope of uranium was extremely dangerous work as Otto Frisch, the physicist in charge of the measurements at Los Alamos, makes very clear. He himself almost suffered a lethal dose of radiation when in an experiment involving a mass of uranium with no reflecting material around it — named, we are told, the Lady Godiva assembly 'for obvious reasons' — Frisch had leant forward and had hastily to withdraw blocks of the uranium compound. 'It was clear to me what had happened,' Frisch graphically writes. 'By leaning forward I had reflected some neutrons back into Lady Godiva and thus caused her to become critical.' Even in the masculine and very serious work of determining the uranium bomb's critical mass, the metaphor of male penetration into female nature with its potentially fatal consequences for the penetrator is strikingly conveyed. (Unhappily, only a week after the end of the war with Japan, a physicist, Harry Daghlian, was fatally irradiated in an experiment similar to the one in which Frisch had come so close to losing his life. The following year on 21 May the physicist Louis Slotin, who had successfully assembled the plutonium weapon for the Trinity test, was likewise fatally irradiated.)[29]

The central problem confronting the Los Alamos scientists was how to bring subcritical masses of either uranium-235 or plutonium into contact quickly enough and thereby create a violent explosion rather than a relatively harmless radioactive fizzle. In the terminology used by the Los Alamos scientists, Jungk explains, the problem was to give birth to a boy and not to a girl.[30] Since the detonating procedure with scarce uranium-235 was reasonably straightforward, the Los Alamos physicists decided that the uranium gun need not be tested before use and that the first uranium bomb under construction, optimistically given a masculine gender and named 'Little Boy', could, when ready, be sent directly to the Pacific for immediate use against Japan. A prior test of the plutonium weapon, however, which involved a highly intricate implosion device, was deemed essential. Optimistically christened 'Fat Boy' or 'Fat Man' and originally scheduled for detonation on 14 July 1945 the test would dramatically symbolise the end of the bomb's long gestation period and would tell the physicists once and for all whether they had fathered a dud or a success, a girl or a boy. Kenneth Bainbridge, the physicist in charge of the so-called 'Trinity' test, who was rather mysteriously asked by Groves's deputy General Farrell to keep Oppenheimer away from the bomb and firing tower until the day of the test, remembers the impracticality of the request: 'No way! The bomb was Robert's baby and he would and did follow every detail of its development until the very end.'[31] Temporarily on leave following the death of his wife from tuberculosis, Richard Feynman relates how, on receiving a telegram informing him 'The baby is expected on such and such a day', he arrived in Los Alamos just in time to witness the birth of the physicists' fully grown monster, the event that, in the words of Kistiakowsky, was 'the emotional climax of wartime Los Alamos'.[32]

The emotional climax of Trinity, as it affected Oppenheimer in the control shelter some 10,000 yards from the explosion, is graphically described in General Farrell's report of the explosion. The metaphor of 'pregnant phallus' does seem particularly appropriate. 'Dr Oppenheimer,' Farrell writes, 'grew tenser as the last seconds ticked off. He scarcely breathed. He held on to a post to steady himself. For the last few seconds, he stared ahead and then when the announcer shouted "Now!" and there came this tremendous burst of light followed shortly thereafter by the deep growling roar of the explosion, his face relaxed into an expression of tremendous relief.' This relief was shared by all present. 'All the pent-up emotions were released in those few minutes,' Farrell continues, and he mentions in particular how 'Dr Kistiakowsky, the impulsive Russian, threw his arms around Dr Oppenheimer and embraced him with shouts of glee.'[33] (It should be noted in fairness to Kistiakowsky that he has indignantly denied that he thus 'lost his self-control and embraced and kissed Oppenheimer'. All he did, he claims, was 'slap him on the back' and remind him that he, Kistiakowsky, had won their bet.)[34] To the delight of the physicists their labours had been successful beyond their most extravagant expectations: their baby was indeed a magnificent boy. 'Atomic fission,' wrote Farrell, 'was almost full grown at birth.'[35] Two days after the test President Truman's Secretary of War, Henry Stimson, attending a meeting of the 'Big Three' at Potsdam, was delighted to receive a cable from Washington which, after decoding, read:

> Doctor has just returned most enthusiastic and confident that the little boy is as husky as his big brother. The light in his eyes discernible from here to Highhold and I could have heard his screams from here to my farm.

The cable, write Hewlett and Anderson, the official historians of the American Atomic Energy Commission, was intended to convey to Stimson that the plutonium bomb was 'as potent as the uranium gun'.[36] It was not unreasonable that the officers who had decoded the message believed that Stimson had really become a father at the age of 77 and wondered if the conference would be adjourned for a day's celebration at such a virile feat![37]

The most secret of wartime projects had, one might say, reached the end of a most successful confinement. The labour of scores of thousands of men and women had been necessary to build the bomb but only a handful of men were present at the monster's secret and most conclusive birth. Since not even the wives of the leading Los Alamos physicists were supposed to know what their husbands were doing or making, the contemptuous observation of the aboriginal woman that 'men make secret ceremonies, women make babies' still appears valid if a rather crucial qualification is added, namely that the secret ceremonies now really and truly worked![38] Indeed this is how the secret ceremony at Alamogordo appeared to the one (male) reporter, William Laurence, privileged to witness at first hand the successful birth:

> The big boom came about a hundred seconds after the great flash — the first cry of a new-born world. It brought the silent,

motionless silhouettes to life, gave them a voice. A loud cry
filled the air. The little groups that hitherto had stood rooted to
the earth like desert plants broke into a dance — the rhythm
of primitive man dancing at one of his fire festivals at the
coming of spring. They clapped their hands as they leaped from
the ground — earthbound man symbolising the birth of a new
force.[39]

Alamogordo was therefore not 'man's rubbish' as the aboriginal
woman had so unkindly described male rituals — at least not in a
technological sense for the test had been stupendously successful.
But in another, more human sense the aboriginal woman's description
appears untruthful only in its generosity to such male endeavour.
For the new magicians of the 'masculine philosophy' had in successfully pursuing nature to her hiding places produced a monster
from which even Dr Frankenstein himself might have shrunk back
in fear before the last irrevocable step had been taken.

Why was this last step taken? In giving his explanation Feynman
has commented: 'You see, what happened to me — what happened
to the rest of us — is we *started* for a good reason, then you're working very hard to accomplish something and it's a pleasure, it's excitement. And you stop thinking, you know; you just *stop*.' The question
I have asked, however, is why did the undoubted pleasure and excitement of building an atomic bomb exclude a continuing political and
moral assessment of the project's aim in the light of changing circumstances? Why, in other words, did the scientists of Los Alamos
not follow Joseph Rotblat's example and leave the project at the time
of Germany's defeat, or at the very least scale down their effort
instead of, in the event, intensifying it?[40] Why were they so prepared
to obey to the letter political directives from above? Part of the
answer, I have suggested, lies perhaps in the 'fact' that the physicists
were not only anxious to stamp and be the first to stamp their
masculine power of intellect upon the world through their historic
building of the atomic bomb but that, driving them relentlessly forward, was a subterranean desire to demonstrate once and for all the
unique creativity of the male vis-à-vis the female. Alas, as Mary
Shelley persuasively suggests in *Frankenstein*, an obsessive male
desire to outdo women in creative ability can only too easily lead to

tragic consequences, especially when that obsession takes the form of loveless, masculine 'penetration' into nature. To his credit, however, Frankenstein did try to 'give birth' to a *living* thing. The Los Alamos scientists, on the other hand, caught up in a harshly masculine world, were attempting to give birth to the most potent instruments of death then conceivable, two nuclear weapons which they affectionately christened with the male names, Little Boy and Fat Man. But, like Frankenstein, the physicists found that the challenge of creating a 'monster' is one thing; the challenge of keeping control over it in a masculine world is quite another.

The Release of the Monster: From Potsdam to Hiroshima and Nagasaki

The masculine world of Potsdam

Whatever the original motives of the Manhattan scientists for making the bomb, General Groves has avowed that there was no doubt in his mind or in the mind of any responsible person he knew that the atomic bomb was a war weapon and, as such, would certainly be used against the enemies of the United States. The world war would thus be brought to its speediest possible end. However, in Groves's eyes the two Axis powers, Germany and Japan, were not the only enemies of the United States as he made clear in testimony at Oppenheimer's 1954 security hearings: 'There was never from about two weeks from the time I took charge of this project any illusion on my part but that Russia was our enemy and that the project was conducted on that basis.' The distinguished mathematician John von Neumann, who had been a member of Groves's 'Target Committee', also shared the General's strategic view: 'I considered Russia as an enemy from the beginning and the alliance with Russia as a fortunate accident that two enemies had quarrelled.'[41] In view of the efforts of some of the Chicago-based scientists to prevent the dropping of nuclear weapons on Japan and, as they saw it, the inevitable start of a nuclear arms race between the United States and the Soviet Union it will be worthwhile to present briefly some principal arguments underpinning the much discussed thesis that the bombings of Hiroshima and Nagasaki were intended as much to intimidate the

Soviet Union as to bring the Far East war to a conclusion satisfactory to the United States. Put at its briefest and starkest this 'revisionist' thesis is that the atomic destructions of Hiroshima and Nagasaki were undertaken in the expectation of compelling the Soviet Union to allow 'free elections' in Eastern European countries, thereby giving rise to governments favourable to America and Britain rather than to the Soviet Union, while at the same time ensuring a Japanese surrender to the United States and consequently avoiding a Soviet share in the occupation of Japan.

It is certainly not difficult to show that the problem of relations with the Soviet Union was uppermost in the minds of American and British leaders as the world war came to an end. The extent of Churchill's foreboding after the Nazi surrender on 7 May 1945 can be gauged by terse sentences expressed in his war memoirs: 'Japan was still unconquered. The atomic bomb was still unborn. The world was in confusion. The main bond of common danger which had united the Great Allies had vanished overnight. The Soviet menace, to my eyes, had already replaced the Nazi foe.'[42] This was apparently a view shared by the American government. As early as March 1945 General Groves had recommended that the Auer company's metal refining works at Oranienburg outside Berlin should be bombed out of existence. Since these works, which would lie in the agreed Russian zone of occupation, produced metallic uranium and could not be dismantled in time before the Russians took over — and moreover the United States had agreed by treaty not to dismantle factories before withdrawing into their zone of occupation — the prudence of Groves's recommendation was appreciated in Washington and approval for the raid granted. On 15 March the factory was bombed into ruins with a saturation attack by over 600 Flying Fortresses.[43]

The day following Roosevelt's death on 12 April 1945, President Truman, who had become Vice-President on 20 January that year, received a briefing on the atomic bomb by James Byrnes, the influential ex-Senator he was to appoint in early July to be his Secretary of State. Some two years earlier Byrnes, in his then capacity as Director of War Mobilisation, had been briefed by President Roosevelt — and he would later write with what 'obvious pleasure' the President had imparted the information — that a secret weapon of incredible destructive power was being developed. Now Byrnes was to relay this information to the man who had so unexpectedly assumed command of the Armed Forces of the United States and who up till then had been told virtually nothing of the Manhattan Project. The new President was astounded to learn from Byrnes, as he recalled later, that the atomic bomb employed 'an explosive great enough to destroy the whole world' and, very significantly, that the new weapon 'might well put us in a position to dictate our own terms at the end of the war'. Subsequently Truman nominated Byrnes to be his special representative on the so-called Interim Committee, then being set up by Stimson with the task of giving advice on policy decisions relating to the existence and use of the atomic bomb. The conviction that had been expressed to President Truman concerning the possible diplomatic force of the atomic bomb was further clarified when, at the end of May, a deputation of three scientists spoke to Byrnes of their anxiety that use of atomic weapons against Japan might precipitate a nuclear arms race between the United States and the Soviet Union. The indefatigable Leo Szilard, who had initiated the meeting, later confessed himself 'completely flab-bergasted by [Byrnes's] assumption that rattling the bomb might make Russia more manageable [in Europe]'![44]

Further explicit evidence of the linkage between Japan, the atomic bomb and the Soviet Union in the planning by senior members of Truman's administration is revealed by the dissimula-tion displayed by Stimson and General Marshall in an important White House meeting on 29 May. This meeting had been called to discuss a major policy proposal brought by the Acting Secretary of State, Joseph Grew, which argued the case that an immediate call be made to Japan to surrender but that the defeated nation be allowed to retain its sacred institution of the Emperor. It was the opinion of the former ambassador to Japan that the 23 and 25 May fire bombings of Tokyo might have convinced a majority of Japanese leaders of the wisdom of accepting such a surrender offer. America, Grew felt, had a lot to gain and little to lose by making such an offer. Were it ac-cepted by the Japanese government the United States would neither need to invade Japan nor require Soviet entry into the Far East war, and consequently a Russian share in the occupation of Japan would be avoided. The negative side of the proposal would be the very considerable risk of provoking a showdown with the Soviet Union (for on 28 May Stalin had told Ambassador Harriman that the Red Army would strike at the Japanese army in Manchuria by 8 August and would expect to share in Japan's eventual occupation). Favourable discussion of Grew's proposal was, however, terminated when General Marshall abruptly declared that while he accepted the document in principle 'publication at this time would be premature'.[45]

Noting in his diary what an 'awkward meeting' it had been since people had been present with whom he could not discuss 'the real feature which would govern the whole situation, namely S-1 [the American code name for the atomic bomb]', Stimson records how he, Marshall and the Assistant Secretary of War 'stayed and discussed the situation of Japan and what we should do in regard to S-1 and the application of it'.[46] Clearly the terms and timing of any genuine surrender call to Japan could not be sensibly discussed independently of the possible use of the atomic bomb and the effect of such use on the Soviet Union. The most depressing possible thesis that suggests itself as a consequence of the abortive White House meeting is that top American leaders deliberately wished to prolong the war until the atomic bomb could be dropped on Japan, with the expectation of thereby bringing the war to an immediate end accompanied by the many 'desirable' consequences which would follow from successful intimidation of the Soviet Union.[47]

Whatever Stimson's ultimate objectives he did in the first week of June explain to President Truman his objections to the saturation bombing of Japanese cities that had been taking place. And sobering objections they are too. It was not just that Stimson did not want the United States to gain the reputation of outdoing Hitler in atrocities, he was also 'a little fearful', he notes in his diary, that the Air Force would have so thoroughly destroyed Japan that 'the new weapon would not have a fair background to show its strength'. Stimson also records in his diary that 'Truman laughed and said he understood'.[48]

On the last day of May the Interim Committee and its Scientific Panel convened to discuss the policy to be adopted towards the Soviet Union regarding S-1, the device which, the Scientific Panel was informed by Stimson, could turn out to be 'a Frankenstein which would eat us up' or the means 'by which the peace of the world would be helped in becoming secure'.[49] When, however,

General Marshall made the tentative (and, in my opinion, very positive) suggestion that the Soviet Union be officially informed of the Manhattan Project and invited to send two scientists to observe the testing of the plutonium weapon, Truman's special representative on the Committee took strong exception. As far as Byrnes was concerned, Stalin should be given no information about the Manhattan Project and that 'the best policy was to push production and research and make certain that the United States stayed ahead'. We are told that no dissent was expressed in the Committee. According to the official historians of the Manhattan Project: 'Such a strong statement by a man of Byrnes's prestige was not to be dismissed lightly. All present indicated their concurrence.'[50] It was only after strong pressure from Chicago scientists that the Interim Committee conceded at its meeting on 21 June that the President might advise Stalin at their coming conference, 'if suitable opportunity arose', that the United States was developing atomic weapons and expected to use such weapons against Japan, but the Committee advised against the giving of any additional information to the Soviet government. The masculine world of Potsdam was being set up.[51]

In their discussion of 6 June President Truman had told Stimson that he had successfully managed to gain a two-week postponement of his coming Potsdam meeting with Churchill and Stalin. Originally scheduled for early July, the meeting had been conveniently re-scheduled to begin on 15 July, one day after the provisional date set for the Trinity test.[52] Obviously the senior Los Alamos physicists could not have been unaware of a political connection between Trinity and Potsdam. Remembering how Oppenheimer had told him in early July of the approaching meeting of the Big Three in Potsdam, the physicist in charge of the Trinity test, Kenneth Bainbridge, recalls how he had understood that 'a successful test was a card which Truman had to have in his hands'. Pressure mounted on the physicists from the Truman administration and the physicists responded as positively as they could. 'Instructions from Washington were that no day was to be lost,' the head of the 'Gadgets Division' writes, 'and it wasn't.'[53] Even safety considerations seem to have been disregarded by the Truman administration. For when on 2 July Oppenheimer requested a three-day delay of the test on the grounds of safety requirements, the request was denied by

Groves who told Oppenheimer that the 'upper crust' wanted the test as soon as possible. Nevertheless, despite the intense efforts of the physicists the plutonium bomb could not be detonated until 16 July, one day before the Potsdam conference saw the first meeting between Truman and Stalin.[54]

The effect of the news of the successful test on the American and British leaders was electrifying. Cables arrived for Stimson on 16 and 18 July and General Groves's detailed report three days later. Churchill records how on 17 July an excited Stimson had told him the 'world-shaking news' by placing a sheet of paper before him bearing just three words, 'Babies satisfactorily born'.[55] When on 21 July Groves's account of the Trinity test arrived, Stimson read out in full the ecstatic report to both Truman and Byrnes. 'They were immensely pleased,' Stimson records in his diary. 'The President was tremendously pepped up by it... He said it gave him an entirely new feeling of confidence and he thanked me for having come to the conference and being present to help him in this way.' When on the next day Churchill read Groves's report the American Secretary of War was regaled with, 'Stimson, what was gunpowder? Trivial. What was electricity? Meaningless. This atomic bomb is the Second Coming in Wrath.'[56] (Perhaps, after all, God knew what he was doing when he sent the Royal Society and the Paris Academy in the 1660s!) According to Churchill, the reception of Groves's report changed Truman into a new man, one who stood up to Stalin, refusing to countenance Polish occupation of East Germany or to recognise the governments established in Rumania, Hungary and Finland. We seemed, wrote Churchill, 'to have become possessed of a merciful abridgement of the slaughter in the East and of a far happier prospect in Europe'.[57] In private, however, Churchill was even less restrained in his enthusiasm for the atomic bomb. Field Marshal Alanbrooke recalls how, the day after reading Groves's report, Churchill was quite carried away by the possibilities the bomb represented in his mind. He was, Alanbrooke comments, 'already seeing himself capable of eliminating all the Russian centres of industry and population without taking into account any of the connected problems, such as delivery of the bomb, production of bombs, possibility of Russians also possessing such bombs, etc. He had at once painted a wonderful picture of himself as the sole possessor of these bombs and capable of dumping them where he wished, thus all-powerful and capable of dictating to Stalin!'[58] Did, however, the Big Two explicitly tell Stalin of the atomic weapons being manufactured at Los Alamos? They did not. At the end of the next day's session (the day after Churchill's extravaganza to Alanbrooke) Truman casually mentioned to Stalin that the United States now possessed a new weapon of unusual destructive power. For his part, Truman recalls, Stalin replied equally casually that he was glad to hear it and hoped the Americans would make good use of the new weapon against Japan. Not a word was said by Truman to Stalin that the new weapon was in fact the atomic bomb![59] Even less was said to the nation that was to have the bomb dropped on it.

After a ten-day delay at Byrnes's insistence, a Declaration to Japan was broadcast from Potsdam on 26 July calling on the Japanese to surrender unconditionally or face the alternative of 'prompt and utter destruction'. At no point in the Declaration was the warning given that, failing Japanese surrender, a new weapon of devastating power would be used and even less was any mention made of the development of atomic weapons. Furthermore Stimson's suggestion that reference be made in the Declaration to the preservation of the institution of the Emperor had been firmly rejected by Truman and Byrnes. Why, then, was no mention made of the existence of atomic weapons? The answer would seem to be that if mention had been made at that time then Stalin would obviously have wanted details. Moreover, if such a mention had been made, especially if accompanied by a concession concerning the continuation of the imperial dynasty, then Japan might possibly have surrendered before atomic bombs could be dropped, so ending the war before Russia could enter it but without allowing Truman and Byrnes to demonstrate to Stalin the power of the new weapons and the readiness of the American administration to use them. If these were in fact the principal reasons why such an uncompromising and inadequate Declaration was made to Japan, then the Declaration achieved what it was intended to. On 28 July Japan officially rejected the Potsdam ultimatum and consequently on 6 and 9 August atomic weapons were dropped on Hiroshima and Nagasaki. Returning from Potsdam aboard the SS Augusta, an exultant President Truman was told of the news of Hiroshima's destruction and triumphantly proclaimed to the sailors around him that this was 'the greatest thing in history'.[60] Three days later on the day that Nagasaki was destroyed the President broadcast to the nation from the White House. In that broadcast Truman told the American people — and the Soviet government — that the Balkan countries were not to be in the sphere of influence of any one world power. It was the first verbal Presidential declaration of 'atomic diplomacy'.[61] On the following day the Japanese government duly offered to surrender to the United States subject only to the condition — despite the atomic bombardment! — that surrender would not 'prejudice the prerogatives of his Majesty as a Sovereign Ruler'. The American government in consultation with the British and Russians now found itself able to hint at an acceptance of this condition and Japan formally surrendered on 14 August. The American government had played its trump card.

Whether Truman and Byrnes, aided by a semi-reluctant Stimson, were as Machiavellian as the above paragraphs suggest they were is a matter of controversy. If they were, they must at times have had doubts in their minds as to the wisdom of the course they were pursuing, not to mention its humanity. Nevertheless, one historian of the Potsdam meeting is unequivocal in his assessment of Potsdam. Writing that the leader of a nation that is already strong and likely to become stronger in the future seeks in general to preserve international conflict and not to end it, Charles L. Mee argues that the question is misconceived as to whether the Cold War could have been avoided if Truman had been less combative, or if the United States had not exacerbated Stalin's paranoia, or if Russia's sphere of influence had simply been accepted. For the assumption is implicit in such questions that Truman wished to avoid conflict and was searching for tactics to assure a tranquil world. But, in Mee's laconic appraisal, 'very little that Truman did could be construed as part of a plan for tranquillity'. Indeed, Mee's analysis of the Potsdam conference leads him to the conclusion that the three principal participants were men 'who were intent upon increasing the power of their countries and of themselves and perceived that they could enhance their power more certainly in a world of discord than of tranquillity'. They were men who, when put to the test, proved manfully equal to the task of rescuing world discord from the 'threatened outbreak of peace'. As for the American aims behind the atomic bombing of Japan, Mee is emphatic:

> No one likes, or wants to confront, the fact — but it is clear
> from the events and conversations during the Potsdam conference
> that the use of the atomic bomb against Hiroshima and
> Nagasaki was wanton murder.[62]

A month after the tragic events of August no less a man than
Henry Stimson had decided that the 'atomic diplomacy' with which
the Soviet Union was being threatened was entirely misconceived
and would do irreparable harm to Soviet-American relations. Before
resigning his post as Secretary of War Stimson accordingly sent a last
memorandum to President Truman pleading with him to reconsider.
These are some of the points the President was asked to reflect on.
Unless the Soviet Union was invited to participate in the exploitation of atomic energy together with the United States and Britain
upon a basis of co-operation and trust, there would inevitably ensue,
Stimson stressed, and indeed it had already started, 'a secret
armament race of a rather desperate character'. The problem of
American-Soviet relations, the President was told, was not merely
connected with but 'virtually dominated by the problem of the
atomic bomb' and it would, Stimson thought, only invite disaster to
continue to negotiate with the Russians 'having this weapon rather
ostentatiously on our hip'. A direct and sincere offer had to be made
as soon as possible by the United States to the Soviet Union and
above all without first making 'a succession of express or implied
threats or near threats in our peace negotiations'. In Stimson's opinion, the old pattern of international relations had to be changed for
the atomic bomb was not simply another though more devastating
military weapon. The bomb, the Secretary of War told his President,
'caps the climax of the race between man's growing technical power
for destructiveness and his psychological power of self-control and
group control — his moral power'.[63] (I am so often irresistibly
reminded of Captain Walton's confiding remark to his sister, 'There
is something at work in my soul, which I do not understand'.)

Stimson's memorandum was to no avail. We shall see at the
beginning of Chapter 4 how it is clearly apparent that President
Truman and his Secretary of State James Byrnes firmly rejected the
last advice they were to be sent from their aged Secretary of War.

However, some six months before Henry Stimson changed his mind, rumblings of concern and apprehension were becoming audible on the part of some of the men who had played, but were playing no longer, a central role in the Manhattan Project. As early as December 1942 physicists at Chicago had received the following telegram from Ernest Lawrence, 'Congratulations to the parents. Can hardly wait to see the new arrival.'[64] They had already emphatically given birth, they had spent a year bringing up their plutonium-making children, and they were now turning round to look critically at those of their colleagues in the last throes of even more decisive labour.

Protest by physicists: too little, too late

If a principal objective of the Truman administration had been to use the atomic bomb in order to intimidate the Soviet Union into accepting American demands at the end of the war, then the aim of some of the Manhattan physicists to try to prevent conflict between the United States and the Soviet Union as a result of misconceived use of the atomic bomb seems in retrospect poignantly irrelevant. Although the concerted efforts of some Chicago physicists to prevent use of the bomb and the disastrous consequences they foresaw are the most well known (and which are summarised below), here and there solitary efforts had already been made by physicists to try to bring the Soviet Union directly into the Project.

The experimental physicist Robert Wilson (who has described himself as 'not particularly liberal' in his Los Alamos days) explained how he had once tried to convince Oppenheimer to go to Washington with the aim of persuading President Roosevelt to invite Soviet scientists to the weapons laboratory: 'Much easier to work things out later,' he had earnestly told Oppenheimer, 'if we had all developed the damned thing together.' He recalls that Oppenheimer, however, seemed to regard him as out of his mind![65] During 1944 Niels Bohr, by common consent the greatest living physicist after Einstein, had even managed to achieve meetings with Roosevelt and Churchill in the attempt to persuade them to co-operate with Russia *before* the bomb was built and tested. Let us only say the meetings were somewhat less than fruitful. In their Quebec conference of

September 1944 President Roosevelt and Prime Minister Churchill added a revealing postscript to their aide-memoire: 'Enquiries should be made,' the two leaders wrote, 'regarding the activities of Professor Bohr and steps taken to ensure that he is responsible for no leakage of information particularly to the Russians.'[66]

The Chicago scientists who, unlike their Los Alamos counterparts, were not involved in the fission bomb's design, constructing and testing consequently found time to debate at considerable length the political implications of the bomb's possible use, especially once the Hanford plants that were producing plutonium were found to be operating successfully. But by the time any of them attempted to take serious action it was already too late. As the European war neared its end the physicist most responsible for setting the Manhattan Project in motion attempted for a second time to write a dramatic letter to President Roosevelt. Ironically, however, Szilard's letter never reached the ailing President but instead it was James Byrnes who found himself reading the following advice from Szilard: 'Perhaps the greatest immediate danger which faces us is the probability that our "demonstration" of atomic bombs will precipitate a race in the production of these devices between the United States and Russia...' Returning to Chicago 'completely flabbergasted' after his disastrous end-of-May meeting with Brynes and more convinced than ever that use of the bomb on Japan would engulf the United States and the world in a new and horrifying arms race, Szilard together with the émigré physicist James Franck and five other Chicago scientists composed the memorandum that would become famous as the Franck Report.[67]

In this short but cogently written report the seven scientists argued their conviction that a surprise atomic attack on Japan would do untold harm to the standing of the United States in the world and would ruin any chances of achieving international control of atomic energy. 'It may be very difficult to persuade the world,' stressed the seven signatories, 'that a nation which was capable of secretly preparing and suddenly releasing a weapon as indiscriminate as the [German] rocket bomb and a million times more destructive, is to be trusted in its proclaimed desire of having such weapons abolished by international agreement.' Russia would certainly be shocked by such an attack on Japan but the consequences would be heightened Soviet suspicion of the United States and the building as quickly as possible of its own atomic armoury. The indiscriminate destruction resulting from an atomic attack would thus not only isolate the United States politically but would, the Franck Report emphatically warned, 'precipitate the race for armaments and prejudice the possibility of reaching an international agreement on the future control of such weapons'.[68]

By 11 June James Franck had taken the report to Washington and, accompanied by Arthur Compton, attempted to deliver it personally to Stimson. The attempt failed when an aide told them (untruthfully) that the Secretary was not in the capital. The report was then left in Washington together with an explanatory note from Compton which, however, turned out to be critical of the report's conclusions.[69] In any case Stimson was never to see the Chicago physicists' memorandum. Four days after Franck's failure in Washington the four physicists comprising the Scientific Panel of the Interim Committee (Arthur Compton, Enrico Fermi, Ernest Lawrence and Robert Oppenheimer) met to discuss the issue of the use of atomic weapons. Despite the fact that Arthur Compton was able to summarise for them the contents of the Franck Report, the Scientific Panel came to the conclusion that there was 'no acceptable alternative to direct military use' and recommended moreover that such use be implemented with no prior warning. The Panel did, however, hesitantly recommend to Stimson that the Russians be informed about the atomic bomb prior to its use against Japan, advice which the Interim Committee saw fit to endorse at its meeting on 21 June.[70] (As we have seen, President Truman did *not* explicitly mention to Stalin the existence of atomic weapons.)

Szilard then attempted to petition the President as he knew was his constitutional right. Signed by over fifty Chicago scientists the petition noted the increasing ruthlessness of aerial bombardment and respectfully requested the President not to escalate the already terrible destruction of Japanese cities with the added horror of atomic bombardment. That nation which first uses atomic bombs, the petition states, 'may have to bear the responsibility of opening the door to an era of devastation on an unimaginable scale'.[71] The Los Alamos physicists, however, with their fingers nearer the trigger singularly failed to take equivalent action — even when requested to do so by

Szilard. Refusing either to sign or to circulate Szilard's petition at Los Alamos, Edward Teller wrote to him on 2 July that the only way of abolishing atomic weapons was to abolish war and that the best way of accomplishing this would be to convince people that the next war would be fatal: 'For this purpose,' he told Szilard, 'actual combat use might even be the best thing' (ironically, this was the position that Szilard himself had held in January 1944!).[72] In a letter to Oppenheimer on 10 July Szilard hinted that the Scientific Director of Los Alamos had more effective ways than he to prevent the use of atomic weapons but declared that just from the point of view of the future public standing of scientists it would be a good thing for at least a minority of scientists to have shown that they put moral considerations above expediency.[73] But Oppenheimer was already working full time on the Trinity test. And after that successful test the physicists of Los Alamos had other urgent matters to think about, namely preparing weapons for use on Japanese cities. Bernard Feld recalls in particular how the members of Otto Frisch's assembly team had immediately drawn lots to decide who should go to the Pacific to assemble the weapons as they came in (and he remembers his disappointment when his name came up only at the fourth or fifth weapon). In any case, Szilard's Chicago petition was a nonstarter. Because James Franck and others had agreed to sign the petition only on the condition that the enterprising Szilard used no unorthodox channels of communication, the petition never reached the President. On 19 July (three days after the Trinity test) Szilard very properly gave the petition to Arthur Compton. Since the Potsdam conference was already under way, speed was of the utmost importance. On 24 July Compton gave the petition to an officer under General Groves who the next day gave it to his superior. It was on 1 August that Groves deposited the petition in Stimson's office.[74] By that time the Los Alamos physicists had dutifully completed the tasks the 'upper crust' required of them and Truman and Stimson were already attending the final day's meeting of the fateful Potsdam conference.

Priority, 'publication' and glory

On 6 August the detonation of the uranium weapon designed and constructed at Los Alamos virtually destroyed the city of Hiroshima, nearly 100,000 of its citizens being killed in just one blast from one bomb delivered from one specially modified B-29 plane. Designed, constructed and assembled by male physicists, the physicists' 'Little Boy' was delivered from the belly of the B-29 bomber manned by an all-male crew. There was, however, a symbolic female presence: the plane from whose belly 'Little Boy' was delivered was called after the pilot's mother, the *Enola Gay*.[75]

The Los Alamos physicists, then, had been the first to make the bomb, the first to test it, and the first to publish it to the world in most dramatic manner conceivable. How did the Manhattan scientists react to the news of Hiroshima's destruction? It is clear that in many cases human rejoicing at the last days of the war combined with human regret and remorse at the great loss of life were allied with or even swamped by masculine exultation at fantastic scientific-military success. A scientist guiltily recalled, after reading an account of the condition of survivors in Hiroshima, how in New York the evening of the day on which Hiroshima was bombed he had enjoyed a 'hastily arranged champagne dinner' with some forty of his colleagues and he recalled too the pride they had felt for their part in ending the war 'and even pride in the effectiveness of the weapon'.[76] At the weapons laboratory in Los Alamos Edward Teller described how before Hiroshima a member of the Women's Army Corps had told him that she was not looking forward to explaining to people at home that her war effort had consisted of driving 'someone name of Teller' from Los Alamos to the airport. Teller relates, however, that the attitude of military personnel at Los Alamos changed completely on the day Hiroshima was bombed. After Hiroshima he always got a smile when he showed his pass on entering the weapons laboratory.[77] . Robert Oppenheimer, on hearing the news of Hiroshima's destruction, apparently called the entire staff of the laboratory together for celebration. 'He entered that meeting like a prize fighter,' recalled one scientist. 'As he walked through the hall there were cheers and shouts and applause all round and he acknowledged them in the fighter's salute — clasping his hands together above his head as he came to the podium.'[78] Otto Frisch, who had himself been once so close to death from irradiation, remembers that he experienced a 'feeling of unease, indeed nausea' as he watched so many of his friends rushing to organise an over-dinner celebration of the death of nearly 100,000 people.[79] 'The only reaction I remember,' Richard Feynman recalls, '... was a very considerable elation and excitement. There were parties and people got drunk.' Thirty six years later Feynman looked back on what he remembers as contemporaneous events in Los Alamos and Hiroshima. 'It would make a tremendously interesting contrast, between what was going on in Los Alamos at the same time as what was going on in Hiroshima,' he commented. 'I was involved in this happy thing, drinking and drunk, sitting on the bonnet of a jeep and playing drums, excitement running all over Los Alamos at the same time as the people were dying and struggling in Hiroshima.'[80]

Three days after Hiroshima's destruction the already tested plutonium weapon, 'Fat Man', was dropped on Nagasaki. Tested the bomb had been but, as General Groves had written to Stimson in his ecstatic report of the Trinity test, 'We are all fully conscious that our real goal is still before us. The battle test is what counts in the war with Japan.' A scientist who had participated in the construction of this already tested bomb recalls the struggle in his own mind between his human and ultra masculine feelings: 'I dreaded the use of this "better bomb". I hoped that it would not be used and trembled at the thought of the devastation it would cause. And yet, to be quite frank, I was desperately anxious to find out whether this type of bomb would also do what was expected of it, in short, whether its intricate mechanism would work. These were dreadful thoughts, I know, and still I could not help having them.'[81] The bomb indeed did what was expected of it.

The reporter William Laurence who had been privileged to watch the Trinity test, was also allowed to witness the bombing of Nagasaki. At Alamogordo he had written eloquently how the Trinity test had appeared to him as a primitive (male) ritual celebrating the birth of a new force — a monstrous weapon of destruction symbolised, however, in terms of a male birth process. His description of the detonation of 'Fat Man' over Nagasaki reveals the same male fascination with birth imagery, in this case the birth of a living monster of almost indescribable destructive power. Watching 'Fat Man' being assembled the day before the bombing, Laurence described how he saw the weapon as 'being fashioned into a living hing, so exquisitely shaped that any sculptor would be proud to have created it'.[82] Forty-five seconds after the plutonium device had been dropped over Nagasaki a huge pillar of purple fire had already reached the altitude of Laurence's plane. 'Awestruck,' Laurence wrote,

> we watched it shoot upward like a meteor coming from the earth instead of from outer space, becoming ever more alive as it climbed skyward through the white clouds. It was a living thing, a new species of being, born right before our incredulous eyes.

A living thing! The male physicists had, virtually without direct female help, made *a living thing*. 'It was a living totem pole,' Laurence emphasised, 'carved with many grotesque masks grimacing at the earth.' Laurence's further description of the evolution of his 'living thing' vividly recalls the description that H.G. Wells had, some thirty years earlier, put into the terrified mind of a survivor of an atomic attack. This is Laurence's ecstatic description:

> Then, just when it appeared as though the thing had settled down into a state of permanence, there came shooting out of the top a giant mushroom that increased the height of the pillar to a total of 45,000 feet. The mushroom top was even more alive than the pillar, seething and boiling in a white fury of creamy foam, sizzling upward and then descending earthward, a thousand geysers rolled into one. It kept struggling in an elemental fury, like a creature in the act of breaking the bonds that held it down. In a few seconds it had freed itself from its gigantic stem and floated upward with tremendous speed... But at that instant another mushroom, smaller in size than the first one, began emerging out of the pillar. It was as though the decapitated monster was growing a new head. As the first mushroom floated off into the blue it changed its shape into a flowerlike form, its giant petals curving downward, creamy white outside, rose-coloured inside. It still retained that shape when we last gazed at it from a distance of about 200 miles. The boiling pillar of many colours could also be seen at that distance, a giant mountain of jumbled rainbows, in travail. Much living substance had

gone into those rainbows. The quivering top of the pillar was protruding to a great height through the white clouds, giving the appearance of a monstrous prehistoric creature with a ruff around its neck, a fleecy ruff extending in all directions, as far as the eye could see.[83]

How ironic that Simone de Beauvoir should write that woman' misfortune is to have been 'biologically destined for the repetition o life' — the mere and uninteresting repetition of life — and tha superiority has been justly accorded in humanity 'not to the sex tha brings forth but to that which kills'.[84] There would seem to exis even in male violence and destruction a repressed desire to give birt and that this repressed desire grotesquely manifests itself even when the killing has reached a new high in efficiency, scientific sophistica tion and terror.

How, finally, did the women of Los Alamos who were not scien tists react to their husbands' success and to their husbands' newly ac quired status as gigantic heroes?[85] An insight may be gleaned from the comments of Laura Fermi, wife of the Nobel laureate physicist 'They behaved as all women would under the same circumstances, she explained. 'Their first bewilderment turned into an immens pride in their husbands' achievement and, to a lesser degree, in thei own share in the project.'[86] If, however, Simone de Beauvoir's claim is true that a man's scientific and technological successes endow him with a 'virile prestige', then the comments of one of the wives woul seem rather grudging. Indicting the male heroes for social inadequac — 'Our good husbands were not too good at being lionised. It embar rassed them and they made no visible effort to improve' — Bernic Brode added provocatively, 'As a matter of fact they gave out com pletely, long before we wives were satisfied.'[87]

As for the effect of the physicists' new status on their children Laura Fermi recounts what seems to me the saddest of stories con cerning her eight-year-old son, Giulio, only two years old when th Fermis had left Italy at the end of 1938. 'In this country,' Giulio' mother relates, 'never hearing anything about his father's work, h underrated his father's role until Hiroshima and the explosion o comments that followed. Until then, Fermi was not an importan man to Giulio. At least, not as important as George's father who wa a Captain in the Army, as Giulio once said. Los Alamos gave a boost to his ego.' Despite such a boost, the proud wife had to acknowledge that 'Giulio himself never looked like the son of an important man'.[88] An important man! Perhaps, on reflection, it is entirely appropriate that J. Robert Oppenheimer, acclaimed as the 'father of the atomic bomb' and proud owner of the Medal of Merit awarded by President Truman, consented after Hiroshima to the honour of being appointed Father of the Year by the National Baby Institution.[89]

Perhaps, though, we might allow nature at Los Alamos through the medium of Edward Teller to make the final comment on what it had seen born at Alamogordo that summer. Recalling his last months at Los Alamos Teller writes: 'One non-technical event of great importance which all of us remember was the water shortage. In the fall of 1945 the snowfall came late, but frost came early... During the war I developed, somewhat to my surprise, two affections: a liking for strangers and the love of green grass. Both were in short supply. In the water shortage of 1945 the grass was dying.'[90]

On the other side of the world, the Manhattan Project had been watched by Soviet scientists with understandable anxiety. They, too, like their Western counterparts had been elated at the news of fission announced in 1939. The disappearance of the names of Fermi, Szilard, Teller and others from physics journals had informed Soviet physicists that fission research had been made a secret in the United States. By September 1942 the State Defence Committee had decided to finance a laboratory to examine the 'uranium problem', appointing Kurchatov as its scientific director. By the end of the European war only limited progress had been made with limited resources. It was, of course, obvious to Soviet experts why the Oranienburg uranium plant had been bombed out of existence: the Soviet Union was not to be allowed to profit in any way from the German atomic bomb project. As the Red Army entered Germany, however, Soviet officials took the opportunity of attempting to recruit into their uranium programme those German nuclear experts who had preferred not to flee westwards, such as Manfred von Ardenne, Peter-Adolf Thiessen and the Nobel laureate Gustav Hertz. (Hertz later explained that the reason he had preferred to go to Russia rather than America was because the United States possessed so many nuclear experts that he thought his work would be more appreciated in the Soviet Union.)

On learning of the successful Alamogordo test the professional vexation Kurchatov and his colleagues felt that America had beaten them to the bomb was overshadowed by their uncertainty and apprehension concerning American intentions. That uncertainty was not to last long. The atomic destruction of Hiroshima and Nagasaki shocked the Soviet leadership as both the Truman administration and its critics within the Manhattan Project knew that it would. But the realisation that the American government was prepared to use atomic weapons when the military situation did not absolutely call for their use brought not the intimidation of the Soviet Union as Truman and Byrnes believed it would, but rather Stalin's decision taken in the middle of August to implement a Soviet 'Manhattan Project' with no expenses spared. Subsequently, in August 1949, almost four years to the day from Stalin's decision, the Soviet Union detonated its first fission weapon.[91]

4. The Creation of the Hydrogen Bomb: 'One of the most fantastic adventures that a scientist can have'

The individual's specific transcendence takes concrete form in the penis and it is a source of pride... Today he still manifests this pride when he has built a dam or a skyscraper or an atomic pile. He has worked not merely to conserve the world as given; he has broken through its frontiers, he has laid down the foundations of a new future... Through the identification of phallus and transcendence, it turns out that his social and spiritual successes endow him with a virile prestige.

Simone de Beauvoir, *The Second Sex*

There is among some people a feeling of compulsion about the pursuit of advanced technologies — a sense that man must be continually proving his virility by pioneering on the frontiers of what is only just possible.

Arnold Pacey, *The Maze of Ingenuity*

It is not my intention to describe in detail the years between 1945 and 1949, the years in which many American physicists agonised over the morality of what had been done and sought to make amends as best they could. These were also the years in which leading American physicists were all but deluged with funds from an 'enlightened' American military and consequently possessed the means to wield considerable power not only over the direction of physics research but also over the lives of thousands of subordinates. The age of 'big physics' had definitely arrived.[1] Enhancing the appeal of physics to both government and military was the steadily worsening political antagonism between the United States and the

Soviet Union. This antagonism reached yet another and major crisis point when in the autumn of 1949 analysis following a B-52 flight showed conclusively that the Soviet Union had exploded its first atomic bomb. The nuclear arms race that had started in 1945 was now proceeding with both superpowers in possession of such monstrous weapons. In the last chapter we saw how the initial decision on the part of physicists to undertake the construction of atomic bombs was only in part, if in great part, caused by fear of Nazi Germany's possible future possession of such weapons. The conse-quences had been catastrophic for Hiroshima and Nagasaki and for the prospect of a just world peace. The consequences had, however, been good for physics. What, we now ask, were the principal reasons behind the controversial decision taken by key physicists in 1949 not merely to renew work on the hydrogen weapon but to undertake a crash programme for its construction, thus escalating the arms race another decisive and deadly step?

The masculine world of 'preventive war'

From the time of the successful Trinity test and particularly after the successful destruction of Hiroshima and Nagasaki, the thought of atomic bombardment of the Soviet Union had apparently found a home in the minds of many Western leaders. We recall how, on hear-ing the news of Trinity, Churchill had enthusiastically envisaged himself as being in a position at some time in the future of destroying at will all important Russian centres of industry and population and thus of dictating terms to the Soviet government. On the day Nagasaki was destroyed President Truman declared in an address to the American people that the Balkan states of Rumania and Bulgaria were not to be under the control of any one power, namely the Soviet Union. The following month at the London conference of foreign ministers Byrnes jocularly told Molotov that if he didn't behave pro-perly 'I am going to pull an atomic bomb out of my hip pocket and let you have it.'[2] A few weeks later Oppenheimer himself complained to the American Secretary of Commerce, Henry Wallace, about Byrnes's brandishing of the atomic bomb as a means of attempting to intimidate the Soviet Union into acceptance of American policy. At the beginning of November Oppenheimer felt concerned enough to complain publicly to the Association of Los Alamos Scientists that one's moral position was very weak indeed if one approached other nations with the bargaining stance: 'We know what is right and we would like to use the atomic bomb to persuade you to agree with us.'[3] Later that month Field Marshal Alanbrooke heard from General Douglas MacArthur, overall commander of American forces in the Pacific, that the Soviet Union was a greater menace than the Nazis had ever been, as exemplified by the story MacArthur claimed to have heard of a Russian commander issuing orders to his troops to rape twice every woman between the ages of 16 and 60 'as an example of the superiority of the Russian race'. MacArthur told Alanbrooke that at least 1,000 atomic bombs ought to be assembled in England and the United States with aerodromes made safe from counter attack by tunnelling into the sides of mountains and that Russia should be atom bombed from both England and the United States (via Okinawa) 'if she started giving trouble'.[4]

To put American policy towards the Soviet Union into a global perspective we have only to bear in mind that America's entry into the world war *ended* the worst economic depression that country had ever known, that during the ensuing combat America lost the relatively small number of some 300,000 troops, and that America emerged from the world war the strongest industrial nation on earth. The nation whose farmers and industrialists had failed to make a satisfactory profit in producing an unfortunate abundance of food and consumer durables had found matters very different with respect to the industrial production of military equipment. The American nation (and American science) had truly thrived on the war. On the other hand, although the Soviet people had all but single handed defeated the Nazi invaders, the country once again lay in ruins as it had in 1920 at the end of the civil war and Western blockade. The following statistics tell their own appalling story. The Nazis had occupied Soviet territory in which nearly 90 million people lived; over 15 million of them were killed. The Nazis destroyed, completely or partially, 15 large cities, 1,710 towns and 70,000 villages; 60 million buildings were destroyed and 25 million people made homeless. Nearly 32,000 industrial enterprises were demolished, 10,000 power stations, 3,000 oil wells, over 1,000 coal mines, 65,000 kilometres of railway track and 86,000 miles of main highway. The Nazis transported to Germany 14,000 steam boilers, 1,400 turbines and 11,300 electric generators. Nearly 100,000 collective farms were sacked. The Nazis either slaughtered or carried with them 7 million horses, 17 million cattle, 20 million hogs, 27 million sheep and goats, 110 million poultry. Some 40,000 hospitals and medical centres were destroyed, 64,000 schools and colleges, 43,000 public libraries with over 100 million books, 44,000 theatres, nearly 3,000 churches and over 400 museums. In the first population census after the war there were, over the age of 18, only 31 million men compared with 53 million women.[5]

In postwar America, however, the necessity of a 'permanent war economy' which had been first argued as early as 1944 by leading industrialists and military chiefs, was now being vociferously advocated. The survival of capitalism in the United States demanded increased arms expenditure and that in turn necessitated the manufacture of a major enemy. The Soviet Union, run by the brutal Stalin and loathed by Western liberals, fitted the bill ideally. (Of course, the many brutal dictators outside the Soviet bloc, especially where American investment was significant, naturally received strong American backing.) An integral part of the now thriving and lucrative American war economy, which is specially relevant to our present concerns, consisted of a very substantial atomic build-up.

As early as October 1947 the American Joint Chiefs of Staff informed the Chairman of the Atomic Energy Commission (AEC) that the Armed Forces needed by January 1953 some 400 atomic bombs of the kind that had destroyed Nagasaki. Dropped on some 100 urban targets, the stockpile might, the Chiefs of Staff thought, be sufficient to achieve the 'killing' of a nation, in particular, the Soviet Union. A year later the Atomic Energy Commission was able to assure the Joint Chiefs that the 400 bombs would be ready by January 1951, two years ahead of schedule.[6] During 1948 calls were constantly made in America for a 'preventive war' against Russia. Thus John von Neumann, for example, who at Los Alamos had always maintained the view that the Soviet Union was America's ultimate enemy, promulgated a very hawkish policy: 'If you say why not bomb them tomorrow, I say why not today? If you say today at five o'clock, I say why not at one o'clock?'[7] Even Bertrand Russell appreciated the 'necessity' of a preventive war against the Soviet Union.

Recognising, however, that immediate war with the Soviet Union would mean the overrunning of western Europe by Russian armies and that therefore atomic bombs, if used, would at first have to be dropped on western Europe and that consequently, despite America's ultimate victory, western Europe would 'be lost to civilization for centuries', Russell nevertheless argued that 'even at such a price... war would be worthwhile [since] communism must be wiped out and world government must be established'. On the other hand, Russell claimed, if professional strategists were correct in their belief that western Europe would be economically and militarily stronger in a few years and that Russia would still not have atomic weapons, then it would be to the advantage of the West to postpone war with the Soviet Union.[8]

Lest the reader might think that the entire western world had gone mad during this period, perhaps I should briefly mention the very sane perspective of the twentieth century's most distinguished scientist, Albert Einstein, who in 1933 had been unable to return to Berlin after a visit to the United States and who had become an American citizen in 1940. Ever since the destruction of Hiroshima and Nagasaki Einstein had undertaken a sustained campaign, both privately and publicly, to attempt to persuade Americans to reverse the foreign policy of their and his government. In January 1948 Einstein described in a letter to an army officer who had challenged his opposition to national conscription how he believed there was a terrible danger that America might succumb to the fearful militarisation which had engulfed Germany half a century earlier. 'We should never forget,' Einstein told the officer, 'that it is totally unlikely that any country will attack America in the near future, least of all Russia, which is devastated, impoverished and politically isolated.' In the spring of 1948 Einstein called on intellectuals to attempt to mobilise opposition towards a preventive war against the Soviet Union and to do so before irrevocable steps had been taken in that direction. A psychoanalyst who advocated 'strong pressure' against the Soviet Union received the message from Einstein, 'I cannot accept your viewpoint, much less the one expressed by Bertrand Russell.' The One World Award Committee was told by Einstein that American rearmament would cause other nations to rearm and hence would bring about the very state of affairs upon which the advocates of armaments sought to base their proposals. In June 1948 the courageous Einstein issued a public statement which succinctly expresses the essence of his position. 'The United States,' he said,

> emerged from the war as the strongest military and economic power and, temporarily, is the only country to possess the powerful atomic bomb. Such power imposes a heavy obligation. To a large extent, the United States is responsible for the ominous competitive arms race which has taken place since the end of the war and which has virtually destroyed the postwar prospects for an effective supranational solution of the security problem.[9]

So Einstein continued his campaign. The development of American policy since the end of the war reminded him increasingly of the events in Germany since the time of Wilhelm II: 'through many victories to final disaster'. At the beginning of 1951 the editor of *The Bulletin of the Atomic Scientists* was informed by Einstein that, in his opinion, 'the present policy of the United States constitutes a more serious obstacle to peace in the world than that of Russia', that it should not be forgotten that the fighting then taking place was in Korea, not Alaska, and that Russia was exposed to a vastly greater threat than the United States and that 'everyone knows it'. While American government policy was apparently directed towards 'preventive war' a concerted attempt existed, Einstein pointed out, to make it appear as though the Soviet Union was the aggressor. The former German citizen who in 1914 had been virtually alone in signing a 'Manifesto to Europeans' which was clearly opposed to a pro-war manifesto signed by a large number of German intellectuals and who in 1933 had become a refugee from Nazism now found himself forced to make a tragic comparison: 'The German calamity of years ago repeats itself: people acquiesce without resistance and align themselves with the forces of evil. And one stands by, powerless.' Yet Einstein was at no time deceived as to the extremely repressive nature of the Soviet regime. While acknowledging the Soviet Union's undoubted social and economic achievements, there was no doubt in Einstein's mind that the Soviet government was 'considerably more brutal and barbarous' to its own citizens than the American government was to American citizens. However, there was also no doubt in his mind that 'the postwar change in power relations among the nations of the world has resulted in the West's being much more aggressive than the Communist world.' It was therefore a lonely and deeply pessimistic Einstein who continually expressed his total dismay and abhorrence at what he described as 'the hatred and fear toward Russia which have been instilled in the American people since the death of Roosevelt'.[10]

(Perhaps I might mention in parentheses that physics for the gentle Einstein was more like a religious quest, a quest for the discovery of harmony in nature, and which had nothing at all to do with the masculine gaining and displaying of power over nature. 'Joy in looking and comprehending,' the ageing Einstein wrote, 'is nature's most beautiful gift.' Like Johannes Kepler more than three centuries before him, and whom he so closely resembled and admired, Einstein searched for harmony in the heavens as a welcome respite from the tumult and discord so characteristic of life on his home planet. If we recall how Clerval had told Frankenstein that the spirit inhabiting the Rhine valley surely has a soul more in harmony with man than the fearsome spirits of the glaciers and icy peaks where Frankenstein had at last come face to face with his monstrous creation, it is perhaps not entirely inappropriate to mention an intriguing aspect of Einstein's character, as related by A. Moszkowski: 'The intense romanticism of Swiss scenery... has never enticed him into its magic circle, and he has nothing to do with the abysmal terrors of glaciers and the world of snow-peaks... In simple contact with Nature he prefers the lesser mountains, the seashore, and extensive plains, whereas brilliant panoramic contours like those of the Vierwaldstetter See do not rouse him into ecstasy.' Speaking of his father, Einstein's eldest son remarked that 'he did not care for large, impressive mountains, but... liked surroundings that were gentle and colourful and gave one lightness of spirit'.[11] But lightness of spirit was something that was hard to come by after Einstein had seen the potentially beautiful play that could be physics give birth to monstrous forces of destruction.)

It was, then, in such a context of extreme hostility to the Soviet Union exemplified by widespread advocacy of and support for 'preventive war' that President Truman announced to the American people on 23 September 1949 that the Soviet Union had recently exploded its first atomic bomb. There have, of course, been many analyses of the response of the American government to the Soviet nuclear test (and to accompanying events of global significance such as the September 1949 Proclamation of the People's Republic of China) and I do not comment on them here. Neither do I comment on the 'internal' military and economic context within which President Truman's decision was taken, particularly the relevance of intense interservice rivalry amongst the American armed forces and the pressure of increased military and industrial demands for the further rearming of the American nation. I have done this at length elsewhere.[12] My aim here is to demonstrate that in so far as leading physicists were concerned, the response of *some* of the principal participants was determined *not only* by how they perceived the Soviet 'threat' — which was, in general, very different from Einstein's perception — but also by masculine motivation vis-à-vis the possibility of building the most horrendously powerful weapon on earth.

The A-bomb's really big brother

It was in part in direct response to 'Joe I' that in October 1949 the General Advisory Committee (GAC) of the Atomic Energy Commission, chaired by J. Robert Oppenheimer, recommended that although the United States ought to accelerate both production and development of fission bombs, it should forego all-out development of the fusion bomb in order to try to prevent an escalation of the arms race to a qualitatively new level. While in a majority Annexe to the GAC Report the four scientific signatories, Oppenheimer among them, expressed their conviction that refusal to develop a hydrogen bomb would offer a 'unique opportunity of providing by example some limitations on the totality of war', in a minority Annexe Enrico Fermi and Isidor Rabi expressed the opinion that the hydrogen superbomb was 'an evil thing considered in any light' and that it would be wrong 'on fundamental ethical principles to initiate the development of such a weapon'. 'My opinion at that time,' confirmed Fermi, 'was that one should try to outlaw this thing before it was born.'[13] The GAC's advice concerning the hydrogen bomb was, however, overruled by President Truman when in March 1950 he approved all-out development of the superweapon. According to Herbert York, the various influential politicians who favoured the H-bomb programme based their views in large part on the lobbying of three nuclear physicists, Edward Teller, Ernest Lawrence and Luis Alvarez[14] (with the nuclear chemist Wendell Latimer and the mathematician John von Neumann also playing important roles). I want to describe and comment briefly on the views of probably the most influential of the three physicists from 1950 onwards, Edward Teller, the man whose quest for paternity at Los Alamos had so conspicuously *not* resulted in a male birth. For the hydrogen bomb, which had been Teller's 'baby', was still very much in gestation when the successful birth of Oppenheimer's babies had so abruptly ended the world war.

In his book *Energy from Heaven and Earth* Teller writes how in 1941 Fermi had first mentioned to him the possibility of constructing a fusion, i.e. a hydrogen bomb. 'It was a challenging question,' Teller writes.[15] It was certainly a challenge that was to preoccupy Teller for the next fifteen years. When in the summer of 1942 he and Bethe travelled to Berkeley to participate in the study group organised by Oppenheimer to look at the feasibility of fission weapons, Bethe remembers how Teller had argued to him that the fission bomb no longer presented serious obstacles and that 'what we really should think about was the possibility of igniting deuterium by a fission weapon — the hydrogen bomb'. In any case, during that summer the participants of Oppenheimer's study group devoted some three quarters of their time to looking at how a superbomb, as they called it, might be triggered by a fission weapon.[16] 'Grim as the subject was,' Hans Bethe remembers, 'it was a most exciting enterprise. We were forever inventing new tricks on the basis of the calculations. The ideas we had about triggering an H-bomb turned out to be all wrong but the intellectual experience was unforgettable.'[17] Teller for his part writes of his difficulty in describing the 'intensity and the fascination of the discussion' concerning 'the Super' and how for him the experience was 'even more challenging' than prewar discussion about the interior of the sun. He explains that even at Los Alamos the purely scientific aspects of the fusion weapon were 'so fascinating that the problem continued to attract attention', especially from him.[18] Indeed, Teller's continued fascination with the problem of the Super was one of the principal reasons why his relations with both Oppenheimer and Bethe became so strained at Los Alamos. For not only had Oppenheimer appointed Bethe as head of the Theoretical Division whereas, Bethe writes, Teller saw himself as having 'seniority over everyone then at Los Alamos, including Oppenheimer', but the consensus of senior scientists at Los Alamos was that all effort should be directed towards realising a workable fission weapon.[19] In verbal testimony at the Oppenheimer hearings Bethe later explained how Teller had become so disgruntled that he had had no choice 'but to relieve him of any work in the general line of the development of Los Alamos and to permit him to pursue his own ideas unrelated to the World War II work with his own group outside of the theoretical division'.[20] These ideas were concerned with the production of the superbomb which, Robert Jungk writes, Teller now called 'his baby', and in particular with the not entirely inconsequential 'proof' that detonation of a Super would not ignite the atmosphere and so totally destroy the earth's entire biosphere. Incomplete though all this theoretical work was, Teller wrote later, the idea of 'the Super bomb survived as a challenge and as a future task for Los Alamos'.[21] Interestingly, even before the war's end Oppenheimer himself had in September 1944 recommended to Washington that 'the subject of initiating violent thermonuclear reactions be pursued with vigor and diligence, and promptly' — a view he had obviously repudiated by 1949.[22]

Teller, however, had not and although during the immediate postwar years he continued to advocate construction of the H-bomb it was not until the autumn of 1949 that Teller's pleadings for a crash programme evoked a sympathetic and active response on the part of powerful politicians with access to the President. During this four-year period, it should be stressed, work on the hydrogen bomb had by no means been at a standstill. According to the Polish-born mathematician Stanislaw Ulam, 'work on the "super" had been going on efficiently and systematically' throughout the postwar years; each year Teller and von Neumann had spent two to three months at Los Alamos helping to design a superbomb, and Ulam recalls that when in the spring of 1949 he had told the Director of Los Alamos, Norris Bradbury, that he had the impression that some people in Washington did not want this work to continue, Bradbury had replied

'I'll be damned if I'll let anybody in Washington or any politicians tell me what work not to do.'[23] Moreover, according to Edward Teller, the restrictive GAC report provoked only an adverse psychological reaction at Los Alamos, especially among the younger 'adventurous' scientists. 'They got mad,' Teller relates. 'And their attention was turned toward the bomb, not away from it.'[24]

However, despite such systematic and recharged work on the Super, as N.P. Davis has written, 'In 1949 the thing that waited... to be born still had long to wait. It demanded a new idea.'[25] That new idea was not immediately forthcoming. In spite of Teller's pleading Hans Bethe had refused to return to Los Alamos after the Soviet nuclear test, convinced by his wife, Rose, and two physicist friends, Weisskopf and Placzek, that the bomb ought not to be built. Even after Truman's decision to authorise an all-out programme, which sent Fermi back to Los Alamos, Bethe still courageously expressed his opposition. However, after the outbreak in June that year of the war in Korea, Bethe decided to participate actively in the new weapons programme, though still primarily hoping 'to clinch the argument that the H-bomb would not work'.[26] At this time, moreover, it really appeared to be the case that no feasible way could be found of triggering a fusion explosion. Although the successful detonation in May 1951 of a device christened 'George' was to confirm that a *large* fission explosion could ignite a *small* quantity of thermonuclear fuel, the converse procedure whereby the physicists hoped to ignite a large quantity of thermonuclear fuel with only a small quantity of fissile material appeared fundamentally unworkable. The effect of this 'bad' prospect on Teller was dramatic. Bethe recalls how 'Teller was completely despondent during this period. He was walking around in deep thought and was terribly moody and got into fights with everybody. He had a really hard time.'[27] Ulam, too, recalls how Teller totally refused to reconcile himself with the negative results that he (Ulam) and others were producing:

I learned that the bad news drove him once to tears of frustration, and he suffered great disappointment. I never saw him personally in that condition, but he certainly appeared glum in those days, and so were other enthusiasts of the H-bomb project.

Subdued and depressed, he would visit our offices periodically
and would attempt to prove us wrong by trying to find
mistakes.

Ulam exempts von Neumann, however, from the category of dismal
Johnnies. As he remarks, von Neumann was always emotionally involved in favour of the construction of an H-bomb and never lost
heart even when the mathematical results conclusively demonstrated
that the original approach was simply not workable.[28]

The breakthrough came in February 1951. A new idea! Who produced that idea, Stanislaw Ulam or Edward Teller, has been a matter
of considerable controversy, as we shall see. But whatever the pro-
prietary rights that idea eventually transformed the entire H-bomb
project. Not immediately, however. When in April 1951 the now re-
juvenated Teller passionately attempted to convince the chairman of
the Atomic Energy Commission, Gordon Dean, of the viability of
the new approach, he found the chairman too distracted by what
Teller discovered after the abortive meeting had been his failed zip-
per and open fly! 'Dean remembered my open fly,' Teller observed
testily, 'but not my ideas.' While it is difficult to believe that a
meeting of such potential significance produced no meeting of minds
because Edward Teller, bursting with enthusiasm for his new idea,
had an open fly which completely threw the chairman of the AEC,
this is nevertheless what Teller relates. Success, however, did come
two months later. At a meeting at the Institute for Advanced Studies
at Princeton, Teller managed to convince all sceptics of the feasibility
of the new approach, including the man who had earlier in Teller's
words, found his 'sloppy dress an insurmountable distraction'.
Teller had won the day. Indeed, response to the theory, he relates,
was 'enthusiastic and unanimous'.[29]

The effect of the theoretical breakthrough on former critics of
the H-bomb was startling. Convinced of the manifest feasibility of
the weapon and urged on by both Teller and Bradbury, Bethe decided
once again to return to Los Alamos this time to participate
wholeheartedly in the new programme. While the programme had
been uncertain, Bethe had comforted himself that Soviet physicists
would be faring no better. Once the programme appeared perfectly
feasible, Bethe decided that it was therefore better to develop the

H-bomb than not to do so.[30] The effect on Oppenheimer was apparently equally dramatic and was described by Oppenheimer himself in his security hearings in 1954. The all-important difference, as conceived by Oppenheimer, was between a technically clumsy and probably unworkable device and a technically 'beautiful' and very workable one. 'The programme we had in 1949,' Oppenheimer explained, 'was a tortured thing that you could well argue did not make a great deal of technical sense. It was therefore possible to argue also that you did not want it even if you could have it. The programme in 1951 was technically so sweet that you could not argue about that. It was purely the military, the political and the humane problem of what you were going to do about it once you had it.' Although his view remained that the H-bomb was a dreadful weapon, nevertheless from a 1951 'technical point of view' the fusion bomb of Teller and Ulam appeared to Oppenheimer 'a sweet and lovely and beautiful job'. This perspective on the desirability of making a 'dreadful weapon' is so startling that it is worthwhile to quote Oppenheimer once more in his view of the basic difference in approach between 1949 and 1951:

> It is my judgement in these things that when you see something that is technically sweet you go ahead and do it and you argue about what to do about it only after you have had your technical success. That is the way it was with the atomic bomb. I do not think anybody opposed making it; there were some debates about what to do with it after it was made. I cannot very well imagine if we [the GAC] had known in late 1949 what we got to know by early 1951 that the tone of our report would have been the same.[31]

If something, then, is technically sweet you go ahead and do it and worry about the consequences afterwards! Stanislaw Ulam, while stressing how difficult it is to decide on someone else's motives, shares with Oppenheimer some doubts as to whether the original opposition to the development of the H-bomb — particularly Oppenheimer's — had been based entirely on 'moral, philosophical or humanitarian grounds'. Oppenheimer seemed to the man who claimed with Teller 'priority rights' on the fusion weapon's design as someone who having started a revolution 'does not contemplate with pleasure still bigger revolutions to come'.[32] Be that as it may, the new manifestly workable design of the H-bomb had rendered its future birth inevitable, as Oppenheimer himself enthusiastically conceded.

Despite the fact that Los Alamos now had a successful design for a workable hydrogen bomb, Edward Teller's relations with his colleagues failed to improve. On the contrary, his long-standing disagreement with Norris Bradbury about how best to run the laboratory deteriorated into a sharp clash over the most effective way to develop the thermonuclear weapon. Finally in November 1951, although it was a 'great disappointment' not to be able to participate in the concluding stage of such a 'magnificent undertaking', Teller left 'the birthplace of the atomic bomb' in order to be able to argue more effectively the nation's need for an alternative laboratory. A year later in November 1952, at the time of the first test of the new fusion device, Edward Teller excitedly watched a seismograph at Berkeley in the hope of observing the shock waves that would result from the successful 'birth' of 'Mike', scheduled for 'delivery' at Eniwetok in the Pacific Marshall Islands. Exultantly watching the seismograph register the expected shock waves from Eniwetok, the delighted Teller sent off a self-explanatory three-word telegram to Los Alamos, 'It's a boy.'[33] An equally delighted Lewis Strauss, Gordon Dean's successor as chairman of the AEC, elevated Edward Teller to a new high status of paternity as 'Father of the H-bomb'.[34]

The three triumphal words of Teller's telegram — 'It's a boy' — described a fusion explosion some 1,000 times more powerful than the fission bomb that destroyed Hiroshima, a bomb that was the end result of the creative spirit of many physicists but in particular of the remarkably talented and creative Edward Teller. It seems entirely appropriate that the horrendously destructive end result of such masculine creativity — the ultimate outcome of masculine repression of and violence towards the feminine — should have been described by Teller in those stark three words, the release of a monstrous force of destruction represented as the birth of a boy! Violence is male. Such, it would seem, is patriarchal history's deadly self-knowledge. The detonation of that hydrogen bomb, moreover, marked yet another major escalation of the arms race. It is salutary to listen to the words of Vannevar Bush at the Oppenheimer hearings as this senior scientist condemned the 1952 test of 'Mike':

I felt strongly that that test ended the possibility of the only type of agreement that I thought was possible with Russia at that time, namely, an agreement to make no more tests. For that kind of agreement would have been self-policing in the sense that if it was violated, the violation would be immediately known. I still think that we made a grave error in conducting that test at that time, and not attempting to make that type of simple agreement with Russia. I think history will show that was a turning point that when we entered into the grim world that we are entering right now, that those who pushed that thing through to a conclusion without making that attempt have a great deal to answer for.[35]

Teller, as we shall see in the next section, has remained a very controversial physicist. What is particularly relevant for us is to note the nature of some of the criticisms made of him. For it has been suggested by some of his colleagues that Edward Teller's role in the creation of the H-bomb was that of a female, not of a male. Hans Bethe relates how he used to say that 'Ulam was the father of the hydrogen bomb and Edward was the mother, because he carried the baby for quite a while'.[36] An even more scathing put-down of Teller is made by a distinguished physicist in the film *A is for Atom, B is for Bomb: A Portrait of Dr Edward Teller*. Bitterly opposed to Teller's postwar policies, the physicist cuttingly remarks that because it was Stanislaw Ulam who had the all-important idea and inseminated Teller with it, Teller should not be called the father of the H-bomb but rather its mother.[37] A resurrected Aristotle might no doubt have more than a little difficulty in understanding the physics of fission and fusion bombs but on the other hand he would comprehend immediately that the masculine spirit that underlay his theory of generation not only underlay the creation of nuclear weapons but was also a weapon by which certain proponents of the nuclear arms race could be attacked where perhaps it hurt most.

Priority, 'publication' and glory

If it was bad enough that in 1951 there existed in the United States one major weapons laboratory making an all-out effort to develop a hydrogen bomb, by the end of 1952 there existed two such laboratories — and furthermore two laboratories in fierce and deadly competition with each other. Edward Teller, we recall, had left Los Alamos in November 1951 in order to help mobilise support for the creation of a second weapons laboratory which in his experienced opinion could and would be run more effectively than that run by Norris Bradbury at Los Alamos. When the General Advisory Committee of the Atomic Energy Commission (with the exception of the new Berkeley member Willard F. Libby) refused to support the proposal for another weapons centre, Teller began to look elsewhere and in particular to the Air Force for support and financial backing. At the same time Ernest Lawrence, Director of the Berkeley Radiation Laboratory, encouraged the young Berkeley physicist Herbert York, who had participated throughout 1951 in the thermonuclear programme, to journey to Los Alamos, Chicago and Washington with the aim of investigating the desirability and feasibility of an alternative laboratory to Los Alamos. The combined proposal coming from Berkeley was for the creation of a second weapons establishment in the university laboratory at Livermore. Faced with mounting pressure from many sides and fearing the intrusion of the Air Force on their monopoly the Atomic Energy Commissioners approved the Berkeley proposal in June 1952. The following September the Livermore laboratory was launched with York as Director and managed by a Scientific Steering Committee with Teller having the power of veto over the Steering Committee's decisions.

Relations between the two weapons laboratories were clearly very strained from the outset and, according to York, rapidly became worse. The popular press gave credit for the successful 'Mike' explosion only to Edward Teller and the Livermore laboratory, an injustice which the Atomic Energy Commission, rigidly adhering to its policy of total secrecy concerning the origins and nature of 'Mike', did nothing to remedy. The 'birth' or 'publication' of 'Mike' had therefore unhappily resulted in glory being accredited principally to one man and certainly to the wrong laboratory! To compound matters further, some senior physicists at Los Alamos, 'while always correct in their attitude to Livermore', nevertheless made it clear that Edward Teller was no longer welcome at the original weapons laboratory. This was to say the least a distinctly unfriendly attitude

hat in the opinion of York greatly contributed to bad feelings between the two establishments. Moreover, when the first Livermore
ests in Nevada in 1953 and at Bikini in the spring of 1954 went very
badly, York rather painfully recalls how 'some Los Alamos scientists
filled the air with horse laughs on those occasions'. One of the fission
ests in Nevada, an embarrassed York acknowledges, barely
destroyed the cab on top of its tower and had the bad form to leave
most of the tower still standing 'for all to see and poke fun at', a
merely decapitated bomb tower presumably not counting as among
the most convincing of phallic symbols. Even worse, the Livermore
laboratory's first attempt at a super explosion at Bikini produced only
a fizzle and plans for a second fusion explosion had to be cancelled.
The Livermore laboratory was giving birth to 'girls'! 'This poor
beginning may have relieved some pressure at Los Alamos,' writes
York, 'but it stimulated us to gird our loins and do better next time.'
And so Livermore and Los Alamos competed with each other as Edward Teller had intended that they should. 'I have little doubt,'
wrote Livermore's first director, 'that the Livermore laboratory was
seen as competition by Los Alamos, and I know for a fact that we at
Livermore saw ourselves as being in competition with them.'[38] By
this time, it might seem, the convenient Russian 'threat' had almost
receded out of the American scientists' view as the two weapons
laboratories raced to outdo each other in virile achievement.[39] For example, York notes 'with some personal chagrin' that while it had
been the Livermore laboratory that had rather rashly promised a
one-megaton warhead that would fit into a small container, it was the
Los Alamos laboratory that had had the necessary expertise at the
time to design and produce one.[40] Nevertheless, no matter how the
credit is apportioned between the two weapons centres — and, according to Teller, science and technology do thrive on competition — the
fact remains that the 1950s saw the development and production of
an impressive variety of nuclear weapons and means of delivery,
ranging from nuclear shells only inches in diameter and 'Davy
Crockett' warheads small enough to be fitted into bazooka-like
devices to all kinds of fission and fusion weapons suitable for the
various missiles then being invented — a rate of 'progress' that twenty
years later a wiser Herbert York, a much wiser Herbert York, would
decide had decreased and not increased the security of the United

States. A decade further on, at the start of the 1980s, this unflaggin
competition between Los Alamos and Livermore would sadly remai
a crucially important feature of America's continuing acceleratio
of the global nuclear arms race.[41]

As part of the initial competition between the Los Alamos an
Livermore laboratories and also contributing to it was the notoriou
'trial' of Oppenheimer conducted by the Atomic Energy Commissio
in the spring of 1954.[42] In this clash of the two fathers — the father
Los Alamos and the A-bomb versus the father of Livermore and th
H-bomb — the American community of physicists was seemingl
torn apart. In the atmosphere of Senator McCarthy's witch-huntin
of 'communists' the Atomic Energy Commission conducted form:
hearings to determine whether or not Oppenheimer was a securit
risk to the United States. 'Indiscretions' committed by Oppenheime
during the war years were once again dredged up but above all ther
existed his initial opposition to development of the superbomb an
his alleged lack of enthusiasm even after President Truman's ap
proval of a crash programme. The principal scientific witnesse
against Oppenheimer were the Berkeley scientists Luiz Alvarez an
Wendell Latimer (Ernest Lawrence who intended to testify again
Oppenheimer was too ill to attend) and, most important of all, Ec
ward Teller. Oppenheimer's actions were often so confused an
complicated, Teller told the board of inquiry, that he would prefer
see the vital interests of the United States in hands which h
understood better and therefore trusted more. While he personall
believed that Oppenheimer would not knowingly endanger the secur
ty of the United States, he could not in all conscience let the matte
rest there: 'If it is a question of wisdom and judgement,
demonstrated by actions since 1945,' Teller declared, 'then I woul
say one would be wiser not to grant clearance.'[43] Clearance was n
granted and all of Oppenheimer's remaining government conne
tions were consequently severed. Politically the new father had won
great victory. The old father had been disgraced and humiliated. B
the cost in personal terms was very high. Teller's devastatin
testimony against Oppenheimer was much resented by a larg
number of American physicists, including several of his forme
friends, and nowhere more than at Los Alamos. Life within th
physics community became exceedingly difficult for Teller. It was

part to try to placate Los Alamos physicists and to win back some measure of scientific peer acceptance that the 'father of the H-bomb' attempted in his fascinating paper 'The Work of Many People' to set matters straight, at least with respect to distributing credit for the development of the H-bomb where credit was due.

In this paper Teller reviews the development of thermonuclear weapons from the discussions of the interior of stars conducted in the 1930s to the 1952 test of 'Mike' and the inauguration of the Livermore laboratory. Complaining that at the present time he was unhappily in the position of being given 'certainly too much credit and perhaps too much blame' for the success of 'Mike' and subsequent explosions, Teller stressed that such an outcome was necessarily 'the work of many excellent people who had to give their best abilities for years and who were all essential for the final outcome'. It was most regrettable, Teller emphasised, that the public is all too often told of a brilliant idea and of a single name associated with it. Concerning that 'brilliant idea' in question and its subsequent execution, I should perhaps quote the apologetic Teller in full as he describes the positive turn of events that followed what had been for him the sad period when it appeared probable that a usable H-bomb was not possible:

> Two signs of hope came within a few weeks: one sign was an imaginative suggestion by Ulam; the other sign was a fine calculation by [Frederic] de Hoffmann.
>
> I cannot refrain from mentioning one particularly human detail in de Hoffmann's work. Since I had made the suggestion that led to his calculation, I expected that we would jointly sign the report containing the results. Freddie, however, had other plans. He signed the report with my name only and argued that the suggestion counted for everything and the execution for nothing. I still feel ashamed that I consented.

According to Teller, then, de Hoffmann at the time appeared to support the belief that 'the idea' is paramount, the execution secondary, which is yet again an example of belief in the supremacy of the supposedly 'masculine' over the supposedly 'feminine' in the process of conception and giving birth. It was four years later that Teller expressed his feeling of shame that Frederic de Hoffmann's name had not appeared on the report together with his own.[44]

Finally, Teller attempted to set matters straight concerning the credit for successful nuclear tests between 1952 and 1955. There was no beating about the bush: 'All the magnificent achievements that have become in the meantime known to the world have been accomplished by Los Alamos.' But words of praise were directed also towards the 'young and vigorous' group of experts in Livermore: 'The more they see that Los Alamos is a long distance ahead of them,' Teller wrote, 'the more eager they are to catch up.' The competition, however, should and would remain friendly, stressed Teller, and he warned that 'disunity of the scientists is one of the greatest dangers for our country'.[45]

In this paper 'The Work of Many People' and in subsequent publications the influential Edward Teller also provides a partial insight into what motivated him in his impassioned advocacy of the Super and of the sophisticated weapons that have succeeded it. For we will not be surprised to learn that even in his published works Teller does not claim that his impassioned advocacy of superweapons was entirely a consequence of the physicist's belief in meeting the 'security' needs of the Western alliance. Teller's credo, in fact, takes us back to the credo of the founding father of the 'masculine philosophy', Francis Bacon, and to Mary Shelley's profound commentary on that masculine philosophy. We need only remember Francis Bacon's battle cry, 'to the effecting of all things possible', and the compulsive, dangerous search into the unknown conducted by Walton and Frankenstein best characterised by Walton's confidence to his sister, 'There is something at work in my soul, which I do not understand.' For immediately Teller refers in his 1955 apologia to the story of the fusion bomb — the superbomb — as the story of 'the adventure of trying to do what at one time seemed impossible'. The paper is moreover sprinkled with such phrases as 'this magnificent undertaking', 'all the magnificent achievements', 'the intensity and fascination of the discussion', 'the spirit of spontaneity, adventure and surprise', 'complete and terrifying success', 'terrible and unprecedented', 'even more challenging', 'a great challenge', 'an even greater challenge' — phrases that illustrate the extent that Teller's soul had, let us say, seemingly identified with the enormity of the H-bomb undertaking. Teller understands, of course, the reasons underlying the passionate rejection of the H-bomb programme on the part of so many people. But Teller plays what he sees as his trump card by reminding such dissenters and faint-hearts of the West's Faustian bargain which has his total approval: 'We would be unfaithful to the tradition of Western civilisation', he asserts, 'if we were to shy away from exploring the limits of human achievement.'[46]

This is the theme with which Teller, declaring himself a 'lobbyist for unborn ideas', often concludes his later publications. Arguing in 1958 that further nuclear testing in the atmosphere was essential in order to perfect the 'clean' bomb, thereby guaranteeing that if a major nuclear war broke out it could be fought without massive worldwide fallout, Teller at the same time reassured his audience that 'random mutations', although almost always harmful, 'have nevertheless been responsible in the long run for all the many magnificent living creatures that nature has produced, including the human species' and that therefore people should not worry about fallout from the *testing* of nuclear weapons since to insist 'that all mutations are harmful... would be to deny the simplest facts of evolution'! After giving this perhaps somewhat less than compelling argument Teller next presents a general reason in favour of continuing nuclear tests. 'The spectacular developments of the last centuries, in science, in technology, and in our everyday life,' Teller writes, 'have been produced by a spirit of adventure, by a fearless exploration of the unknown.' Whatever, then, the many specific political and military reasons why such 'experiments' should continue, there also exists, Teller writes, 'this very general reason — the tradition of exploring the unknown'.[47] In one of his very latest publications — his 1979 book *Energy from Heaven and Earth* — Teller states that he is sometimes asked whether he is sorry that he has worked on nuclear weapons. He answers that he is not. He was privileged indeed to have had the opportunity of participating in 'one of the most fantastic adventures that a scientist can have'. Teller's final verdict is that 'the atomic adventure was not the first, nor the last, nor the greatest adventure in history. But it was great and it was inevitable.'[48] Whatever the verdict on the building of the fission weapon, the building of the superweapon was, however, clearly not inevitable. That it was built was very much in part a consequence of the 'magnificent obsession' of Dr Edward Teller.

In this connection it is certainly interesting to note the views of Herbert York concerning what he now recognises as overall American responsibility for the increasing momentum of the arms race and for his own involvement as the first Director of Livermore and later as the Director of Defense at the Pentagon. For while acknowledging in 1970 that the United States has been responsible 'for the majority of the actions that have set the rate and scale of the arms race' and for leading 'the entire world in this mad rush toward the ultimate absurdity', York claims that it is not because Americans and their leaders are 'more aggressive' or 'less wise' than anyone else but simply because Americans 'are richer and more powerful, that our science and technology are more dynamic, that we generate more ideas of all kinds'. These are, moreover, the answers that he repeats in his 1976 account of the decision to build the hydrogen bomb, putting forward the proposal that American 'technological exuberance' is the principal culprit.[49]

What, however, are the reasons advanced by York to explain his own very active participation in the thermonuclear crash programme? He agrees that at the time he feared the goal of world revolution as proclaimed by the Sino-Soviet bloc. But there were other reasons. For he was inspired by the 'scientific and technological challenge of the experiment itself; it was to be the very first occasion in which a thermonuclear reaction took place on the surface of the earth'. York recalls how he had played only a peripheral role in the Manhattan Project, learning about the Trinity test only a week or so after it had taken place, but that this time his role in the Promethean quest would indeed be a central one. He was, in addition, just as Feynman had been before him, excited at the prospect of working personally with men who were 'legendary yet living heroes' to young physicists as were Teller, Bethe, Fermi, von Neumann, Wheeler, Gamow and others. Finally, because the controversy over the hydrogen bomb had taken place in secret — confined like nearly all such nuclear disputes to the manoeuvrings of a very select few — York had heard of its substance only second hand from Teller and Lawrence and it was not until a quarter of a century later that he was able to see (and agree with) the GAC Report arguing against an all-out effort to construct the superweapon. Writing rather guiltily of how 'heady and exciting' the thirty-year-old Berkeley physicist had found the negotiations he was conducting in Los Alamos, Chicago and Washington concerning the founding of a second weapons laboratory, the York of some twenty-five years' additional wisdom asks compassionate readers to bear in mind how several biographical publications also 'clearly express the excitement scientists and other humans commonly find in such huge history-making events'.[50]

Obviously, what York is referring to is the syndrome of masculine motivation with which this book is concerned: the scientific and technological challenge of achieving the first thermonuclear reaction on earth, larger-than-life heroes and huge history-making events, and personal fame and glory. The pregnant phallus metaphor does not, however, occur in York's writings except for the odd word or phrase such as 'a strong and virile response to "Joe I" ' and York's description of the technological argument for a second weapons laboratory being 'so strong in its thrust' as to leave the decision makers powerless. We may also note York's comment that in due course 'outer space' exploded on the political scene and replaced atomic energy as the 'sexiest' technological area.[51] York's two critiques of the arms race are in any case descriptions of masculine motivation at work even if York does not explicitly see things this way. He does, though, while agreeing that the many individuals promoting the arms race 'derive either their incomes, their profits, or their consultant fees from it', insist that much more important than money as a motivating force are the individuals' 'own psychic and spiritual needs'. Indeed, in York's opinion, 'the majority of the key individual promoters of the arms race derive a very large part of their self-esteem from their participation in what they believe to be an essential — even a holy — cause'.[52] It is the thesis of this book, however, that these 'psychic and spiritual needs' and 'self-esteem' are in large part masculine in nature: the quest to be the first to penetrate into nature's virgin secrets, the aim of shaking nature to her foundations, the desire to achieve peer and world-wide acclaim, and, above all, the compulsive need to affirm virile masculinity through the ongoing pursuit of technological superiority over all rivals, 'friendly' and otherwise, in the dangerous and therefore very manly business of nuclear weapons development. That such a need is inherently destructive goes without saying. Even where the wisdom of years gains precedence over successful masculine ambition, the damage once done cannot easily be undone in a masculine society Like Dr Frankenstein, Dr Oppenheimer and other scientists before him, Dr York was to find out too late that the challenge of making a monster is incomparably easier than the challenge of keeping it permanently and safely under lock and key, not to mention the challenge of persuading it just to quietly disappear as if it had never been.

Big masculine science

How has masculine science been faring in the last two decades? And what is its present state of health? A few random observations will suggest that it is very much alive and well, to say no more.

It is the opinion of Herbert York that in the 1960s space became 'sexier' than atomic energy. Missiles and phallic power? Grotesquely Stanislaw Ulam, whose idea 'conceived' the hydrogen bomb and who subsequently became a power behind missile technology remarks proudly how in a high-powered committee he had got a proposal to collect and reuse missile rockets laughed out of court with the withering comment, 'This sounds to me like a proposal to use the same condom twice.' Very appropriately, it would seem, a teacher of English, Peter Abbs, states that nuclear missiles 'with their sleek phallic forms' appear to him to be 'the ultimate symbol of male intelligence divorced from religious impulse and feminine cherishing' 'Psychologically,' he writes, 'missiles are the engine of rape.'[53] Be it noted that 'fratricide' is the term used by American missile experts to describe the mishap in which the intended nuclear explosion resulting from a successful missile strike against the enemy unfortunately destroys accompanying missiles yet to reach their targets Missiles and phallic power? When that most acclaimed triumph of American technology, the space shuttle, was successfully launched in April 1981 Michael Smith noted in *The Guardian* that 'the shuttle... represents far more than another piece of space hardware to the Americans. Columbia is a virility symbol.' But where virility is male violence, it would unfortunately seem, is never very distant Two days later Alex Brummer reported in *The Guardian* how Senator John Glenn, America's first man in space, was talking 'in visionary fashion of laser beams and particle weapons being deployed by the shuttle and its successors, which would be able to intercept intercontinental ballistic missiles heading for the United States and its allies'.[54] Significantly Edward Teller claims in his editorial in the February 1981 issue of *Physics Today* that 'there is hardly anything lasers cannot do' and he writes how 'defense against incoming missiles is more challenging, more important and more in accordance with what we wish to do' than further development of nuclear weapons. And to the question concluding his editorial, 'What will be the relationship between our new government [of President Reagan] and physics?', Teller answers, 'I believe that the initiative will lie with the physicists.'[55]

The initiative will lie with the physicists! Perhaps so. However, the incoming President's message to the astronauts aboard the space shuttle suggested that those physicists attempting to intensify — and destabilise — the arms race might be met considerably more than half way by the President whereas those sane physicists attempting to contain and end the arms race might not be met at all. 'Thanks to you,' the two astronauts were informed, 'we all feel as giants once again. We feel the surge of pride that comes from knowing we are the first and we are the best and are so because we are free. As you hurtle from earth in a craft unlike any other constructed, you will do so in the feat of American technology and American will.'[56] Ironically, some two weeks before President Reagan broadcast this message to the astronauts he had barely survived an assassination attempt carried out by a twenty-five-year-old male, John Hinckley, who, apparently, was attempting 'to show his manliness to his screen love... when he shot the President, his press secretary and two guards'.[57] Which of the two, however, it might well be asked, deserves to be credited with the more masculine, or rather the more irrational, indeed the more psychotic behaviour, President Ronald Reagan or Mr John Hinckley? The answer is far from immediately obvious. The whole spectrum of masculine activity from the politically acceptable activity of building bigger and better bombs, missiles and laser weapons in order to display virility to the world, to the politically unacceptable activity of assassinating great male figures in order to display virility to a supposedly admiring female friend is a spectrum of activity that humanity could desperately do without.

In that masculine spectrum lies, of course, a multiplicity of activities both directly or indirectly connected with the nuclear arms race. I do not in this book discuss the so-called 'peaceful' uses of nuclear reactors — they can in principle always be used for producing the plutonium from which implosion fission weapons are made[58] — but a few comments will not be out of place. Just as nuclear weapons are male creations that are specifically designed to have violent explosive power — and (in the past) have been honoured with masculine status — so nuclear weapons for peaceful purposes are male restructurings of 'female' nature that, while potentially dangerous, indeed lethal, can be made to produce harnessable energy if kept under ever-vigilant manly control. 'I am come in very truth,' wrote Francis Bacon, 'leading to you Nature with all her children to bind her to your service and make her your slave.'[59] We recall how Otto Frisch at Los Alamos had almost received a fatal dose of radiation when by leaning too far over the unshielded 'Lady Godiva' assembly he had almost set off an uncontrolled chain reaction. In the same way heavily shielded 'female' reactors are still in principle and in practice potentially lethal devices if allowed to get out of control. 'The myth of the dualistic nature of woman as either asexual virgin-mother or prostitute-vamp,' writes Andreas Huyssen, 'is projected onto technology which appears as either neutral and obedient or as inherently threatening and out-of-control'.[60] Such a male projection seems particularly apt with respect to nuclear reactors. It is interesting how Edward Teller, in discussing 'weak' radiation effects from properly behaving reactors, seems to believe that he is addressing only male readers and 'lightheartedly' compares the Dresden III nuclear reactor at Illinois with female sleeping partners. Quoting an AEC report to him which reassures him that while 'you get more radiation from [leaning against] Dresden III than from [sleeping with] your wife', Teller also quotes the AEC warning 'against the habit of sleeping each night with two girls, for then you would get more radiation than you get from Dresden III'.[61] All very amusing, manly, and instructive.

Instructive also is the experience of a professor of anthropology at the University of California, Laura Nader, who participated on the Committee on Nuclear and Alternative Energy Systems project of the National Academy of Sciences. When after six months of committee meetings and memoranda she remarked that nobody in her 'Synthesis Panel' had ever used the word 'solar' she was told by two male participants that 'solar's been an orphan child' and that 'solar's not very intellectually challenging'. Commenting that male professionals in the United States strike her as 'very macho', Nader writes that it would appear that for something to be 'intellectually challenging' to such professionals it has preferably to be 'complicated, hazardous, difficult and risky' and which in addition requires 'high technology and big money'. Conservation, she has discovered, is considered feminine, an appraisal which she appropriately concludes renders 'nuclear a very masculine endeavor'. For such male professionals, she writes, 'conservation isn't sexy. It's not hazardous; it's not risky: it's obvious'. And she concludes pessimistically: 'We have gotten to the point in our society where we can no longer entertain obvious solutions.'[62]

Perhaps not only in American society. According, for example, to Dr Ramanna of the Atomic Energy Commission in India, the successful introduction of the fast breeder reactor will be the most significant step forward in the country's nuclear programme. 'Nothing can be more exciting for us than these breeder reactors,' Dr Ramanna is quoted as saying, 'it will be like taming the tiger.'[63] Nuclear technology constitutes, indeed, a masculine endeavour. Fondly recalling features of the fast neutron plutonium reactor, called Clementine, which had been successfully developed by Los Alamos physicists, Norris Bradbury, Director of Los Alamos until 1970, regretted the laboratory's failure to overcome the next 'tough' challenge of developing out of the research reactor, Clementine, 'a very different breed of cat', a power plutonium reactor. As for the possibility of generating electricity by harnessing fusion rather than fission power, which would be an inherently safer form of atomic energy, Bradbury reported after his retirement on the immense difficulties so far encountered: 'I hope Nature isn't kidding us here; I don't suppose she really is. The energy is there, but it certainly is very difficult to extract and it's going to be very expensive to extract.'[64] Very difficult and very expensive! Perhaps rather more so than safety requirements the two criteria of difficulty and expense are, it seems to me, amongst the more important criteria that have to be satisfied in masculine societies before a major national project can be seriously contemplated and then launched. Better still, of course, if the project serves not only to increase the political power and economic wealth of a privileged few but also to increase the military might of the nation, i.e. the coercive physical power associated with and controlled by a select male elite.

What masculine men do not want are simple and logical solutions to the world's problems and certainly not all of them want a simple and logical solution to the world's most dangerous problem which is the nuclear arms race. Lord Zuckerman, for seven years Chief Scientific Adviser to the British Government, expresses his puzzlement over why the view has been so difficult to put across that for many years now there has been no sense in further elaboration of weapons systems. The basic reason, he declares, is that, strangely, it is not because the sane view sounds 'soft and defeatist, but because it is too simple and too logical'. He stresses that since the postwar arms race began the world has 'without doubt become a more perilous place than it has ever been in human history'. But he does not appreciate that, if my argument is correct, this is by no means undesirable to the masculine mentality. 'The men in the nuclear weapons laboratories of both sides have succeeded in creating a world with an irrational foundation,' he laments. 'They have become the alchemists of our times, working in secret ways which cannot be divulged, casting spells which embrace us all.'[65] I agree (disregarding the unjustified slur on the alchemists of early modern Europe). But what in my opinion Zuckerman does not perceive or disagrees with is the thesis which I hope this chapter has served to underline, namely that the spectacular creation of increasingly sophisticated scientific weaponry is the insane and on-going achievement of a masculine mentality that is not only flourishing in very influential places both inside and, of course, outside the scientific establishment but whose bearers have so far managed to place themselves quite beyond the control of 'ordinary' people.[66]

5. When the Ice Breaks: 'Some questions have to remain unanswered. At some point we have to stop'

In preindustrial Europe, celibacy, far from being condemned as it was in the oriental societies, was generally praised. For priests, monks, and nuns, celibacy actually became a rule of life. Until modern times in Europe intellectualism was inconceivable except in a state of celibacy... Until the end of the Middle Ages, the school of medicine at Paris did not allow married men to graduate. At Oxford and Cambridge until the end of the nineteenth century, married men were not admitted among the fellows of the colleges.

> C.M. Cipolla, *Before the Industrial Revolution*

Only in socialist society will science become the genuine possession of all mankind. New paths of its development are opening before it, and there is no limit to its victorious advance, either in infinite space or in everlasting time.

> Boris Hessen, *The Social and Economic Roots of Newton's 'Principia'*

Twentieth-century science and in particular the nuclear arms race are obviously phenomena of an industrialised and industrialising world in which the masculine objective of ever-increasing power over nature has been its seemingly inexorable driving force. The ongoing achievement, however, of such ever-greater domination over nature exacts, as we have seen, a very heavy penalty on its proponents and practitioners.[1] For since human beings are themselves products of a natural (evolutionary) process and are themselves 'nature', then in so far as masculine men need to and do view women, non-human species and the 'inanimate' world as 'other', as 'nature', and therefore as 'mere matter' for conquest and exploitation, they are able to do so consistently only if they bifurcate the cosmos into a Cartesian-like conceptual duality of masculine and feminine, associating drives towards conquest with masculine characteristics and the objects of such drives with feminine ones. The heavy price, of course, that masculine men have to pay for ever-increasing domination of nature is their own self-mutilation as they necessarily proceed to subjugate and conquer the feminine within themselves, such as the need to relate, to enter into dialogue and, above all, to be receptive. What remains after such masculine subjugation and conquest of the feminine is, as we shall see in this chapter, the ideal of ever-more powerful masculine mind in ever-increasing control of the rest of the cosmos. If that, however, is the long-term cosmic objective, what the world is witnessing at present is, in cosmic terms, the relatively minor struggle between supermasculine men for control of the earth and exploitation of its natural resources. It is, I suggest, within such a context that we might best view the nuclear arms race. It is a particularly menacing consequence of masculine competition and ambition to control and subdue what is 'other'. At the same time the nuclear arms race — the drive towards death — is the most appropriate symbol of the masculine drive to repress totally what is 'feminine' within the male consciousness. Beyond the nuclear arms race — if there is to be a beyond — there looms the prospect of a totally masculinised world. In the first part of this chapter, I attempt to illustrate what this might entail by examining some of the writings of three prominent twentieth-century men, the novelist H.G. Wells, the marxist scientist J.D. Bernal, and the nuclear physicist Freeman J. Dyson. The activities of Dyson in opposing a test-ban treaty and contributing to the design of the neutron bomb, at least in part because of a masculine *weltanschauung*, before totally changing course and becoming an important campaigner for the 1963 test-ban treaty will then refocus the discussion on to the specific problem of the nuclear arms race and the chance we have either of persuading our Captain Waltons to turn back or of ourselves taking hold of the rudder of spaceship earth. I begin my elaboration of the masculine *weltanschauung* with a brief look at the influential novelist and science fiction writer, H.G. Wells.

'Towards the immense and awful future of our race'

We recall from Chapter 2 how Leo Szilard, who in 1939 had drafted the catalytic letter to President Roosevelt, had seven years earlier read H.G. Wells's *The World Set Free* and had subsequently received most interesting advice from Wells's German publisher, Otto Mandl. The rather doubtful burden of this advice was that successive world wars could be avoided only if men provided themselves with abundant opportunities for heroism and confrontation with danger by undertaking the magnificent adventure of conquering outer space. Szilard's response had been that *if* this was so, then only the controlled release of nuclear energy would enable mankind to embark on such a heroic and necessarily hazardous mission. Some twenty years later the Polish-born mathematician, Stanislaw Ulam, who had worked at Los Alamos on both atomic and hydrogen weapons, would help set in motion a project to use atomic bombs as propellants for space craft. Recalling the influence of Jules Verne and H.G. Wells on his pre-adult thinking, Ulam would write that 'even in my boyish dreams, I did not imagine that some day I would take part in equally fantastic undertakings'.[2] Although Ulam's project ultimately failed, H.G. Wells's dream of space exploration is already being realised. While it remains to be seen whether or not humanity will escape an atomic world war — and Wells lived just long enough to witness the awful events of August 1945 — it is fascinating to note what this remarkable man himself had to say in 1913 about the future of humankind following the disastrous atomic world war that he envisaged for the mid-1950s, a world war ominously preceded, in Wells's story, by a catastrophic financial crisis and the massive unemployment that accompanied it.

Humanity, we can be thankful, is not entirely wiped out by the ensuing nuclear devastation but its leaders finally learn the necessary lesson and, according to Wells, world government is at last established on the earth. Of particular interest to us, educational reconstruction is placed in the hands of a committee of men and women dominated for a period of time by Marcus Karenin, a Russian physically but not mentally crippled from birth who at the end of the novel is stoically awaiting a dangerous operation to relieve his painful physical condition. At a newly established station for surgical work high in the

Himalayas, perched on a granite terrace surrounded by a towering wilderness of ice and snow (we return to the ominous texture of *Frankenstein*), Karenin optimistically tells the men and women keeping him company of his hopes for mankind's future.

Karenin's first task is to rebuke a fellow patient and poet for so ardently rejoicing in the wave of lovemaking that has apparently swept the world during the present period of reconstruction: 'I know your songs, Kahn, your half-mystical songs, in which you represent this old hard world dissolving into a luminous haze of love — sexual love.' But Kahn, imaginative though he is, is too young to comprehend that 'the power that has brought man into these high places under this blue-veiled blackness of the sky and which beckons us on towards the immense and awful future of our race, is riper and deeper and greater than any such emotions'. Let young people sing and rejoice and be lovely and wonderful but adult humanity will inevitably detach itself from such immature goings-on and take the path that is 'the eternal search for knowledge and the great adventure of power'. The institutions of the world that exaggerate the differences between the sexes must be changed so that woman, previously specialised for love and reproduction, will become unspecialised and hence 'as parts of and contribution to the universal mind of the race' will join with man as fellow-travellers along the new, exciting and hazardous path of the future.[3]

Abolish women! This cannot and must not be. It is Karenin's turn to be rebuked and the chief administrator of the surgical station, Rachel Borken, sets him straight:

Apart from sex we are different from you. We take up life differently. Forget we are — females, Karenin, and still we are a different sort of human being with a different use. In some things we are amazingly secondary. Here am I in this place because of my trick of management, and Edith [an already famous cytologist] is here because of her patient, subtle hands. That does not alter the fact that nearly the whole body of science is man made; that does not alter the fact that men do so predominantly make history, that you could nearly write a complete history of the world without mentioning a woman's name. And on the other hand we have a gift of devotion, of inspiration, a distinctive power for truly loving beautiful things, a care for life and a peculiar keen close eye for behaviour. You know men are blind beside us in these last matters. You know they are restless — and fitful. We have a steadfastness. We may never draw the broad outlines nor discover the new paths, but in the future isn't there a confirming and sustaining and supplying role for us? As important perhaps as yours? Equally important. We hold the world up, Karenin, though you may have raised it.

While Karenin quickly replies that he agrees with Borken, he nevertheless insists that women must in future learn to think of themselves not as women — and hence in relation to men — but in relation to the sun and stars. They have to cease to be men's adventure in order to accompany men on a great mutual adventure. In any case, the human beings of the future will go on to mould bodies and feelings and personal reactions as boldly as they now carve mountains and direct the oceans and air currents. Man will admit no limit to his power of self-modification for there will be no limit to either his knowledge or his power. Science will therefore provide the means to settle one old dispute for ever. 'If woman is too much for us,' Karenin laughs good-humouredly towards Borken, 'we'll reduce her to a minority, and if we do not like any type of men and women, we'll have no more of it.' Bodies will be discarded with all their animal limitations and the spirit of man will be free to soar to a new future. 'In a little while men who will know how to bear the strange gravitations, the altered pressures, the attenuated unfamiliar gases and all the fearful strangeness of space will be venturing out from this earth,' declared Karenin. 'This ball will be no longer enough for us; our spirit will reach out.' What will be the fate of the first space-travellers? 'They may succeed out there; they may perish, but other men will follow them...'[4]

Karenin knew that he might well die as a result of the operation, as indeed he does. But, as the sun disappeared behind the mountains, Karenin's last words were defiant ones addressed to an old adversary. Man would soon be setting out from earth, first stop the moon and then, eventually, the conquest of the sun. 'I shall put my foot on your spotted face and tug you about by your fiery locks,' warned Karenin. 'Old Sun... well may you slink behind the mountains from me, well may you cower...'[5]

Perhaps we should not read too much into the good-humoured earnestness of Wells's Karenin. Yet it might give us at least pause for thought. There is to be a masculinisation of life in three ways: the aim of human life is to be the conquest of matter throughout the universe, human beings are to become as far as possible pure (immortal) mind shedding as much of their earthly hindrances as possible, and woman, freed from the role of reproducer, is to participate as man's equal in the great male adventure of conquering the universe. There is, in other words, to be the concrete realisation of a Cartesian-like cosmos, a cosmos of disembodied (masculine) mind in ever-increasing control of mindless (feminine) matter. In this cosmos Dr Frankenstein will not make the mistake of leaving Elizabeth, nor for that matter would he have the opportunity of returning to Elizabeth; for an intellectualised, mentalised Elizabeth will be constantly at his side, contributing her part to whatever mad mission the two are at work on.

A new species and the future triumph of masculine mind

A distressed and disconsolate H.G. Wells lived for only one year after the destruction of Hiroshima and Nagasaki. A world-famous scientist who lived to see the full realisation of the atomic age, who wrote frequently on the future of man and the responsibilities of scientists, a scientist who influenced many others, not least with his 1929 essay *The World, the Flesh and the Devil* (which was reprinted in 1970 with the author's approval), is John Desmond Bernal. If one seeks a horror picture of a totally masculinised future, sketched with clarity and honesty, one need search no further than this very first book by Bernal. Its subtitle, *An Inquiry into the Future of the Three Enemies of the Rational Soul*, conveys the essence of the masculine thesis that the author promulgates with such passionate conviction. The three enemies of the rational soul have indeed met their match in J.D. Bernal, as a brief exposition of his famous essay quickly demonstrates.

It is science, we learn from Bernal, that will lead the way to a future free from material scarcity. Very soon, the reader of *The World, the Flesh and the Devil* is told, for every place in which we can imitate nature, 'we shall be able to improve on her in ten'. This would mean the realisation of a world no longer inimical to full human growth and one capable of supporting a much enlarged population. This future population, however, while secure from want and enjoying ample leisure would still be restricted to the earth's surface and subject to possible adverse climatic changes. But not for long. The earth will quickly be left behind. 'Already ambition is stirring in men to conquer space as they conquered the air,' writes Bernal. Indeed, man will not rest content, believes Bernal, until he has colonised most of the sidereal universe to the extent of invading and organising the stars themselves for his own purposes. Just as Karenin called out his friendly warning to the setting sun, so Karenin's successor very simply affirms that 'the stars cannot be allowed to continue in their old way'. Nothing less than conquest of the entire material universe is, then, Bernal's answer to the challenge from the first of the rational soul's enemies, namely material scarcity and the prison that is the earth.[6]

Because the rational soul is housed in a body subject to decay and disintegration — the rational soul's second enemy — Bernal suggests that after a suitable period of time occupied in the 'larval' activities of dancing, poetry, lovemaking, and, occasionally, reproduction, man can and will terminate such ordinary life by having his brain transferred to a shock-proof metal container that not only keeps the brain alive and functioning but allows it through highly complex sensory imputs and motor mechanisms to be totally mobile and manipulative of the environment. 'It is brain that counts,' states Bernal, 'and to have a brain suffused by fresh and correctly prescribed blood is to be alive — to think.' The complex surgical operations would eventually be carried out, Bernal writes, 'by mechanisms controlled by the transformed heads of the [medical] profession', though in the earlier and experimental stages, of course, the operations would still have to be done by 'human surgeons and physiotherapists'. The end result would be the transformation of a mortal man into a not yet immortal but very long-lived 'completely effective, mentally directed mechanism'. Although Bernal agrees that the new man must undoubtedly appear to the uninitiated as a strange, monstrous and inhuman creature, nevertheless this future man is claimed by Bernal to be the logical outcome of the type of humanity that exists at present, normal man being an evolutionary dead end. The new men will enjoy the advantage of not only being able to connect up with each other in a very direct way, literally sharing each other's feelings, but will be able to form multiple organisms and hence truly achieve immortality. Finally, Bernal affirms, 'the nature of life-processes themselves will be far more intensively studied' and eventually life will be created — at first only for experimental purposes and then for quite other reasons. 'Men will not be content to manufacture life,' states Bernal, 'they will want to improve on it'. We are asked to agree, therefore, that the flesh — the second of the rational soul's enemies — poses no serious obstacles to the advancement of intelligence in the cosmos.[7]

The most serious obstacle to the rational soul's progress is posed by its third and most elusive enemy, the devil, namely human desires and motives. For if humans do not *want* the changes which Bernal suggests will certainly be *possible* in the future, then the changes will not happen. 'Whether an age or an individual will express itself in creative thinking or in repetitive pedantry,' writes Bernal, 'is more a matter of desire than of intellectual power, and it is probably more the nature of their desires than of their capacities that will determine whether or not humanity will develop further.' But what will be the future of desire in a materially sufficient world? Bernal, struggling with the Freudian hypothesis that science is but a consequence of a sublimation of sexual desire, expresses uncertainty. Although there is a real danger, he suggests, that a golden age could settle permanently on the world so reducing life to a static, idyllic, Melanesian existence of eating, drinking, friendliness, lovemaking, dancing and singing, Bernal expresses confidence, like Karenin before him, that this will not happen. For a sound intellectual humanity, enjoying a full adult sexuality, will certainly not be content with indefinitely repeating itself in circles but will need a 'real externalisation in the transforming of the universe and itself'. While obviously there is a danger that a breakdown in mechanical civilisation could bring about a wide-ranging revulsion to further mechanisation, especially of the kind Bernal envisages, so that the opportunity for further progress would consequently be lost, Bernal sees a way out of the dilemma. The conflict between the 'humanisers' and the 'mechanisers' could conceivably be resolved by the splitting of the human race into two parts, one part developing a fully balanced humanity and a second part, consisting of the mechanisers, groping their way unsteadily beyond humanity.[8]

Looking forward, then, to an increasingly mechanised future despite the ever present existence of 'very sane reactionaries' who will always advise against further progress, Bernal suggests in his penultimate chapter that the sexual instincts of the new man will be sublimated in part into scientific research and in large part into the aesthetic quest to determine the desirable form of the humanly controlled universe. Because emotion will in the future be under rational control it will thus present no danger to progress. Of course, while it certainly would be dangerous to the future of progress if feelings were presently controllable since a great majority of men would probably be content to remain in a state of more or less ecstatic happiness, we are assured that the man of the future will undoubtedly have discovered that happiness is not an end of life. What, however, is the purpose of life according to Bernal? Bernal closes the chapter with what can only be described as an apotheosis of the Faustian spirit:

> We must not assume static psychology and a further static knowledge. The immediate future which is our own desire, we seek; in achieving it we become different; becoming different we desire something new, so there is no staleness except when development itself has stopped. Moreover, development, even in the most refined stages, will always be a very critical process; the dangers to the whole structure of humanity and its successors will not decrease as their wisdom increases, because, knowing more and wanting more they will dare more, and in daring will risk their own destruction. But this daring, this experimentation is really the essential quality of life.

To dare and, in doing so, to risk self-destruction. This is the essential quality of life![9]

In his final chapter Bernal discusses how a possible dimorphism of humanity may be brought about, namely how one part of humanity may transform itself into a new progressive species while the greater part of humanity unprogressively remains human. The key group of humans will be the scientists, Bernal suggests, perhaps by being forced into positions of political power as a result of the consequences of their own insatiable curiosity while aided in no small part by the indifference and lethargy of the masses. Unable to assess or control what is going on in the scientific corporations of the future, perhaps for a while not even caring, humanity as a whole might wake up too late to the fact that something important and terrifying had happened. 'From one point of view,' Bernal writes, 'the scientists would emerge as a new species and leave humanity behind; from another, humanity — the humanity that counts — might seem to change *en bloc*, leaving behind in a relatively primitive state those too stupid or too stubborn to change.'[10] Should there not be sufficient room on earth for the two species, the progressive beings might have to reduce accordingly the numbers of the unprogressive. On the other hand, assuming that the colonisation of space is already well under way the progressive beings could simply manage the earth as a human zoo with its gently meandering inhabitants unaware that they exist merely for purposes of observation and experiment. Bernal concludes his book by expressing the hope that because the latter solution is both possible and probable it will not be rejected for those reasons. Are there enough human beings, he asks, sufficiently mature to allow primitive desires for a mysterious future to be changed by recognition of the new possibilities into correspondingly progressive desires — desires that will ensure the concrete realisation of the new possibilities? Bernal does not know the answer to his question but it is clear where his sympathies lie.

The author of *The World, the Flesh and the Devil* clearly follows H.G. Wells's Karenin in all but two aspects. Where Karenin sees all of humanity transforming itself into what amounts to a new male species intent on colonising the universe, Bernal envisages the greater likelihood of only a minority of humanity wishing to make and making the daring decisive leap. Also while Karenin discusses and proposes a solution to 'the woman question', Bernal does not (although asserting as an aside that 'devotion to children has never been the mainspring of human activity').[11] It is apparent, however, that either women remain as women in the human zoo or they become masculinised as 'completely effective, mentally directed mechanisms' in company with the minority of progressive males. Bernal therefore hopes for, predicts and advocates a masculinised cosmos. Male mind and intellect will triumph over female matter and emotion, indeed the mind of the future will direct the matter of the entire cosmos, no less! Moreover, there need be no fear for the safety of the future Dr Frankensteins in their continual quest for ever-greater knowledge and power. For the deliberate risk of self-destruction is the very measure of the Dr Frankenstein's progressiveness![12]

The visions of both Wells and Bernal are fantasies. In the one, peace is attained on earth after a horrendous world war involving atomic weapons, in the other world unity is simply assumed to follow the increasing scientisation of human society. However, the very ethos of both futures which is the masculine one of ever-extending control of the material universe indicates the intrinsic implausibility of each. Males intent on dominating everything non-human, while arranging for women to become supporting males, are hardly likely to agree not to compete among themselves for power. That uncontrollable masculine drive — 'there is something at work in my soul, which I do not understand' — will in general inevitably include other males within its ambit, and the 'ideal' Baconian activity of co-operative, collective penetration and impregnation of female matter is always likely to be a non-starter.

I can best illustrate this thesis by looking at the concrete example of a world-famous scientist — and admirer of Bernal's first work — who has eloquently and courageously written of his life during three very turbulent decades. What I shall try to indicate, according to my reading of Freeman J. Dyson's own account of his activities, is that it is not until Dyson explicitly queries the Baconian injunction, 'the effecting of all things possible', that he is able to desert his captain and join the rebelling sailors demanding, in this case, the abolition of nuclear tests in the atmosphere. In so following Dyson's career we are given a further perspective on the events that have preoccupied us in this book: the construction of atomic weapons, the bombing of Hiroshima and Nagasaki, the construction of hydrogen weapons and the mentality that underlies this nuclear terror.

The Faustian bargain rejected

As a young man not yet twenty years of age, the mathematically gifted Dyson had joined Bomber Command in 1943 as a civilian scientist in the Operational Research Section. The war, Dyson remembers, was to bring him to reject one by one all his moral principles. Before the war he had been a pacifist, a follower of Gandhi, but after the commencement of war he convinced himself of the necessity of violent resistance to Hitler although he believed such resistance should stop short of the use of bombing. A few years later he had convinced himself that even indiscriminate bombing of cities was morally justified since it was helping to win the war. A year later, although he no longer believed in the war-winning efficacy of indiscriminate bombing, he nevertheless continued to work at Bomber Command on the grounds that he was morally justified in his efforts to save the lives of bomber crews. After the terrible destruction of Dresden during the last spring of the war Dyson writes that he could no longer find any excuses at all for his war work. Yet in August 1945 he was still working at Bomber Command and ready to join a British fleet of 300 bombers, called Tiger Force, which Churchill was to send to the Far East to assist in the American bombing of Japanese cities. In Dyson's words:

> We were to be based on Okinawa, and since the Japanese had almost no air defenses, we were to bomb, like the Americans, in daylight. I found this new slaughter of defenseless Japanese even more sickening than the slaughter of well-defended Germans. Still I did not quit. By that time, I had been at war so long that I could hardly remember peace. No living poet had words to describe that emptiness of the soul which allowed me to go on killing without hatred and without remorse. But Shakespeare understood it, and he gave Macbeth the words:
>
> > I am in blood
> > Stepped in so far, that, should I wade no more,
> > Returning were as tedious as go o'er.

The journey to the Far East was not necessary. When the bombing of Hiroshima was announced at Dyson's breakfast table in the form of a giant newspaper headline 'New Force of Nature Harnessed', Dyson remembers how he approved of the big and impersonal headline proclaiming childhood's end, how he did not bother to go to the office that day, and how he looked forward to the pleasure of one day meeting the obviously outstandingly competent men who had built atomic weapons while he, Dyson, had been messing around with old-fashioned bombs. Throughout the war years, Dyson writes, he had never forgotten Eddington's 1935 warning of the grim possibility of harnessing atomic energy for destructive purposes.[13]

In 1949 the pleasure Dyson had looked forward to in August 1945 became a reality when he enrolled as one of Hans Bethe's graduate students at Cornell University. Together with Bethe, there were the ex-Los Alamos physicists Robert Wilson, Philip Morrison, Richard Feynman and many others. Dyson remembers with amazement how quickly he had fitted in with 'this bunch of weaponeers' and he recalls the endless conversation of his colleagues about their Los Alamos days, their pride and nostalgia, their talk of how Los Alamos had been for them a great experience, a time of hard work and comradeship, and a time of great happiness. Commenting on his colleagues' indignant but understandable repudiation of Oppenheimer's notorious assertion that 'the physicists have known sin', Dyson nevertheless found himself forced to agree with Oppenheimer. Los Alamos had been 'a great lark' for his Cornell colleagues. They did not just build the bomb, Dyson claims. They *enjoyed* building it. They had the best time of their lives in building it. That is what, in Dyson's opinion, Oppenheimer was referring to when he said they had sinned. And, Dyson asserts, Oppenheimer was right.[14]

In 1956, after outstanding achievements in 'pure' physics, Dyson was invited by Frederic de Hoffmann, ex-Los Alamos physicist and newly appointed president of General Atomic, to join him and Edward Teller and some other thirty or forty people in the attempt to design a safe nuclear reactor as a commercial venture for this fledgeling division of the General Dynamics Corporation. For nineteen years, Dyson writes, ever since reading Eddington's description of the possible *peaceful* uses of atomic energy, he had waited for the chance of making Eddington's dream come true. This joint venture was to prove not only a limited commercial success for General Atomic but, significantly for Dyson, was to introduce him to Theodore Taylor, another ex-Los Alamos physicist who had successfully pioneered 'a new art form, the design of small efficient bombs that could be squeezed into tight spaces'.[15]

In 1958, the year after Sputnik, Dyson was invited by Taylor to participate in a very special project, funded in its early days by

General Atomic with the support of de Hoffmann and then by the Department of Defense. Originally suggested three years earlier by Stanislaw Ulam and a fellow mathematician, this project was no less than the design and construction of a spaceship to be propelled through space by the detonation of atomic bombs dropped periodically from the spaceship itself. Accepting Taylor's invitation, Dyson began his full-time year in the pursuit of this incredible goal with the writing of 'A Space Traveler's Manifesto'. 'From my childhood,' readers of the manifesto learn, 'it has been my conviction that men would reach the planets in my lifetime, and that I should help in the enterprise.' And help Dyson certainly did. Indeed, Dyson writes that the fifteen months he spent working on Project Orion — as the project was to be called — were the most exciting and in many ways the happiest of his scientific life. Nuclear weapons were to be given a peaceful application in a truly significant project. During this time, however, an impassioned debate was taking place in the United States concerning the advisability or otherwise of negotiating a treaty with the Soviet Union to ban all nuclear testing. Hans Bethe, Dyson's old friend, supported a comprehensive test ban whereas Edward Teller, Dyson's new friend, was resolutely opposed. Dyson himself was adamant in his views: 'My affection and respect for Bethe never wavered,' we read, 'but in the debate I was heart and soul on Teller's side. Orion could not survive without bomb tests.' The project could not survive without bomb tests! In the short run, Dyson explains, it was necessary to show sceptics that the spaceship could take the blast from a nuclear explosion and remain intact; in the long run it was necessary to design fission-free nuclear bombs — and this could be done only by much testing — so that radioactive fallout from a space flight would be reduced almost to zero. It was this commitment to the 'peaceful and pure' Project Orion that not only would take Dyson to the Livermore Laboratory for two weeks in the summer of 1959 for the purpose of trying to design fission-free weapons but would also, at least in part, motivate him to write an article for the influential journal *Foreign Affairs* arguing passionately against the desirability of a test-ban treaty with the Soviet Union. Siding totally with Teller, Dyson strongly objected to the label of warmonger ascribed to Teller merely because, Dyson writes, 'of his passionate desire to explore *to the end* the thermonuclear technology that he had pioneered' (emphasis added).[16]

As Dyson now acknowledges, although he was at Livermore only because he 'wanted to explore the universe' and certainly not because there was thought of murder in his heart, nevertheless the fact remains that at Livermore he helped to design what would later become known as the 'neutron bomb'. After that experience, he writes, he could never again 'honestly say that the bombs we wanted to use for Orion had nothing to do with bombs that are designed for killing people'. In his *Foreign Affairs* article, 'The Future Development of Nuclear Weapons', Dyson went on to suggest that a permanent test ban would be a dangerous illusion because future improvements in weapons technology (particularly the fission-free weapons that Orion so badly needed!) would create irresistible pressure towards secret or open violation of any such ban. These pressures would come about because the country perfecting fission-free weapons would enjoy the military advantages of being able to fight 'tactical nuclear wars' and ultimately perhaps enjoy both the military and non-military advantages of long-range, economical space travel.[17]

In retrospect, Dyson writes, it is easy to see that his article was mistaken in at least four ways. He writes that technically he misjudged the time scale for the development of fission-free weapons, militarily he was wrong in thinking of tactical nuclear war as a feasible way to employ military forces, politically he was wrong in stating that a test ban would surely be ineffective as a means of preventing development of fission-free weapons, and morally he was wrong in not questioning the morality of supplying the American military with new weapons (Dyson explains, not referring to his second world war experiences or to Hiroshima and Nagasaki, that 'Vietnam has taught us that our own weapons are not always wisely used'). The article, Dyson concludes in retrospect, was a desperate attempt to salvage an untenable position with 'spurious emotional claptrap'.[18]

What, then, motivated Dyson to write what was, he now agrees, such a desperately misconceived article? Was he behaving similarly to the Los Alamos 'bunch of weaponeers' who had redoubled their efforts to make the atomic bomb before the war ended? Did his passionate commitment to the 'peaceful and pure' Project Orion turn Dyson into a passionate Coldwarmonger, anxious to keep the Cold

War boiling so that his own pet project would thrive as a consequence? Cautioning that it is difficult to be fully aware of one's own
motives, Dyson gives the following explanation:

> I cannot excuse this [article] on the grounds that it was written
> as a last desperate attempt to save Orion from extinction. Ob-
> viously there was more to it than that. It was written, in so far
> as I can be aware of my own motives as an act of personal loyalty
> to Edward Teller and to his colleagues with whom I worked at
> Livermore. I was deeply impressed by the fragility of the efforts
> at Livermore to design radically cleaner explosives. Inside the
> barbed-wire fence at Livermore, all the serious thinking was be-
> ing done by five or six gifted young people, who worked under
> depressing conditions of physical and mental isolation. They
> might at any moment decide to quit. Outside the fence, the
> whole society was indifferent or actively hostile to their efforts.
> My article was in some sense an act of psychological atonement
> which I owed to Edward Teller for the fact that I was leaving
> him and going back to Oppenheimer at Princeton. I wanted to
> show my friends at Livermore that there was at least one person
> outside the fence who cared.

Six years after Dyson wrote his *Foreign Affairs* article, the Air Force
officially ended Project Orion. While Air Force personnel had tried
for six years to devise military applications of the Orion system in
the end they discovered what, according to Dyson, 'we had known
from the beginning, that no reasonable military application of the
Orion system exists'. This was, however, very definitely not the
point of view stated in the *Foreign Affairs* article.[19]

In the summer of 1963 Freeman Dyson joined the test-ban team
of the Arms Control and Disarmament Agency (ACDA) and at the
end of August spoke to the Senate Foreign Relations Committee
against Edward Teller in favour of ratifying the proposed test-ban
treaty. How had such a remarkable change come about? We learn
from Dyson that during 1961 and 1962 the United States and the
Soviet Union exploded more bombs than ever before, so producing
an alarming increase in the amount of radioactive fallout in the Northern Hemisphere. According to the study Dyson then made, the
number of nuclear weapons tests carried out since 1945 had doubled

every three years or so. Noting that it takes roughly three years to plan and carry out a bomb test, Dyson then reasoned that if each bomb test raised two new questions which have to be answered some three years later by two further bomb tests there could be only one sane conclusion. 'Some questions have to remain unanswered. At some point, we have to stop.' It was in that summer of 1962, Dyson writes, that he accepted for the first time the inevitability of a test ban. A year later, as a member of the ACDA test-ban team Dyson supported the inclusion of 'peaceful' nuclear explosions in the test-ban treaty in order to ensure agreement with the Soviet Union. In doing so, Dyson was adding his signature to Orion's death warrant and he knew it. 'Some questions have to remain unanswered. At some point we have to stop.' Dyson had reached, for him, a parting of the ways and he chose the path of science in the service of humanity, not the path of humanity in the service of masculine science and scientists.[20]

In *Disturbing the Universe* Dyson confirms that on no account would he consider reviving Project Orion if by some miracle the necessary funds were suddenly to become available (and 'peaceful' nuclear testing permitted). For, by its nature, the Orion spacecraft inevitably leaves a radioactive mess behind it. Moreover, not only has the public attitude to environmental pollution changed in the twenty years since Orion's inception but so has Dyson's. Orion will therefore not be resurrected, at least not by Dyson. The commitment to space travel, however, remains with Dyson, burning as brightly as ever.[21]

It is sobering to read Dyson's present reflections on the nature of human beings, military scientists and the future of space travel. Pessimistically Dyson is forced to the conclusion that a fascination with violence lies somewhere deep in the hearts of all of us and that grown-up people are only over-grown children who still like to play with dangerous toys. It seems to me that in this particular case it might have been better if Dyson had written men for people and boys for children. However, Dyson affirms that the intellectual arrogance of his profession is responsible for the devotion of scientific strategists to offensive weapons, rather than defensive; for defensive weapons, according to the mentality of military physicists, could never be described as 'technically sweet'. As for Edward Teller,

Dyson writes that possessed by an indomitable urge to light a thermonuclear fire on earth the Hungarian physicist was surely following in the footsteps of Faust. In Dyson's opinion:

> Nuclear explosives have a glitter more seductive than gold to those who play with them. To command nature to release in a pint pot the energy that fuels the stars, to lift *by pure thought* a million tons of rock into the sky, these are exercises of the human will that produce an illusion of illimitable power [emphasis added].

Once again it seems to me that Dyson would have come nearer the mark had he substituted the word 'masculine' for 'human' in the second sentence.[22]

Despite, however, the gravity of the nuclear arms race and its threat of nuclear holocaust, Dyson puts forward the view that there exists a still graver threat to humanity, a threat arising not from nuclear physics but from developments in biology. For although nuclear war would destroy civilisation it would not, Dyson believes, exterminate the human species. On the other hand, the possibility of deliberately distorting or mutilating the genetic apparatus of human beings does raise the spectre of abolition of the human species. Ten years earlier, like Bernal before him, Dyson had seen space travel as not only providing people with the perpetually dangerous frontier they ultimately need but, more importantly, as providing a place where the scientific adventurers of the future 'can be safe from prying eyes, free to experiment undisturbed with the creation of radically new types of human beings, surpassing us in mental capacities as we surpass the apes'.[23] In *Disturbing the Universe* this view is repeated and reinforced. Human beings will inevitably travel into space and eventually they and their descendants will expand as a million species occupying every ecological niche available to them. Men will play God but as local deities not as lords of the universe. There will be insanity as there is now and some rulers will no doubt be as crazy as H.G. Wells's Doctor Moreau on his little island. But in the long run, Dyson believes, the sane will adapt and survive better than the insane. Should this wave of human and post-human expansion throughout the universe meet other forms of life, the hope is expressed that the ecologies of our neighbours will not be disrupted or overwhelmed since the universe is undoubtedly large enough to provide ample living space for all of us. 'The expansion of life over the universe,' summarises Dyson,

> is a beginning, not an end. At the same time as life is extending its habitat quantitatively, it will also be changing and evolving qualitatively into new dimensions of mind and spirit that we cannot imagine. The acquisition of new territory is important, not as an end in itself, but as a means to enable life to experiment with intelligence in a million different forms.[24]

The nuclear arms race and masculine science

We have seen, then, that 'pure' physics, the nuclear arms race, space travel and 'the secret of life' all interconnect. Freeman Dyson's first love was space travel, his first major scientific success came in the 'pure' physics of relativistic quantum mechanics, and the need to produce 'clean' bombs for the Orion Project led to his working at Livermore and to a contribution to the making of the neutron bomb (and at least in part to his Cold War article in *Foreign Affairs*); while at the back of it looms the spectre of the discovery of 'the secret of life' and of limitless, unwatched experiments in the creation of new life forms in the immensity of conquered space. Perhaps within half a century — no one can know the time span for sure — new and entirely man-made complex forms of life will exist both on the earth and at great distances from it. 'Little Boy' and 'Fat Man', 'George' and 'Mike' will then have been put in their proper place.

The worst, then, is still to come. Unable to create life, men of science have demonstrated the power of their intellects in creating weapons that obliterated Hiroshima and Nagasaki and will obliterate civilisation if the nuclear holocaust is launched. Assuming that this holocaust is prevented or sufficiently delayed, the masculine penetration into the secrets of nature that yielded first the discovery of the philosopher's stone will eventually yield 'the secret of life'. Very eloquently Max Delbrück, a year after the end of the war, ruefully recalled his excessive optimism of 1938 while yet promising great things to come:

Perhaps you would like to see this childish young man after

eight years and ask him, just offhand, whether he has solved the riddle of life yet? This will embarrass him, as he has not got anywhere in solving the problem he set out to solve. But being quick to rationalise his failure, this is what he may answer, if he is pressed for an answer: 'Well, I made a slight mistake. I could not do it in a few months. Perhaps it will take a few decades, and perhaps it will take the help of a few dozen people. But listen to what I have found, perhaps you will be interested to join me.'[25]

Appropriately enough, J.D. Bernal writes in a 1968 foreword to *The World, the Flesh and the Devil* that the greatest discovery in all modern science has been the discovery by molecular biologists of the double helix, that now famous structure which explains in physical, quantum terms, Bernal optimistically writes, the basis of life and gives some idea of its origin. Certainly the techniques of molecular biology, and especially those associated with 'recombinant DNA', have brought the creation of complex new life-forms within the realm of feasibility. Rather despairingly the biologist and Nobel laureate George Wald observes: 'It is all too big, and is happening too fast.' Very confidently, on the other hand, the ex-physicist and Nobel laureate Walter Gilbert rejoices: 'We have moved from a period in which we could only look at bacteria... to a period of construction... And this gives us the ability to take an abstract science and actually make it function in the world. That's one of the things I find extraordinarily exciting now.'[26] At the same time, male space travel has already started and assuming that civilisation escapes or sufficiently postpones nuclear holocaust the masculine mentality that constructed and perfected fission and fusion weapons will soon be setting out to colonise the cosmos, implanting in every available ecological niche 'improved' forms of itself and the new forms of life that it has created. It is all a very depressing prospect.

A depressing prospect, that is, for those of us who are insufficiently masculine to enjoy the thrill of the arms race, the excitement of participating in it directly, of playing 'game strategy', or of working our way up the hierarchy of security until we achieve that *special* security clearance.[27] Insufficiently masculine to look forward to becoming increasingly disembodied, ever-more powerful brains controlling ever-greater areas of the material universe. No one who has looked closely at modern science will fail to see at least some similarity between the activities of Mary Shelley's Dr Frankenstein and the activities of leading scientists in producing increasingly sophisticated offensive weapons to those of 'pure' researchers penetrating into the 'recesses of nature' in search of 'the secret of life'. The arms race, above all, appears to be a particularly masculine phenomenon. The American politicians, industrialists, military strategists, weapons scientists and vicarious participants of the arms race seem to me to enjoy their dangerous 'sport' of keeping well ahead of the Soviet Union, quite apart from the very considerable economic benefit that many of them derive from it; they take decisions that accelerate the arms race believing that the Soviet Union will have to do its best to respond in kind (and no doubt some of them would even be prepared as a last resort to provide assistance to the Soviet Union should any dropping out be contemplated or should the Soviet Union threaten to fall hopelessly behind). For their part, the Soviet participants seem to be almost equally determined to keep up; together with legitimate defence needs there are also bureaucratic interests at stake as well as masculine pride. Of course, for both sides the existence of a menacing external enemy can be utilised to justify the perpetuation and even the intensification of social injustice at home and a ready excuse is thereby always conveniently at hand for diversion of resources that ruling groups would otherwise find difficult not to employ in reducing social and economic inequities. In particular, as American capitalist and ruling circles understood so well from 1944 onwards, the inequitable social relations of industrial production in the United States could not survive general disarmament, hence the successful call for and establishment of a 'permanent war economy'. The nuclear arms race does most certainly have its uses in maintaining, not to say increasing, the wealth and power of the already wealthy and powerful and nowhere is this more true than in the United States.[28]

It is my opinion, then, that the principal driving force of the nuclear arms race is not the brute fact of scarce material resources, important though it is, but masculine motivation — in essence, the compulsive desire to lord it over other people and non-human nature, and then manfully to confront a dangerous world. While, for example, the 'more balanced' strategists of neither side *intend* to try to destroy the other militarily since outright military victory is now inconceivable even given the first strike capability which is being built up by the United States, it is the perpetually increasing risk of nuclear war and of the prospect of nuclear disaster that give to these masculine participants in the contest a very special thrill and sense of ultimate power, importance and meaning. As the accuracy of American missiles increases so that Soviet silos can be destroyed by direct hits with a warning time of only a few minutes, so it will become increasingly 'rational' for the Soviet Union to strike first before its own missiles are destroyed by an American first strike. Of course, to avoid American nuclear retaliation following a Soviet pre-emptive first strike the Soviet leadership will not be slow to see the 'wisdom' of providing its armed forces with its own highly accurate first-strike missiles. As soon as submarine-based missiles are as detectable and destroyable as land-based silos, then the nuclear arms race will have reached an all-time high in instability as silos are increasingly 'hardened' against enemy 'penetration' and each side deliberates the wisdom of a first strike.[29] What a game for real men! Were, on the other hand, the economy of the Soviet Union to collapse during this insane competition, then no doubt after a period of masculine exultation American promoters of the arms race would weep over the body of their erstwhile antagonist as the monster wept over Dr Frankenstein's. A great deal of purpose, meaning and excitement would have gone from their lives. The next adversary to be conquered in ceaseless battle would be their own bodies and the cosmos. There is another possibility (apart from the one of aiding the Soviet Union). Rather than just see their 'enemy' collapse economically, perhaps there are some supermasculine competitors in the United States who would prefer to launch an all-out nuclear attack on the Soviet Union after which (as they see it) they would emerge from their special bunkers, heroic and victorious, to confront the exciting challenge of rebuilding a horribly devastated world.

It is, we must bear in mind, masculine motivation that is at issue, not human. Thus I have several times suggested that substitution of the word 'human' by the word 'masculine' in various passages I have quoted would have rendered them more accurate, as, for example, in Freeman Dyson's account of the Faustian mentality or when Emilio Segrè declared that the Trinity test would stand as a great monument of human endeavour for a long time to come. The same 'error', as I see it, occurs in the writings of several analysts and opponents of the arms race. Where John Gofman, for example, states that 'among humans, we observe cases of insatiable appetites for power', I would want to emphasise that the majority of such obsessive humans are males.[30] Frank Barnaby, for example, has argued that while academics, bureaucrats, military men and industrialists financed by the military budget do not want even to risk war, they do want to keep their jobs, improve their professional status, personal power and prestige, and increase their profits — on the face of it, he writes, 'all very human and understandable motives'.[31] With respect to professional status, power, prestige and profit, I again believe that masculine would be a more accurate description of the motives. Similarly, in a perceptive letter to *The Guardian*, A.J. Lane has talked of two driving forces underlying the crises of the century, one being the career structure of politicians, weapons technologists and military men, the other force being 'the restlessness and drive, the impatience with stability, that characterises the human being, that takes us to Everest and to the Moon, and to the discovery of penicillin, but that also explains agression and acquisitiveness and commercial and political exploitation and the current almost pleasurable thrill with which atomic war is being contemplated by many in disregard of the known consequences.'[32] Again, it seems to me that it would be considerably more accurate to replace the words 'the human being' by the words 'the male' or, perhaps even more accurately, by the words 'a small proportion of mostly Western males'. Of course, I do not mean to imply that women cannot and that some do not share such masculine characteristics — they can and some do. What I am affirming is that such masculine characteristics are overwhelmingly displayed by men, not by women, while conceding that females are often all too ready to feel pride in the masculine accomplishments of their males and accord them the masculine status they covet. One recalls the pride Laura Fermi states that she and other Los Alamos wives felt after the destruction of Hiroshima had demonstrated to them the masculine accomplishments of their husbands. 'Quite often, even by staunch feminists,' Paul Hoch regrets, 'the male is still evaluated as either fatal or feeble, a fascinating beast or a dreadful bore.'[33] Masculine motivation, then, is displayed overwhelmingly by men, but in women masculine men can and do all too easily find an appreciative, admiring audience.

The thesis of this book has been that masculine motivation came into its own with the rise of the masculine philosophy in the seventeenth century, a rise greatly aided, of course, by the concurrent development of capitalism. It was indeed with remarkable foresight that Francis Bacon recognised that successful institutionalisation of the 'new science' would inaugurate the 'truly masculine birth of time' and so make possible the 'dominion of man over the universe'. We recall how masculine scientists were liberated from troublesome thoughts of incest by the declaration of the 'death of mother nature', thus leaving them free to seek ever-deepening penetration of male mind into the secrets of female nature and in this way to achieve the 'fathering' of technologies qualitatively superior to anything that female nature is capable of producing. On the other hand, for those masculine scientists in total retreat from sexual woman and *mysterious* female nature, the aim of the masculine philosophy was viewed as and declared to be the ever-increasing control of (male) mind over the barren, passive (female) matter of the cosmos. Much of twentieth-century physics seems indeed to be the final maturation of what was so convincingly begun in the seventeeth century. In our discussion of both 'pure' and military physics we have many times noted an obsession with power, control and epoch-making triumphs on the part of important protagonists, objectives often being explicitly presented in terms of 'pregnant phallus' metaphors such as the storming of female nature to her inmost citadel with the concomitant fathering of both nuclei and nuclear weapons. In the final 'asexual' future envisaged for mankind — should there be a future at all — a dramatic image is to be found of ever-experimenting, ever-developing intelligence increasingly taking over the running of the material universe. 'Man's place in the physical universe is to be its master,' writes the Nobel laureate Willard Libby. 'It is his place, by controlling the natural forces with his intelligence, to put them to work to his purposes and to build a future world in his own image.' 'Man's place in the physical universe,' Libby modestly claims, '[is] to be its king through the power he alone possesses — the Principle of

Intelligence.'[34]

Scientists seem at times to be uneasily aware of the militaristic, aggressive, sexual metaphors they and their protagonists have often used and continue to use. We recall how Rutherford's biographer, A.S. Eve, in bypassing the very apt description of Rutherford supplied by the astrophysicist G.E. Hale, tried to liken Rutherford, as Thompson likened Percy Shelley, to a male philosopher at rest in the lap of patient nature twining her loosened tresses to see how she will look nicest in his song — a rather far cry from the Rutherford whose powerful advance had, in the imagery of G.E. Hale, forced nature to retreat from trench to trench, and from height to height, until she was making her last unavailing stand in her inmost citadel. Although in the same apologetic vein Professor Sir Andrew Huxley in his 1977 presidential address to the British Association regretted the use of militaristic metaphors to describe scientific inquiry, he nevertheless unproblematically referred to nature as female in character. 'My own inclination,' he told his audience, 'has been to think of the progress of science as resembling the exploration of a newly discovered continent. Nature is there, not like an enemy resisting our advance, but waiting for us to find our way through her jungles and across her mountain passes.'[35] While in this metaphor nature is likened to a female continent passively awaiting the imprint of the active male explorer, if my reading of pioneering treks through jungles and across mountain passes serves me well, a virgin continent must still be reckoned as posing unexpected dangers that the intrepid male explorer must be prepared to meet and overcome. Indeed, however non-aggressively the quest to know nature is described, one image persistently occurs, namely that nature is regarded as female and that scientific inquiry progressively renders female nature known and in doing so progressively places nature at the theoretical and manipulative disposal of the scientific investigators. In his memorable television interview entitled 'The Pleasure of Finding Things Out' Richard Feynman vividly describes how 'wild' nature is progressively rendered knowable by scientific inquiry. 'What is wonderful,' he stated, 'is that, as we expand our experience into wilder and wilder regions of experience, every once in a while we have these integrations when everything is pulled together into a unification which turns out to be simpler than it looked before.' As to whether female nature can be known in her inmost citadel or whether there is no such citadel, Feynman expresses his unconcern. 'Nature's there,' he stated, 'and she's going to come out the way she is.'[36] According to Jacob Bronowski, every good scientific experiment is 'a challenge to nature', a challenge which compels nature 'to declare herself for or against our model of her', a challenge that ideally takes place in a laboratory setting where 'we try to strip the test to its naked essentials, yes or no'. This is no easy task, for, as Willard Libby has explained, 'the experienced scientist knows that nature yields her secrets with great reluctance and only to proper suitors'. But the secrets of nature so gained, Bronowski affirms, truly give men the power they seek and rightly need — 'the power by which men struggle to shake off the restrictions in which nature (outer and inner) imprison every other animal'. And men have been strikingly successful: 'We command nature as no animal does,' Bronowski explains, 'because we are able to see her objectively, that is, to analyse her into objects, and to acknowledge that the facts with which she confronts us are as they are — whether we like it or not.'[37]

Such images vividly portray science, at least in part, as a masculine activity whose objective is penetrating, unveiling and knowing the secrets of a decidedly female nature. In the first instance, one might (I think erroneously) regard such science as merely another sphere of masculine activity (interconnecting with the political, industrial and military spheres) in which men are able to assert masculinity through retreat into a competitive male-dominant world in principle devoid of the threat of woman as sexual being and of the challenge of woman as creator of life. Indeed, the biologist Richard Lewontin in his harsh review of James Watson's *The Double Helix* even goes as far as to denote the interaction between man and nature as secondary to science! Recognising that the requirement for great success in science is great ambition and, moreover, an ambition 'for personal triumph over other men, not merely nature', Lewontin flings down a gauntlet: 'Science is a form of competitive and aggressive activity, a contest of man against man that provides knowledge as a side product. That side product is its only advantage over football.'[38] And he admits that Watson is perfectly candid on this issue! But what a momentous side-product it is that is produced by this battle of man against man and of both against nature so properly called the masculine philosophy' by the first Secretary of the Royal Society. Moreover, as a consequence of that side-product achieved through mental penetration into the secrets of female nature, the man of science is, as we have seen, able to initiate that which no amount of successful penetration into female human companions will ever achieve, namely the male creation of fantastic technologies and ultimately the male creation of life.[39]

In short, the deeper the mental penetration into female nature, the greater the mental virility the man of science is able to claim. This observation also affords a partial interpretation of the well-known and significant hierarchy of prestige that exists within the natural sciences, a hierarchy which crudely speaking proceeds downwards from the 'hardest' of the natural sciences, paradigmatically physics, through chemistry to the 'softest' of the sciences such as biology.[40] For given the fundamentally reductionist assumption informing the natural sciences, namely that the world can ultimately be understood in terms of the properties and interactions of its very smallest constituent parts, it is clear that the 'hard' discipline of physics, which studies the physical properties of atoms and their constituent parts, requires greater penetrating power than the softer discipline of chemistry which studies molecules and the yet softer discipline of biology which studies the behaviour of living beings and the chemical functioning of their constituent parts. We may, for example, sympathise with the chemist George Kistiakowsky who, while wishing to regard himself at Los Alamos as a 'brother physicist' like the rest, recalls the experience of Oppenheimer publicly informing the distinguished chemist that he was an 'outstanding third-rate physicist'.[41] As for biology, the ex-physicist Francis Crick and co-discoverer with James Watson of the structure of the DNA molecule writes simply that 'the ultimate aim of the modern movement in biology is in fact to explain *all* biology in terms of physics and chemistry'. His fellow Nobel laureate, James Watson, agrees that 'complete certainty now exists among essentially all biochemists' that all characteristics of living organisms including, of course, hereditary phenomena, will eventually be 'completely understood in terms of the coordinate interactions of small and large molecules'.[42]

Within each discipline, moreover, there also exists a hierarchy of prestige for the same basic reductionist reason. For example, within physics, the study of elementary particles is typically regarded as more prestigious than other branches of physics and within biology the study of gene structure and replication is more prestigious than the study of macroscopic biological systems, such as ecology.[43] Furthermore, within each discipline or sub-discipline the more theoretical is the practice, i.e. the more 'mental' and less contaminated with 'female' matter it is, the greater is the prestige accruing to the practitioners. Thus within physics, theoretical physics is widely regarded as more prestigious than experimental, in other words, as 'harder' and more 'penetrating'. All credit, then, to the theoretical physicist S.A. Goudsmit who complained at a History of Science Congress in 1962 that theoretical physicists were too often given an unfair share of the credit and, as an example, how sad he felt to see that textbooks had now chopped off even the hallowed name of Rutherford from the once widely used term, the Bohr-Rutherford atom.[44] Pure mathematics, on the other hand, while admirably devoid of contamination with female matter and therefore a prestigious discipline within the sciences is also devoid of physics' mental penetration into female matter and therefore not only lacks physics' virile prestige but has an ambiguous status, being neither art nor science.[45]

Of course, while within the sciences and within each science there exist hierarchies of masculinity, science as a whole is clearly regarded as masculine by its practitioners vis-à-vis the arts or non-scientific practice. We may recall the opinion of C.S. Sherrington who, writing at the beginning of the twentieth century, declared of medicine (very much at the 'soft' end of the masculinity spectrum) that it possesses two aspects, a scientific, rational and therefore male aspect constantly struggling to triumph over a non-scientific, trial-and-error and therefore female aspect. His words are worth quoting in full:

Who will refute me if I assert that medicine is as well as an art a science? Somewhere it is said that woman is the last thing that man will ever civilise. So the scientific aspect, the male-face of the two-visaged medicine, thinks of that female face, the empiric, with whom his lot is linked. He feels that his other half is the last thing science will ever render wholly rational. By dint of patient toil he improves her practice, showing her a reason every now and then.[46]

From this point of view one can begin to make more sense of the passionate condemnation by defenders of the 'rationality' of science of those investigators of the history of science who have dared to suggest or have been interpreted as suggesting that non-rational or even irrational factors may play an important role in the development of scientific theories. Thus when the philosopher of science Imre Lakatos asserts that 'in [Thomas] Kuhn's view scientific revolution is irrational, a matter for mob psychology' and that 'in the light of better rational reconstructions of science one can always reconstruct more of actual great science as rational', Kuhn himself is moved to reply that 'no process essential to scientific development can be labelled "irrational" without vast violence to the term' and that to interpret his account of the history of science as a defence of irrationality in science is 'not only absurd but vaguely obscene'.[47] What is at stake here? Reviewing the proceedings of a confrontation in the late 1970s between philosophers of science on the one hand and historians on the other, a distinguished member of the latter discipline, Stephen Brush, has explained that the combined discipline of history *and* philosophy of science is going through a protracted and difficult birth and that in his opinion 'the most important question may be which [of the two parents] is the father, which the mother, and what will be the gender of the offspring?'![48]

Not surprisingly there are practitioners in the history of science — never mind the philosophy of science — who regard their discipline as a 'hard' one and who believe and advocate that historians of science should confine themselves to exploring the development of the 'hard' content of science either omitting or keeping in a subordinate context the intrusion of 'soft' content and issues. Again, passions run high. Thus at a meeting in the early 1980s of the American Association for the Advancement of Science the historian of science Charles Gillispie deplored what he perceived to be a continuing trend away from 'hard' history of science towards a social history characterised at its worst, it would seem, by prolonged emphasis on the merely personal and anecdotal. 'These scholars,' he stated, 'have a lust for just the sort of thing most rigidly ruled out of court in the science we do now — the irrational and the personal.' One could hardly have a stronger denunciation of a 'feminine' content to the history of science! And where does such a 'feminine' history of science lead? According to Gillispie, improper emphasis by historians of science on social implications without adequate and proper regard for the technical content of the science has produced a 'depiction of scientists as hucksters of weapons and research'![49]

Clearly, modern science is predominantly a 'masculine philosophy' that has a concealed if mutilated 'feminine' aspect. Just as masculine men attempt to conceal and continue to repress the feminine within themselves, so masculine practitioners of science and its associated disciplines attempt to conceal and strive to eliminate the 'soft' content of what they practise and analyse. Again like masculine men, they are able to offer little defence of what they do and advocate other than the ground that 'hardness' is somehow good and 'softness' is not! Those historians of science, however, who strive to understand the human context of science are able to offer a more compelling reason. What is most important for them is not first and foremost the well-being of modern science but the well-being of people. Their focus is on human beings and they practise their discipline with the hope of acquiring a richer understanding of human beings. 'It is important,' explains one 'moderate' historian of science, 'for our understanding of who and where we are.'[50] And, I would add, more important still for our understanding of where we are heading and how to introduce a means of steering and changing course. Masculine science, masculine history of science, and masculine philosophy of science have somehow to be made more human so that the well-being of humanity, men and women, becomes their prime concern and, together with this concern, the well-being of the biosphere. This is clearly seen by the philosopher and historian of science Paul Feyerabend. Disputing the (masculine) claim that there is essentially one 'rational' method by which scientific progress is achieved, Feyerabend declares that not only is such a claim unrealistic but that it is pernicious because 'the attempt to enforce the rules is bound to increase our professional qualifications at the expense of our humanity'.[51] Modern science or humanity? It seems an unfortunate and totally unnecessary choice. But as readers will recall, the young J.D. Bernal envisaged the human species ultimately splitting into two, a 'progressive', scientific (masculine) part consisting of increasingly non-human mentally-directed mechanisms and the 'reactionary' remainder groping their way towards a fuller humanity. In the ideal Cartesian universe that is the ultimate refuge of the masculine man of science, there will exist no longer the feminine distraction of women, home and children, the constant reminder of masculine insufficiency, and nor will there exist sexual woman to tempt and to threaten — the universe will consist of male mind in increasing control of the matter of the universe, mind threatened with destruction only as a result of its own miscalculations in its on-going experimentation with itself and with silent, passive, unquestioning matter.

Masculine society and sexual repression

It is undoubtedly not coincidental that the civilisation that produced science and industrialisation has been historically one of the most sexually repressive civilisations on record. As is well known, the Christian tradition has been basically hostile to sexuality and to women as sexual beings since its very earliest days. Saint Augustine lamented the fact that man has no control over his penis and that during orgasm not only are uncontrollable movements made by the man but that he also temporarily loses his power of rational thought. In the earliest period of the Church before the Synod of Macon voted by a majority of one that women possessed souls and were therefore human beings like men to the period of early modern Europe when some eighty per cent of the victims of the witchcraze were women, the Church branded sexual women as men's downfall and pronounced sexual intercourse legitimate only if procreation was the intended aim.[52] Even such a man as John Donne described early in the seventeenth century not only how Adam and all his male descendants had been corrupted by Eve but how each man shortens his own life with each act of sexual intercourse:

> For that marriage was our funerall:
> One woman at one blow, then kill'd us all.
> And singly, one by one, they kill us now.

> We doe delightfully our selves allow
> To that consumption; and profusely blinde,
> Wee kill our selves to propagate our kinde.[53]

During the seventeenth century when the 'masculine philosophy' was being established, we recall that witch-hunting and the ferocious interrogation of the witch-hunters' mostly female victims reached their peak. In the Enlightenment of the following century, the ideology of progress vociferously promulaged by a small but influential elite meant, as Jordanova has noted, that the growth of what was seen as a 'humane, rational, and civilised society' could also be interpreted as 'a struggle between sexes, with men imposing their value systems on women in order to facilitate social progress'.[54] During the eighteenth century the first 'scientific' treatises were published decribing the calamitous effects of masturbation on both its male and female practitioners and in the nineteenth century, following the discovery of chloroform as an anaesthetic, doctors were able to undertake remedial surgery, especially on women sufferers of untoward desire, including clitoridectomy and ovariotomy. As late as the last decade of the nineteenth century we read of the clitoris of a seven-year-old 'masturbator' being excised by the consulting surgeon of a hospital in Ohio.[55] While one cannot but be impressed by the accomplishments of Western men of science during this period and of the associated technological achievements of their industrial counterparts one is nevertheless forced to speculate concerning their conscious or unconscious motivation and in particular to ask why a culture that had so singularly failed to accept sexuality in men and even less in women so often interpreted scientific inquiry in terms of sexual metaphors. Even more is one led to doubt that the bearers of a culture that had come to such overall grief in the relationship between men and women would manage to find sufficient wisdom to apply the 'masculine philosophy' in a way that would promote and enhance the humanness of the culture.

Interestingly, in an article published in *The Bulletin of the Atomic Scientists* which speculates on the origins of violent behaviour, the author James W. Prescott suggests that the most violent societies are those most repressive of female sexuality and that, in his words, 'the great barrier between man and woman is man's fear of the depth and intensity of female sensuality'.[56] Could male dread of female sexuality be greatly reduced or even eliminated, then, hopefully, sexual behaviour on the part of men could and would become more joyously passionate than would presently appear to be the case, more sensuous and playful, and the drive to penetrate and possess correspondingly reduced. Both in lovemaking and in scientific inquiry, the sensibility underlying Francis Thompson's description of Percy Shelley might then turn out to be more accurate than the sensibility underlying G.E. Hale's description of Ernest Rutherford. The emergence of sexually liberated women and non-fearful, sexually unrepressed men would also presumably mean the disappearance of compulsive heterosexuality and at the same time a greater generosity or readiness on the part of people to exchange or give sexual caresses. The Swedish psychiatrist Lars Ullerstam has written movingly of the unmet sexual needs of various groups of people and how these could be satisfied in a less sexually repressive society by men and women prepared to provide, either freely or for a reasonable fee or as employees in a National Health Service, sexual help, reassurance and comfort.[57] In a report on female and male 'erotic Samaritans' in a Birmingham Institute, one woman described her surprise at how aroused she became the first time, at how much she felt able to give, at 'the element of fun in the sex', while another declared that 'it's like being a nurse in some ways' and that 'it's good to feel you're helping someone'.[58] It seems to me that if humankind is ever going to realise a more human world, one necessarily free from the armoury of war and the brutality of oppression, then the world will certainly be one characterised in great part by sexual loving and sexual generosity.

The question then arises as to how men in general are to be liberated from the insecurity of masculinity and the over-compensation in achievement, combined with an aggressive sexuality, that this insecurity generates and reinforces. In Chapter 1 it was suggested that any society in which a sexual division of labour exists is one in which men and women are conditioned into becoming, and into striving to become, masculine and feminine rather than fully human and moreover that men in such societies will necessarily tend to display the undesirable masculine characteristics with which this book has been concerned. The solution to the problem of the sexual division of labour would appear to be an obvious one. Not only must social institutions be provided that make it possible for women to act in the 'male' public sphere but men must also play their part, and indeed wish to play their part, in the 'female' sphere of domestic concern and caring institutions. In other words, both men and women must be allowed to become fully human beings rather than predominantly masculine and feminine beings. Interestingly, Prescott, too, argues for the necessity of such a fundamental change in the typical pattern of child-caring: 'men must share with women the responsibility for giving affection and care to infants and children,' he states.[59] In his opinion, beneficial changes in society must surely follow as the father assumes a more equal role with the mother in child-caring and particularly as the father becomes more affectionate towards his children. Boys who receive tender physical affection from their fathers will not associate gentle, sensuous touching with 'unmanliness' and an immense pressure to act tough and to be tough will consequently not be felt. Not excluded from participation in childbirth and from the care of infants and children, the male will be under less pressure to define for himself a masculine domain of behaviour from which women are excluded and which he then tends to associate, consciously or unconsciously, with pregnant phallus metaphors.[60] As Bruno Bettelheim encouragingly writes: 'The more men are enabled to acknowledge the positive wish to create life, and emphasise their contribution to it, the less need will there be to assert their power through destructive inventions'.[61] Moreover, enjoying a stronger human identity and a weaker masculineone, the adult male will feel correspondingly more secure and less resentful against women for possessing the 'feminine' qualities that he has either repressed or is socially not allowed to display. Consequently he will feel less need to behave in a sexually aggressive way towards women. Finally, as male sexual violence disappears so will the institutions that help to maintain the sexual and social oppression of women. Clearly these are all immensely complex matters and I merely make here what seem to me to be very plausible assumptions.[62] My overall point of view is that not until the sexual division of labour is abolished for both men and women and sexual repression ended or greatly reduced at all ages will it be possible to put an end to the manufacture of ghastly weapons of war, nuclear or otherwise. As Amory

Lovens and L. Hunter Lovens have wisely pointed out in their book *Energy/War*, while many reflective nuclear physicists must have so often wished for a magic wand that would make all nuclear fission impossible, yet even if such a wand were waved, it would still be necessary to put into reverse 'the psychic premises of eons of homocentric, patriarchal, imperial culture'.[63]

Of course, it may after all be the case that in any social system there will always be large numbers of men who are 'inherently' prepared to do anything to maintain and, if possible, increase their income, wealth and power, provided they can get away with it, from betraying relatives, friends and colleagues in home and work situations to participating in the design, manufacture and strategic planning of weapons of mass murder. Perhaps von Neumann is correct in his bleak assertion that it is 'just as foolish to complain that people are selfish and treacherous as it is to complain that the magnetic field does not increase unless the electric field has a curl'.[64] The basic premise underlying this book, however, is that von Neumann's assertion is unfounded and that there exists enough humanness in the overwhelming majority of people either to compel (predominantly) masculine leaders and pacemakers to reverse the race to total disaster or for people to oust their leaders from power and assume through new democratic organisations and institutions a direct responsibility for bringing about a more livable, classless world.

For we, like the crew of Captain Walton's ship, must decide to turn back. Moreover, the ice that has to break, the ice that seemingly blocks any deviation from the path that leads to certain disaster, is ice that will thaw at our change of will. We have reached the point where to go on is to guarantee nuclear holocaust while to turn back is to offer humanity at least a chance of avoiding holocaust and at least a possibility of realising a world in which sufficiently human beings will not be ashamed of the activities and achievements of their species. In Britain and other western European countries the way back seems particularly obvious, seen clearly as long ago as the 1950s and now a policy increasingly advocated by hundreds of thousands of men and women who belong to or who support the revitalised Campaign for Nuclear Disarmament. This policy is that we should *unilaterally* renounce the possession and manufacture of nuclear weaponry and concentrate solely, if weapons are needed at all, on the manufacture of basically defensive armaments such as anti-tank weapons. Certainly, it is my belief that Soviet leaders never had any intention of invading Western Europe except as a deterrent to try to prevent a nuclear blitz of the Soviet Union in the late 1940s and 1950s. Even if they should have or were in the future to present a non-nuclear western Europe with a choice of nuclear devastation or Soviet military occupation — which I emphatically believe would never be the case — then Soviet occupation of western Europe for a number of decades until the invaders had been socially and culturally absorbed by the natives would be far from among the worst possible paths that humanity could follow and certainly far preferable to the path of an ever-escalating arms race that can have only one end. With western European and other countries opting out of the nuclear arms race, world moral pressure would be that much greater on the humanness of leaders both in the United States and the Soviet Union to begin to reassert their humanness and to initiate the process of mutual step-by-step disarmament. For in the present world context I believe that were the Soviet Union to disarm unilaterally, then it would be at a far greater risk of nuclear attack from the United States than the United States would be from the Soviet Union were America to disarm unilaterally. One should not forget that at one time numerous men including such very different and distinguished people as John von Neumann and Bertrand Russell either advocated or were not opposed to a nuclear blitz against the Soviet Union, the latter being in addition apparently prepared to accept the destruction of western Europe as an unwelcome but unavoidable consequence.[65] However, a nuclear disarmed western Europe and, as a consequence, less repressive eastern European Soviet satellite states would set an example to both the United States and the Soviet Union and would be able to impose increasing moral pressure on both countries to begin nuclear disarmament and to ensure, principally through their joint efforts, a world organisation not only able to prevent aggressive acts between nations but to begin the long process of realising an increasingly just, sustainable and participatory world society (in the appropriate words of the World Council of Churches).[66] There seems to be no other path to a reasonable world than collaboration between the presently hostile superpowers and the first steps along such a path could be initiated by the refusal of the peoples of western

Europe to follow the present path, which ends at the nuclear abyss.

Clearly, renunciation of nuclear weaponry would liberate vast resources throughout western Europe and particularly Britain for the rebuilding of rundown areas and for the renovation of processes essential to civilised life. Equally clearly, however, the constructive use of resources presently allocated to the manufacture of offensive weapons as part of the arms race and in part for repressive purposes both at home and in Third World countries would require the bringing about of profound social and economic changes, changes that lead away from emphasis on industrial production for the principal benefit of large privately owned organisations and instead towards the realisation of egalitarian, classless and democratic societies. The institutionalisation of competitive behaviour characteristic of capitalist societies and which helps to give masculine behaviour its present pre-eminent status would be recognised as humanly undesirable and would in the process undergo appropriate dismantling. Capitalist science and technology would cease to be.[67] Of special concern here, education in science, and particularly in physics, would undergo dramatic change.

In a more human society, one would automatically expect a 'higher' education in physics to be characterised by not only a much larger percentage of women studying the subject than at present but also by a significant amount of time devoted to understanding how physics can help play its part in identifying and solving world problems, in particular to understanding why physicists became so involved in military and destructive processes and the connected question of why physics, and especially nuclear physics, became one of the most masculine of activities.[68] It follows that one measure of the non-masculinity of an education in physics at a particular institution is the extent to which such questions are seriously studied by staff and students. Indeed, if a physics department does not include serious and searching discussion of the 'social responsibility of scientists' *as an integral part of its curriculum*, then any claims the department might make for the espousal of social responsibility are essentially a sham. It is quintessentially masculine to attempt to impart as much technical expertise as possible and leave totally unexamined the social relevance and possible implications of that expertise. Overall, a human science would be very different both in social organisation and in values, aims and research priorities from the masculine science so characteristic of today's world. 'If we would know life,' advises the American biologist Barry Commoner, 'we must cherish it — in our laboratories and in the world.'[69] I should perhaps emphasise that in my opinion the world desperately needs not the absence of science but the practice of human science, a science informed throughout by the search for a just, livable and life-enhancing world. Certainly, however, humanity could be without a science that sends some forty per cent of its graduate research and development 'output' to work in designing and producing yet further military weapons, so keeping the arms race on the boil. Indeed, as Frank Barnaby writes, while some 400,000 scientists are presently employed in military aspects of science, the number of scientists actively working towards disarmament is depressingly small. 'It is hard to avoid the conclusion,' Barnaby gloomily writes, 'that scientists are on the whole little interested in the potential social consequences of their work, even when these consequences are as disastrous as a nuclear war.'[70] But these scientists have lived and live in a harsh, competitive, masculine world and into the bargain were given an 'education' in masculine science, not human science. All the more credit, then, to those scientists who, in increasing numbers, are overcoming the effects of their 'education' and, despite social and economic pressures, are asserting their basic humanity to oppose the claims of the Coldwarmongers and begin the practice of a human science.[71] In his article appropriately entitled 'A Human Reconstruction of Science' the Harvard historian of science Everett Mendelsohn has admirably summarised what some guidelines might be for such pioneers of a human science — guidelines that themselves need to be explored and debated. 'A reconstructed science,' he has written,

> would value truth, but also compassion. It would have an in-
> built ethic that would defend both being and living; that is,
> knowledge would be non-violent, non-coercive, non-exploitative,
> non-manipulative; knowledge that would set out to pursue har-
> mony with nature rather than dominion over nature; knowledge
> that would include subjective experience, that is interior
> knowledge; that would finally renounce the Faustian quest to
> achieve the limits of the universe or total knowledge; that would

work to construct models that would be more explanatory and more inclusive — science practised among and derived from the public. What if we were to say that we would not undertake to develop what could not be understood and publicly absorbed, that we were intent on building a science not confined to academics and institutions? This is only the beginning of a list. It would have to go beyond this in new directions. But this certainly would remake and reshape scientific activity. Change of this sort would represent a revolution — a revolution no less in magnitude than that of the seventeenth century — a revolution in science. But I would say that the crisis of knowledge that we face is no less great today than that which faced the pioneers of the new science of the seventeenth century.[72]

The reconstruction of knowledge would obviously not be confined to 'higher' education but indeed would begin in the infant-parent relationship and be consolidated in the basic education given to children at both primary and secondary levels. A relevant measure of the non-masculinity of a particular institution would be the extent to which both boys and girls are given the opportunity to learn, and are encouraged to learn, all subjects from mathematics to cooking and from needlework to physics. It would clearly be a very masculine education indeed were boys encouraged to learn only traditionally masculine subjects from mathematics to woodwork and the girls encouraged to learn all subjects, those traditionally considered masculine and also those traditionally considered feminine. For not only would the boys not be encouraged to develop a human identity but the girls would be placed in an impossible position vis-à-vis the boys, having to choose between masculine and feminine identities or struggling to attain a human identity with little prospect of finding a human male partner and certainly no prospect of living in a human world. Such a hypermasculine education would lead towards an increasingly masculine future in which women become mere masculinised assistants to masculine supermen and — in declining numbers — feminine keepers of the home and caring institutions. We could reasonably hope and expect, on the other hand, that when a human world decides to begin exploring the cosmos, its space voyagers therefore leaving behind them a world in which injustice, poverty and degradation have been everywhere eliminated, such an undertaking will be carried out by human men and women whose desire to embark on such a vast adventure springs principally from anticipation of the joys of better knowing this incredible universe in which we find ourselves. Such fully human men and women would take the capacity to love and to care to other parts of the universe and would be able to reciprocate wherever they find beings of a similar disposition in the cosmos — and able to beat a hasty retreat where not![73]

Interestingly, six years after the publication of *Frankenstein*, Mary Shelley published another major novel, *The Last Man*. It is as if in this novel she responds to the questions, What will happen if we do not stop and turn back? If we do not cease making war on each other and on the natural world? For in *The Last Man* we are told how 'nature, our mother, and our friend' eventually turns on humankind 'a brow of menace'.[74] A virulent strain of the plague never before known and before which medical science is powerless gradually reduces the human population to a handful of survivors. By the closing pages of Shelley's novel only one solitary human being, accompanied by a dog, remains to wander humanless over the surface of the earth. It is a description of death, torment and degradation that reviewers in the opening decades of the nineteenth century found unacceptable to civilised society. In the closing decades of the twentieth century, however, readers of *The Last Man* will see only too close a similarity between the plight of the survivors of a nuclear world war on a radioactive, contaminated and polluted earth with the plight of the dwindling number of survivors of a plague-stricken earth. Indeed, the filmed record of a conference organised by 'Physicians for Social Responsibility' that took place in San Francisco in 1980 is entitled, 'The Last Epidemic: Medical Consequences of Nuclear Weaponry and Nuclear War'![75]

This book has been concerned with the question, what is there in our nature that makes us either build atomic weapons or accept their threatened use? In the opening pages of *The Last Man*, Mary Shelley's sole survivor, Lionel Verney, poses a very related question, 'What is there in our nature that is for ever urging us on towards pain and misery?'[76] In *Frankenstein*, Captain Walton gives an answer of sorts: 'There is something at work in my soul, which I do not understand.' It is clear, however, that Mary Shelley believes that something is a consequence of the Captain's past and continuing flight from the feminine within himself. Because of such repression and the need to maintain it, Captain Walton, Dr Frankenstein and any number of masculine men seek to express a distorted nature in great history-making exploits revealingly described in 'pregnant phallus' metaphors, exploits that will supposedly bring them acclaim and glory. Even Adrian in *The Last Man* comes fully to life only when faced with the heroic challenge of protecting England against the deadly plague. 'Strange ambition this!' Mary Shelley writes. 'Yet such was Adrian. He appeared given up to contemplation, averse to excitement, a lowly student, a man of visions — but afford him worthy theme, and — ... so did he spring up from listlessness and unproductive thought to the highest pitch of virtuous action. With him went enthusiasm, the high-wrought resolve, the eye that without blenching could look at death.'[77] Thus Mary Shelley might be describing the ivory tower masculine scientist come to life in the heroic cause of defending Western civilisation against the Soviet 'menace'. She might also be warning ardent masculine campaigners for nuclear disarmament to beware of needing the conflict in order to become and remain fully alive! Perhaps Mary Shelley's mother, Mary Wollstonecraft, put the masculine dilemma as its briefest in her classic *Vindication of the Rights of Women*: 'The welfare of society is not built on extraordinary exertions,' she maintained; 'and were it more reasonably organised, there would be still less need of great abilities, or heroic virtues.'[78] Indeed yes. But what full-blooded male would really want to live in a reasonably organised world?

Afterword

In an article entitled 'Birth Reborn' Ann Paul has described her filming of an unusual maternity unit run by a Dr Michel Odent in a small town, Pithiviers, in northern France.[1] In this unit the mothers-to-be themselves take control of how they give birth, assisted by six midwives working in teams of two, 48 hours at a stretch. The philosophy that characterises the unit, as Ann Paul had heard Michel Odent explain in London, is that giving birth is a sexual experience, that our sexual, intellectual and emotional life is part of a whole, and 'the right place to give birth would be the right place to make love'. Some time later she and a film crew were watching a woman giving birth in Pithiviers. 'We stood together and witnessed our first natural birth through the small glass window of a door leading into the birthing-room and tears unashamedly flowed down our faces. The room was softly lit and very warm, there was no furniture, only a large platform scattered with cushions — and a sheet on the floor. In the room a young naked woman was being supported under the arms by her husband while Odent and a midwife stood by and whispered encouragement — the baby was very nearly there.' Painkilling drugs are never used at Pithiviers, Paul writes, and the expectant mothers know that this is a condition of their being able to give birth in Odent's unit. 'Instead,' Paul reassures, 'the woman in labour relies on the secretion of her own natural hormones, endorphines, which reduce the pain and also give a sense of well-being. All the women I watched giving birth experienced this sense of well-being; they seemed ecstatic, as if on another level of consciousness.' Post-natal depression is almost unknown. Paul concluded: 'We came to "observe" and ended up "sharing" in the celebration of love.' Pithiviers and the loving births described by Ann Paul seem a long, long way, sexually, intellectually and emotionally from Los Alamos and Livermore and the violent births of the weapons physicists' creations, 'Little Boy' and 'Fat Man', 'George' and 'Mike'. Perhaps in what Pithiviers both is and symbolises there is yet hope for the world.

Notes

Place of publication is London, unless otherwise stated.

Introduction

1. My three books referred to are: *Liberation and the Aims of Science: An Essay on Obstacles to the Building of a Beautiful World* (1973; Edinburgh: Scottish Academic Press, 1980), *Witch-Hunting, Magic and the New Philosophy: An Introduction to Debates of the Scientific Revolution, 1450-1750* (Brighton, Sussex: Harvester Press, 1980), *Science and Sexual Oppression: Patriarchy's Confrontation with Woman and Nature* (Weidenfeld Nicolson, 1981).

2. Annette Kolodny, *The Lay of the Land: Metaphor as Experience and History in American Life and Letters* (Chappel Hill: Univ. of North Carolina Press, 1975), p.149.

3. P. Chilton, 'Nukespeak: nuclear language, culture and propaganda', in Crispin Audrey (ed.), *Nukespeak: The Media and the Bomb* (Comedia Publishing Group, 1982).

1. Compulsive Masculinity: 'Something at work in my soul, which I do not understand'

1. See especially Nancy Chodorow, *The Reproduction of Mothering: Psychoanalysis and the Sociology of Gender* (California UP, 1978). For an interesting review and discussion, see Elizabeth Long, *Telos*, No 43 (Spring, 1980) and Judith Lorber, Rose Laub Coser, Alice S. Rossi and Nancy Chodorow, 'On *The Reproduction of Mothering:* A Methodological Debate', *Signs* 6 (Spring, 1981). For an overview of the problem of masculinity see Paul Hoch, *White Hero, Black Beast: Racism, Sexism and the Mask of Masculinity* (Pluto, 1979).

2. See my discussion in *Science and Sexual Oppression*, Ch.2, pp.30-44, 54-59.

3. See especially Wendy Hollway, ' "I just wanted to kill a woman" Why? The Ripper and Male Sexuality', *Feminist Review*, No 9 (October, 1981), pp.33-40. In a discussion of the portrayal of violence against women in contemporary fiction, *Cosmopolitan*'s fiction editor, Anne Boston, has written in *The Bookseller* (15 May 1982), p.1865:

'The level of wishfulfilment revenge exacted by male authors on their female creations is something staggering... I find myself dropping books in a state of shock, wondering (no doubt naively) how on earth men think up such stuff? Do they really hate us *that* much?' See also Jessica Benjamin, 'The Bonds of Love: Rational Violence and Erotic Domination', *Feminist Studies* 6 (1980) pp.144-74. For a discussion of the views of Freud and Marcuse with respect to the two supposedly 'instinctual' drives, Eros and Thanatos, see my *Science and Sexual Oppression*, Ch.1.

4. *Science and Sexual Oppression*, Ch.2, pp.44-6, 51-2.
5. Colin M. Turnbull, 'Mbuti Womanhood', in Frances Dahlberg (ed.), *Woman the Gatherer* (Yale UP, 1981), p.210.
6. Yolanda and Robert Murphy, *Women of the Forest* (Cambridge UP, 1974), p.94.
7. V.W. Turner, 'Three Symbols of Passage in Ndembu Circumcision Ritual' in M. Gluckman (ed.), *Essays on the Ritual of Social Relations* (Manchester UP, 1962), pp.144, 161, 173.
8. See L.R. Hiatt, 'Secret Pseudo-Procreation Rites among the Australian Aborigines' in L.R. Hiatt and C. Jayawardena (eds), *Anthropology in Oceania* (Brighton, Sussex: Angus & Robertson, 1971), pp.80, 88; see also L.R. Hiatt, 'Queen of the Night, mother-right, and secret male cults' in R.H. Hook (ed.), *Fantasy and Symbol: Studies in Anthropological Interpretation* (New York: Academic Press, 1979). On the phenomenon of womb-envy, see especially Margaret Mead, *Male and Female* (1950; Harmondsworth: Penguin, 1967), pp.110-11.
9. See Mary A.C. Horowitz, 'Aristotle and Woman', *Journal of the History of Biology* 9 (1976), pp.183-213.
10. H.C. Erik Midelfort, 'Heartland of the Witchcraze: Central and Northern Europe', *History Today* (February, 1981), p.28. See Francis Bacon, 'The Masculine Birth of Time or The Great Instauration of the Dominion of Man over the Universe', in Benjamin Farrington, *The Philosophy of Francis Bacon* (Liverpool UP, 1970). For a particularly instructive discussion of Bacon and the new science, see Evelyn Fox Keller, 'Baconian Science: A Hermaphroditic Birth', *The Philosophical Forum* 11 (1980), pp.299-308.
11. 'Thoughts and Conclusions' in Farrington, p.92; *The New Organon*, Bk.1, Aphorism 109 in J. Spedding et al. *Works of Francis Bacon* (1879-1890), Vol.4, p.100; 'The Refutation of Philosophies' in Farrington, p.129; 'Thoughts and Conclusions', p.83.
12. *De Augmentis Scientiarum*, Bk.4, Ch.1 in Spedding (note 11), Vol.4, p.373; *The New Atlantis* in Spedding, Vol.3, p.156; *The New*

Organon, Bk.2, Aphorism 51 in Spedding, Vol.4, p.245.

13. Henry Power, *Experimental Philosophy* (1664; New York: Johnson Reprint, 1966), p.82.

14. Bruno Bettelheim, *Symbolic Wounds: Puberty Rites and the Envious Male* (Thames & Hudson, 1955), p.136, quoted by E.F. Keller (note 10) and Norman O. Brown, *Life against Death: The Psychoanalytic Meaning of History* (Sphere, 1968), p.245. Bettelheim continues: 'It should be noted also that the phallic stage with its aggressiveness (hence fear of retaliation), its overevaluation of the penis in particular and of masculinity in general, is accompanied by anxiety about losing the penis.'

15. Bacon, *The Advancement of Learning*, Bk.2, Ch.7, in Spedding (note 11), Vol.3, p.357.

16. Carolyn Merchant, *The Death of Nature: Women, Ecology and the Scientific Revolution* (Wildwood House, 1982), p.189.

17. J. Collins, *Descartes' Philosophy of Nature* (Oxford: Blackwell, 1971), p.26.

18. See, for example, the discussion in Monica Sjöö and Barbara Mor, *The Ancient Religion of the Great Cosmic Mother of All* (Trondheim, Norway: Rainbow Press, 1981), esp. p.70.

19. Quoted in L.D. Cohen, 'Descartes and Henry More on the Beast Machine', *Annals of Science*, 1 (1936), p.50.

20. R.S. Westfall, 'Newton and the Hermetic Tradition', in A.G. Debus (ed.), *Science, Medicine and Man in the Renaissance* (Heinemann, 1972), p.184.

21. Descartes, *Discourse on Method* (Indianapolis, New York: Liberal Arts Press, 1956), p.40.

22. T. Birch (ed.), *The Works of Robert Boyle* (London, 1772), Vol.5, pp.532 and 179.

23. Farrington (note 10), pp.131, 72, quoted by E.F. Keller (note 10), p.301.

24. Henry Power, extract in Marie Boas Hall (ed.), *Newton and Newton's Laws* (New York: Harper, 1970), p.127.

25. Bacon, in Spedding (note 11), Vol.4, p.407.

26. *The Compleat Midwifes Practice Enlarged* (London, 1659), quoted by Hilda Smith, 'Gynecology and Ideology in Seventeenth-Century England', B.A. Carroll (ed.), *Liberating Women's History* (University of Illinois Press, 1976), p.103.

27. Margaret Cavendish, 'From the World's Olio', in Joan Goulianeros (ed.), *By a Woman Writ* (Indianapolis, New York: Bobbs-Merrill, 1973), p.55.

28. N. Malebranche, *Recherche de la Vérité* (1673), in G. Rodis-Lewis (ed.), *Oeuvres de Malebranche* (Paris: Libraire Philosophique J. Vrin, 1962), Vol.1, p.267.

29. Jeffrey B. Russell, *A History of Witchcraft: Sorcerers, Heretics and Pagans* (Thames & Hudson, 1980), p.116.

30. Edward MacCurdy (ed.), *The Notebooks of Leonardo da Vinci* (Cape, 1954), Vol.1, pp.94 and 64.

31. W.M. Conway (ed.), *The Writings of Albrecht Dürer* (Peter Owen, 1958), p.172.

32. Thomas Browne, *The Religio Medici and Other Writings* (Dent, 1931), p.65.

33. Malebranche is quoted by C.U.M. Smith, *The Problem of Life* (Macmillan, 1976), p.266.

34. Derek J. de Solla Price (ed.), *Natural Magic* (1658; Basic Books, 1957), Bk.9, Chs.28 and 29. I am indebted to Keith Hutchison for this information.

35. See my *Witch-Hunting, Magic and the New Philosophy*, pp.132-4. In a modern equivalent of such a put-down the psychologist Paul Meehl describes 'insignificant' research in the following way: 'Meanwhile our eager-beaver researcher... has produced a long publication list and been promoted to full professorship. In terms of his contribution to the enduring body of... knowledge, he has done hardly anything. His true position is that of a potent — but — sterile intellectual rake, who leaves in his merry path a long train of ravished maidens but no viable scientific offspring'; quoted by Michael J. Mahoney, *Scientist as Subject: The Psychological Imperative* (Cambridge, Mass: Ballinger, 1976), p.151.

36. 'Publisher to the Reader' in R. Boyle, *Experiments and Considerations Touching Colours* (1664); A.R. Hall and M.B. Hall (eds.), *The Correspondence of Henry Oldenburg* (University of Wisconsin Press, 1965-73) Vol.4, p.77; Sprat, *History of the Royal Society* (1667; Routledge, 1959), p.124; Glanvill, *The Vanity of Dogmatizing*, Introduction by Stephen Metcalf (1666 edn; Brighton, Sussex: Harvester Press, 1970), p.162; Oldenburg, Vol.1, p.113.

37. *Diary and Correspondence of John Evelyn* (1859), Vol.3, p.348; T. Birch (note 22), Vol.2, p.8; I. Barrow, *The Usefulness of Mathematical Learning* (1774; Frank Cass, 1970), pp. xxix, xxx; H.W. Turnbull et al. *The Correspondence of Isaac Newton* (Cambridge UP, 1959-77), Vol.2, p.474.

38. Quoted by Gad Freudenthal, 'Early Electricity between Chemistry and Physics' in J.L. Heilbron (ed.), *Historical Studies in the Physical Sciences* (University of California Press, 1981), Vol.11, Part 2, p.229. For a fuller account of the masculinity of the scientific revolution in early modern Europe see my *Science and Sexual Oppression*, Ch.3.

39. Ludmilla Jordanova, 'Natural Facts: A Historical Perspective on

Science and Sexuality', in Carol P. MacCormack and Marilyn Strathern, *Nature, Culture, Gender* (Cambridge UP, 1981), pp.45 and 54; see also Merchant, *The Death of Nature* (note 16), pp.189-91.

40. John Davy (ed.), *The Collected Works of Sir Humphry Davy* (1839-40), Vol.8, pp.275, 282, 276.

41. *Ibid.*, pp.177, 175.

42. The edition of *Frankenstein* I have used is that published by Oxford University Press in 1969 (now available as a World's Classics paperback, 1980) which follows the text of the version published by Mary Shelley in 1831. For the original 1818 edition and the substantial changes made by Mary Shelley for the 1831 edition see James Rieger (ed.), *Frankenstein* (University of Chicago Press, 1982). Note that with respect to the 1818 edition, Rieger writes (p. xviii) that Percy Shelley's 'assistance at every point of the book's manufacture was so extensive that one hardly knows whether to regard him as editor or minor collaborator'. In my reading of *Frankenstein* I have been very much influenced by Peter Dale Scott's essay 'Vital Artifice: Mary, Percy, and the Psychopolitical Integrity of *Frankenstein*' in George Levine and U.C. Knoepflmacher (eds.), *The Endurance of Frankenstein: Essays on Mary Shelley's Novel* (University of California Press, 1979). For a very different interpretation from the one presented here, see Ellen Moers, 'Female Gothic: The Monster's Mother', *New York Review of Books* 21 (21 March, 1974), pp.24-8 and reprinted in Levine and Knoepflmacher. My thanks to Ian Miles for several years ago telling me what a good novel *Frankenstein* is.

43. *Frankenstein*, pp.20, 21-2.

44. *Ibid.*, pp.39, 40, 42.

45. *Ibid.*, pp.44, 47, 48.

46. *Ibid.*, pp.52, 54, 55.

47. One is irresistibly reminded of the theme of Carolyn Merchant's book, *The Death of Nature* (note 16).

48. *Frankenstein*, pp.69, 97.

49. *Ibid.*, p.166.

50. *Ibid.*, pp.214, 215, 217, 219.

51. *Ibid.*, p.56.

52. Adrienne Rich, 'From an Old House in America', *Poems, Selected and New 1950-1974* (New York: Norton, 1975), quoted by Peter Dale Scott (note 42), p.202.

53. E. Schrödinger, 'Science, Art and Play' (1935), in *Science, Theory and Man* (New York: Dover, 1957), p.29. Schrödinger continues: 'It is the duty of a teacher of science to impart to his listeners knowledge which will prove useful in their professions; but it should also be his intense

desire to do it in such a way as to cause them pleasure.'

54. See especially the last section of Ch.3 of my *Liberation and the Aims of Science*, which concludes (and this is still my opinion): 'In a civilised world physics would certainly be a delightful play, bringing at peak moments beauty, pleasure and joy into the lives of those who choose this way to dialogue with nature. But this is not a civilised world and the [potentially] beautiful play called physics has given birth to monstrosities.'

55. C.S. Lewis, *The Abolition of Man* (1947; New York: Macmillan, 1977), p.69;

56. Vaughan, *The Complete Poems*, ed. A. Rudrum (Harmondsworth; Penguin, 1976), p.171; E.F. Keller (note 10), p.307.

2. The Discovery of the Philosopher's Stone: 'They penetrate into the recesses of nature and show how she works in her hiding places'

1. Margaret Gowing, *Britain and Atomic Energy 1939-45* (Macmillan, 1964), p.87; Freeman J. Dyson, *Disturbing the Universe* (New York: Harper & Row, 1979), p.7.

2. For a description of the physics of these four decades, see, for example, the first chapter of Gowing's book which is written by Kenneth Jay; G.K. Conn and H.D. Turner, *The Evolution of the Nuclear Atom* (New York: Elsevier, 1966); Thaddeus J. Trenn, *Transmutation, Natural and Artificial* (Heyden & Son, 1981); and E.N. Jenkins, *Radioactivity: A Science in its Historical and Social Context* (Wykeham, 1979).

3. T.H. Huxley, *Evolution and Ethics and Other Essays* (Macmillan, 1925), pp. 85-6.

4. Sir William Crookes, *Report of the British Association for the Advancement of Science* (1899), p.27.

5. Quoted in M. Howorth, *Pioneer Research on the Atom: The Life Story of Frederick Soddy* (New World Pubs, 1958), p.83. See also Lawrence Badash, 'How the "Newer Alchemy" was Received', *Scientific American* 213 (1966), pp.88-95, and T.J. Trenn, *The Self-Splitting Atom: The History of the Rutherford-Soddy Collaboration* (Taylor & Francis, 1977), p.42.

6. See Joe D. Burchfield, *Lord Kelvin and the Age of the Earth* (Macmillan, 1975), p.164. F. Soddy, *Matter and Energy* (1912), p.245; Soddy 'Transmutation, The Vital Problem of the Future', *Scientia* XI (1913), p.196 (see also note 10 below).

7. C. Moureu, *Chemistry and the War* (1924), quoted by Spencer R. Weart, *Scientists in Power* (Harvard UP, 1979), p.38.

8. Weart, *Scientists in Power*, p.49.

9. *Ibid.*, p.86.

10. F. Sherwood Taylor, *The Alchemists* (1952; Paladin, 1976), p.179. Even after the second world war physicists continue to write of nuclear physics as the new alchemy. For example, in his essay, 'Atoms and Nuclei' in J.L. Crammer and R.E. Peierls (eds.), *Atomic Energy* (Penguin, 1950), p.44, Hans A. Bethe writes: 'So now, at last, the dream of the alchemists is fulfilled, not only in theory but also in practice; one element can be transformed into another in quantities which are of practical importance.'

    Similarly in a chapter entitled 'The Renaissance of Alchemy' Edward Teller writes in his book with Allen Brown, *The Legacy of Hiroshima* (Macmillan, 1962), p.96: 'Surprising similarities exist between the alchemist of medieval times and the atomic scientist of today. The alchemist tried to transmute base metals into gold; scientists have made materials that have not been on the earth since the Day of Creation. Alchemists strived to build a perpetual motion machine that would require no fuel; scientists have developed nuclear reactors that feed on almost nothing but which are, unfortunately, expensive to run...'

11. Robert Reid, *Marie Curie* (1974; Paladin, 1978), p.41.

12. Marie Curie, *Pierre Curie* (1923; New York: Dover, 1963), pp.36, 19, 36, 69.

13. R. Reid, *Marie Curie*, pp.83, 94, 110.

14. Eve Curie, *Madame Curie* (1938; Heinemann, 1962), p.236.

15. *Pierre Curie*, opening quotation; see also Reid, p.120.

16. *Marie Curie*, p.124.

17. See, for example, Ian I. Mitroff, Theodore Jacob, and Eileen Trauth Moore, 'On the Shoulders of the Spouses of Scientists', *Social Studies of Science* 7 (1977), pp.303-27.

18. See A.S. Eve, *Rutherford* (Cambridge UP, 1939), p. ix; L. Rosenfeld and E. Rudinger, 'The Decisive Years 1911-18' in S. Rozental (ed.), *Niels Bohr: His Life and Work as Seen by his Friends and Colleagues* (Amsterdam: North Holland, 1967), p.51.

19. *Marie Curie*, p.124.

20. But also some difficulty! In particular, the seemingly plausible claim that scientific theories are 'progressively capturing more and more truth about the world' is an exceedingly difficult one to justify. For a recent eloquent attempt at justification, see William Newton-Smith, 'Is Science Rational?', *Social Science Information* 19 (1980), pp.469-99 and *The Rationality of Science* (Routledge & Kegan Paul, 1981); for an alarmingly convincing exposition of the difficulties yet to be over-

come, see Larry Laudan, 'A Confutation of Convergent Realism',
Philosophy of Science 48 (1981), pp.19-49.

21. Ernest Rutherford, *The Transformation of the Atom* (BBC, 1933),
p.28. A.S. Eve, *Rutherford*, p.102; Rutherford, *Radioactivity* (Cambridge UP, 1904), p.338.

22. M. Howorth, *Pioneer Research on the Atom* (note 5), p.123.

23. F. Soddy, *The Interpretation of Radium* (1909), p.244.

24. H.G. Wells, *The World Set Free: A Story of Mankind* (Macmillan,
1914), pp.22, 31, 38.

25. *Ibid.*, p.88.

26. Thaddeus J. Trenn, 'The Central Role of Energy in Soddy's Holistic
and Critical Approach to Nuclear Science, Economics and Social
Responsibility', *British Journal for the History of Science* 12 (1979),
p.267.

27. A.S. Eve, *Rutherford*, p.254; quoted by T.J. Trenn, 'The Justification
of Transmutation: Speculations of Ramsay and Experiments of
Rutherford', *Ambix* 21 (1974), p.73. According to A.H. Compton,
Rutherford wrote to an American friend of his success at artificial
transmutation, claiming that 'its influence on history might eventually
be greater than the war that had just been fought': see M. Johnston
(ed.), *The Cosmos of Arthur Holly Compton* (New York: Knopf, 1967),
p.29.

28. A.S. Eddington, 'The Internal Constitution of the Stars', *Report of the
British Association for the Advancement of Science* (Murray, 1920), p.13.

29. J.B.S. Haldane, *Daedalus or Science and the Future* (Kegan Paul,
1923), pp.3-4.

30. For Moureu's remarks, see Weart, *Scientists in Power* (note 7), pp.17,
38. On Rutherford and Hankey, see R.W. Clark, *The Birth of the
Bomb* (Phoenix, 1961), pp. xiii, 153 and S. Roskill, *Hankey, Man of
Secrets* (Collins, 1974), Vol.3, p.428. Rutherford (note 20), p.25.

31. See Maurice Goldsmith, *Frédéric Joliot-Curie, A Biography* (Lawrence
& Wishart, 1976), pp.59-60; Pierre Biquard, *Frédéric Joliot-Curie: The
Man and his Theories*, tr. by G. Strachan (1961; Souvenir Press,
1965), p.163.

32. Arthur Eddington, *New Pathways in Science* (Cambridge UP, 1935),
p.163; Frederick Soddy, 'Foreword', Sir Daniel Hall et al. (eds.), *The
Frustration of Science* (1935; New York: Books for Libraries Press,
1965) and see Trenn (note 26), p.273; Rutherford, *The Transformation
of Energy* (Papers of the Greenock Philosophical Society, 1936), p.16.

33. Spencer R. Weart and Gertrud Weiss Szilard (eds.) *Leo Szilard: His
Version of the Facts: Selected Recollections and Correspondence* (Cambridge, Mass.: MIT Press, 1978), Ch.1.

34. For an absorbing account of the discovery of uranium fission, see Hans G. Graetzer and David L. Anderson, *The Discovery of Nuclear Fission: A Documentary History* (New York: Van Nostrand, 1971). For Otto Hahn's own account, see his 'The Discovery of Fission', *Scientific American* 205 (1958), 76-84.

35. Quoted by Weart, *Scientists in Power*, p.95.

36. David Irving, *The Virus House* (William Kimber, 1967), pp.32-4, 43; published in the United States as *The German Atomic Bomb* (New York: Simon & Schuster, 1967). Irving is a right-wing historian whose sympathies apparently lie with the efforts of Nazi scientists to make the atomic bomb. His overall thesis and documentation contrast sharply with Robert Jungk's thesis in *Brighter than a Thousand Suns* (1956; Penguin, 1960), namely that German scientists were reluctant on moral grounds to make the bomb for Hitler. See especially the review by Eugene Rabinowitch and the ensuing discussion in *Bulletin of the Atomic Scientists* (June, 1968), pp.32-9 in which Rabinowitch strongly disagrees with Irving's conclusion 'that what was missing in the German project was efficient military leadership'.

37. See, for example, Simone de Beauvoir, *The Second Sex* (1949; Harmondsworth: Penguin, 1972), pp.79, 95, 691; see also especially note 35 of Ch.1.

38. Sir W. Crookes (note 4), pp.4, 19, 33.

39. Sir Henry Tizard, 'The Rutherford Memorial Lecture' in *Memorial Lectures delivered before the Chemical Society, 1933-1942*, Vol.4 (The Chemical Society, 1951), p.183. In his essay 'Reflections of a European Man of Science' the Nobel laureate Max Born refers to Rutherford as 'the great physicist, Lord Rutherford, the father of contemporary nuclear research', in Werner Heisenberg, Max Born, Erwin Schrödinger and Pierre Auger, *On Modern Physics* (New York: Clarkson N. Potter, 1961), p.70.

40. A.S. Eve, *Rutherford*, pp.39, 40, 56.

41. E. Rutherford, 'The Transmutation of the Elements', *Discovery* 14 (April, 1933), p.105; quoted by Ruth Moore, *Niels Bohr: The Man and the Scientist* (Seven Oaks, Kent: Hodder & Stroughton, 1967), p.114.

42. Eve, *Rutherford*, p.231. On Hale, see D.J. Kevles, 'George Ellery Hale, the First World War, and the Advancement of Science in America', *Isis* 59 (1968), pp.427-37.

43. See Lawrence Badash (ed.), *Rutherford and Boltwood: Letters on Radioactivity* (Yale UP, 1969), p.351.

44. Quoted by H.R. Robinson, 'Rutherford: Life and Work to the Year 1919, with Personal Reminiscences of the Manchester Period' in J.B. Birks (ed.) *Rutherford at Manchester* (Heywood, 1962), p.85.

45. Eve, *Rutherford*, p.319.
46. Eve, *Rutherford*, p.122; Badash, *Rutherford and Boltwood*, p.109; Soddy, *The Interpretation of Radium*, p.234.
47. Quoted by E.N. da C. Andrade, 'The Birth of the Nuclear Atom', *Proceedings of the Royal Society* A244 (1958), p.444.
48. Eve, *Rutherford*, p.199; Born, *Atomic Physics* (Glasgow: Blackie, 1946), 4th edn, p.58.
49. Howorth, *Pioneer Research* (note 5), p.328. For a classic discussion and interpretation of priority disputes in science, see Robert K. Merton, 'Priorities in Scientific Discovery' in Bernard Barber and Walter Hirsch (eds.), *The Sociology of Science* (Collier Macmillan, 1962). With respect to priority disputes, Merton writes, p.449: 'What is true of physics, chemistry, astronomy, medicine and mathematics is true also of all the other scientific disciplines, not excluding the social and psychological sciences. As we know, sociology was officially born only after a long period of abnormally severe labour. Nor was the postpartum any more tranquil. It was disturbed by violent controversies between the followers of St. Simon and Comte as they quarrelled over the delicate question of which of the two was the father of sociology and which was merely the obstetrician.'

Merton leaves somewhat unanswered the question as to who the mother of sociology might have been! On pp.459-60 Merton lists the Fathers of the Sciences and Sub-Sciences. As he notes, p.460, 'On occasions, the presumed father of a science is called upon, in the persons of his immediate disciples or later adherents, to prove his paternity...'
50. A.S. Russell, 'Lord Rutherford: Manchester, 1907-19: A Partial Portrait', in Birks, *Rutherford at Manchester*, pp.89, 100; 'Madame Curie Memorial Lecture' (1935), *Chemical Society Memorial Lectures 1933-42* (note 39), p.46. I am indebted to Professor Colin A. Russell for the latter reference.
51. Rutherford (note 41), p.105; Eve, *Rutherford*, p.432; F. Thompson, *Shelley* (1914), p.46.
52. Victor F. Weisskopf, 'Niels Bohr and International Scientific Collaboration', in Rozental, *Niels Bohr* (note 18), p.262; 'Niels Bohr (A Memorial Tribute)', *Physics Today* 16 (1963), p.59; W. Heisenberg, *Physics and Philosophy* (New York: Harper, 1962), p.42; Heisenberg, *Physics and Beyond: Memoirs of a Life in Science* (Allen & Unwin, 1971), pp.68-69; Weisskopf, 'Physics and Physicists the Way I knew them', in C. Wiener (ed.), *The History of Twentieth-Century Physics* (New York: Academic Press, 1977), p.437.
53. Goldsmith, *Frédéric Joliot-Curie* (note 31), pp.32, 41. Francis Perrin

writes that Irène Curie 'found great joy in motherhood and, despite the hours spent in the laboratory, devoted much time to her children until their adolescence', in C.G. Gillispie (ed.), *Dictionary of Scientific Biographer* (New York: Scribner, 1973), Vol.7, p.158.

54. Biquard, *Frédéric Joliot-Curie* (note 31), p.36.

55. Goldsmith, *Frédéric Joliot-Curie*, p.54.

56. W.F. Libby, 'Berkeley Radiochemistry' in G.H. Bishop et al, *The Excitement and Fascination of Science* (Palo Alto, California: Annual Reviews, 1965), pp.247, 252, 248. The ex-Manhattan physicist John A. Wheeler writes that the conclusion that plutonium was fissile was soon 'to lead to a preposterous dream: by means of a neutron reactor such as never before existed, manufacture kilograms of an element never before seen on earth' in 'Some Men and Moments in Nuclear Physics: The Interplay of Colleagues and Motivations', R.H. Stuewer (ed.), *Nuclear Physics in Retrospect* (Minneapolis: U. of Minnesota Press, 1979), p.276.

57. Otto Frisch and Lise Meitner, 'Disintegration of Uranium by Neutrons: A New Type of Nuclear Reaction', *Nature* 143 (1939), pp.239-40.

58. Niels Bohr, 'Light and Life' (1932) in N. Bohr, *Atomic Physics and Human Knowledge* (New York: Science Editions, 1961); see Robert Olby, *The Path to the Double Helix* (Macmillan, 1974), pp.227-37.

59. As related by Otto R. Frisch, 'The Interest is Focusing on the Atomic Nucleus' in Rozental, *Niels Bohr*, pp.146-7.

60. Weart, *Scientists in Power*, p.72; Derek J. de Solla Price, *Science since Babylon* (Yale UP: 1962), p.83.

61. Stokes is quoted by Lawrence Badash, 'Radioactivity before the Curies', *American Journal of Physics* 32 (1965), p.129; see Reid, *Marie Curie*, p.70.

62. Rutherford's letter to his mother is quoted by E.N. da C. Andrade, *Rutherford and the Nature of the Atom* (Heinemann, 1965), p.55. On the dispute with Soddy see Eve, *Rutherford*, pp.99-101, and Howorth, *Pioneer Research* (note 5), pp.105-06: Rutherford's book entitled *Radioactivity* was published early in 1904 with Soddy's book of the same title appearing in May the same year.

63. On Bohr's impatience, see L. Rosenfeld and E. Rudinger, 'The Decisive Years 1911-18', in Rozental, *Niels Bohr*, p.51; J. Rud Nielson, 'Memories of Niels Bohr', *Physics Today* 16 (1963), p.23.

64. See Norman Feather, 'The Experimental Discovery of the Neutron', in *Proceedings of the 10th International Conference of the History of Science* (Paris: Hermann, 1964), pp.139-43; Goldsmith, *Frédéric Joliot-Curie* (note 31), p.42.

65. M. Goldsmith, *Frédéric Joliot-Curie*, p.42.
66. Weart, *Scientists in Power* (note 7), pp.45-6; Goldsmith, *Frédéric Joliot-Curie*, pp.53-5.
67. See Emilio Segrè, 'The Consequences of the Discovery of the Neutron' in *Proceedings of the 10th International Conference of the History of Science*, pp.151-5.
68. For Hahn's displeasure, see Weart, *Scientists in Power*, pp.53, 300 note 45; for the December haste of Hahn and Strassmann, see Irving, *The Virus House* (note 36), p.27; Weart, p.63.
69. For Szilard's action in the United States, see Weart and Gertrud Weiss Szilard (note 33), Ch.2 and Weart, *Scientists in Power*, Ch.5, 'The Secret of the Chain Reaction'; Kowarski is quoted by Weart, p.72; Herbert Anderson, 'The Legacy of Fermi and Szilard', *Bulletin of the Atomic Scientists* (September, 1974), p.60. For an instructive account of Szilard's attempts to achieve scientists' self-censorship, see also Christopher Chyba, 'The Recombinant DNA Debate and the Precedent of Leo Szilard' in S.A. Lakoff (ed.), *Science and Ethical Responsibility: Proceedings of the U.S. Student Pugwash Conference, 1979* (Reading, Mass.: Addison Wesley, 1980).
70. Irving, *The Virus House* (note 36), p.33.
71. For the wartime activities of Fritz Haber, see *From my Life, the Memoirs of Richard Willstäter*, tr. L.S. Hornig (1958; Elmsford, New York: Benjamin, 1965), pp.264-7, 281. In his Haber Memorial Lecture (note 39), p.146, J.E. Coates writes: 'The war years were for Haber the greatest period of his life. In them he lived and worked on a scale and for a purpose that satisfied his strong urge towards great dramatic vital things.' For a fascinating insight into the lives and beliefs of German physicists during this period, see Russell McCormmach, *Night Thoughts of a Classical Physicist* (Harvard UP, 1982).
72. Otto Hahn, *My Life*, tr. by E. Kaiser and E. Wilkins (1968; Macdonald, 1970), pp.118-30.
73. For Rutherford and Haber, see Max Born, *My Life: Recollections of a Nobel Laureate* (Taylor & Francis, 1978), pp.261-2, and Mark Oliphant, *Rutherford: Recollections of the Cambridge Days* (New York: Elsevier, 1972), pp.58-60.
74. For Haber's resignation, see Alan D. Beyerchen, *Scientists under Hitler: Politics and the Physics Community in the Third Reich* (Yale UP, 1977), pp.41-2 and Joseph Haberer, *Politics and the Community of Science* (New York: Van Nostrand Reinhold, 1969), pp.136-42.
75. Haberer, p.135.
76. Oliphant, *Rutherford*, p.58; Irving, *The Virus House* (note 36), p.34.
77. R.H. Stuewer (ed.), *Nuclear Physics in Retrospect: Proceedings of a*

Symposium on the 1930s (Minneapolis: University of Minnesota Press, 1979), pp.11, 319.

78. Weart, *Scientists in Power*, pp.272-3.

79. The path to the fission weapon was a tortuous one. On 16 March 1939 Niels Bohr conjectured to Rosenfeld, Teller, Wigner and Wheeler that because only the rare isotope of uranium (U-235) is readily fissile and because it would be an immensely complex and expensive task to separate a sufficient quantity of U-235 from natural uranium, the manufacture of an atomic bomb was not a practical proposition. However in the late spring of 1940 American physicists realised that in a uranium reactor it would be possible to produce a new fissile element, plutonium, and hence that the manufacture of fission weapons would be feasible provided only that uranium chain reactions could be generated on a sufficiently large scale (see note 56). In addition early in the spring of 1940 Rudolf Peierls and Otto Frisch, then working in England, had calculated that the amount of uranium-235 necessary in order for a violent explosion to occur, the so-called critical mass, was less than a kilogram and would result in an explosion of staggering magnitude. Their memorandum to the British government brought into being the so-called Maud Committee and set in motion the British atomic bomb project. In the United States the Manhattan Project, to which the British team contributed, would successfully attempt to make both plutonium and uranium (U-235) weapons.

3. Alamogordo, Hiroshima and Nagasaki: 'Almost full grown at birth'

1. Victor F. Weisskopf, 'Nuclear Fission — A Peril and a Hope', originally given as a talk to the American Physical Society, *Anticipation* (World Council of Churches), No. 26 (June 1979), p.59.

2. Szilard's letter is printed in full in S.R. Weart and G.W. Szilard, *Leo Szilard: His Version of the Facts* (Cambridge, Mass.: MIT Press, 1978), pp.94-6; 'My Life as a Physicist' in V.F. Weisskopf, *Physics of the Twentieth Century: Selected Essays* (Cambridge, Mass.: MIT Press, 1972), p.14.

3. On Weisskopf's suggestion that Heisenberg be kidnapped, see Martin J. Sherwin, *A World Destroyed: The Atomic Bomb and the Grand Alliance* (New York: Knopf, 1975), p.50; R.P. Feynman, 'The Pleasure of Finding Things Out', *The Listener* (26 November 1981), p.635; see also Feynman, 'Los Alamos from Below', in Lawrence Badash, Joseph O. Hirschfelder, and Herbert P. Broida (eds.), *Reminiscences of Los Alamos, 1943-1945* (Dordrecht, Holland: Reidel, 1980), p.105.

4. Feynman, 'The Pleasure of Finding Things Out', p.635. On 8 May Feld had receive a telegram from his younger brother who had been listed for the previous six months as missing in action during the advance into Germany: see Ian Low, 'Science for Peace', *New Scientist* (24 July 1975), pp.208-11; Weisskopf, 'The Los Alamos Years', in I.I. Rabi et al. *Oppenheimer* (New York: Scribner, 1969), p.27.

5. E. Segrè, *Enrico Fermi, Physicist* (U. of California Press, 1970), p.145.

6. Oppenheimer's testimony, *In the Matter of J. Robert Oppenheimer* (Washington: Atomic Energy Commission, 1954), pp.32-3.

7. Philip M. Stern with the collaboration of H.P. Green, *The Oppenheimer Case: Security on Trial* (St Albans, Herts: Rupert Hart-Davis, 1971), p.90; J.R. Oppenheimer, 'Physics in the Contemporary World', *The Open Mind* (New York: Simon & Schuster, 1955), p.88.

8. Groves, *Now It Can Be Told: The Story of the Manhattan Project* (André Deutsch, 1963), p.415.

9. Truman is quoted by L. Giovanniti and F. Freed, *The Decision to Drop the Bomb* (Methuen, 1967), p.28. See also Elting E. Morrison, *Turmoil and Tradition: A Study of the Life and Times of Henry L. Stimson* (Boston, Mass.: Houghton Mifflin, 1960), pp.616-18.

10. Max von Laue, quoted by David Irving, *The Virus House* (note 36 of Ch.2) p.16. It should be noted that the interned German scientists were incredulous that the Allied scientists had managed to get so far ahead of them. Otto Hahn took the opportunity to call Heisenberg and his interned colleagues 'second raters'.

11. Arthur Compton, *Atomic Quest* (Oxford UP, 1956), p.108; Edward Creutz is quoted in Martin Sherwin (note 3), p.48.

12. Compton, pp.139, 143, 144, 139.

13. Compton, *Atomic Quest*, pp.160, 184. In *The Cosmos of A.H. Compton* (note 27 of Ch.2), p.52, Compton writes, 'My life has been a thrilling adventure.'

14. Quoted by Nuel Pharr Davies, *Lawrence and Oppenheimer* (Cape, 1969), p.127.

15. As reported by Stephane Groueff, *Manhattan Project: The Untold Story of the Making of the Atomic Bomb* (Collins, 1967), p.221. See also Bethe's own account in Jeremy Bernstein, *Hans Bethe, Prophet of Energy* (New York: Basic Books, 1980), pp.72-3. E. Segrè, *Enrico Fermi* (note 5), p.151.

16. See Oppenheimer's letter to Rabi printed in A.K. Smith and C. Wiener (eds.), *Robert Oppenheimer: Letters and Recollections* (Harvard UP, 1980), p.250. E. Segrè, *Enrico Fermi*, p.145.

17. Feynman, 'Los Alamos from Below' (note 3), pp.106, 109, 128-9. On scientific heroes, see Pnina G. Abir-Am, 'Essay Review: How

Scientists View Their Heroes: Some Remarks on the Mechanism of Myth Construction', *Journal of the History of Biology* 15 (1982), pp.281-315.

18. Oppenheimer's farewell speech to 5,000 scientists and their wives of the Association of Los Alamos Scientists, 2 November 1945, in Smith and Wiener, *Robert Oppenheimer* (note 16), p.316.

19. *In the Matter of J. Robert Oppenheimer* (note 6), p.13.

20. Segrè, *Enrico Fermi*, pp.145, 149.

21. Groves's communication to Stimson is printed in full in Martin Sherwin, *A World Destroyed: The Atomic Bomb and the Grand Alliance* (New York: Knopf, 1975), p.308.

22. J.O. Hirschfelder, 'The Scientific and Technological Miracle at Los Alamos', in L. Badash et al. *Reminiscences of Los Alamos* (note 3), pp.69, 67.

23. *In the Matter of J. Robert Oppenheimer* (note 6), p.469.

24. The expression 'tremendous intellectual power' is used by Hans Bethe in his biographical memoir, 'J. Robert Oppenheimer, 1904-1967', *Biographical Memoirs of Fellows of the Royal Society* 14 (1968) 391-416; the expression 'intellectual sex appeal' is quoted by Jungk in *Brighter than a Thousand Suns* (Penguin, 1960) p.125; David Bohm is quoted by Peter Goodchild, *J. Robert Oppenheimer* (BBC, 1980), p.30; Lawrence is quoted by Herbert Childs, *An American Genius: The Life of Ernest Orlando Lawrence* (New York: Dutton, 1968), p.333; for the fun made of Gregory Breit's title see N.P. Davis, *Lawrence and Oppenheimer* (note 14), p.125 and Oppenheimer's testimony, *In the Matter of J. Robert Oppenheimer* (note 6), p.27.

25. Compton, *Atomic Quest*, p.130.

26. Jungk, *Brighter than a Thousand Suns* (Penguin, 1960), p.128.

27. For comments on the 'baby boom' in Los Alamos, see J. Bernstein, *Hans Bethe*, p.82, V.F. Weisskopf, 'The Los Alamos Years', p.26, and Bernice Brode, 'Tales of Los Alamos' in L. Badash et al. (note 3), pp.141-2.

28. George B. Kistiakowsky, 'Reminiscences of Wartime Los Alamos', in Badash et al. (note 3), pp.51, 60.

29. O. Frisch, *What Little I Remember* (Cambridge UP, 1979), p.161. On the deaths of Daghlian and Slotin, see Frisch, pp.160-1, and Jungk, p.177. Note that Slotin called the experiment 'twisting the dragon's tail'. See also S. Alsop and R.E. Lapp, 'The Strange Death of Louis Slotin', in Charles Neider (ed.), *Man against Nature* (Weidenfeld & Nicolson, 1956).

30. Jungk (note 26), p.180. Oppenheimer's wife, Kitty, gave birth at Los Alamos to a girl, christened Katherine but known as Tony or Toni.

Bernice Brode writes (note 27, pp.141-2), 'So many babies were born that the hospital had at one time nearly half its capacity used as nursery. The whole town wanted to come and see the babies, especially when a little Oppenheimer was born. The sign "Oppenheimer" was placed over baby Tony's crib and people filed by in the corridor for days to view the boss's baby girl.'

31. K.T. Bainbridge, 'A foul and awesome display', *Bulletin of the Atomic Scientists* (May 1975), p.43.

32. R.P. Feynman, 'Los Alamos from Below' (note 3), p.130; Kistiakowsky, 'Trinity — a reminiscence', *Bulletin of the Atomic Scientists* (June 1980), p.19. James W. Kunetka in *City of Fire* (Englewood Cliffs, New Jersey: Prentice-Hall, 1978), pp.165-6, writes: 'Many men who couldn't be at Trinity... decided to try for a view of the shot from the roads around Trinity or from the Sandria Mountains outside Los Alamos... The bomb, after all, was the baby of the Laboratory, and there was little the Security Office could do to dampen parental interests.'

33. General Thomas F. Farrell's description of the Trinity test, sent by General Groves to Stimson on 18 July 1945, is reproduced in Sherwin, *A World Destroyed* (note 21), pp.311-2.

34. Kistiakowsky (note 28), p.60.

35. Farrell in Sherwin, *A World Destroyed* (note 21), p.312. Oppenheimer's (pre-arranged) message to his wife was, 'You can change the sheets.'

36. Richard G. Hewlett and Oscar E. Anderson, *A History of the United States Atomic Energy Commission, Vol.1: The New World, 1939-1946* (Pennsylvania State UP, 1962), p.386.

37. Charles L. Mee, Jr., *Meeting at Potsdam* (André Deutsch, 1975), p.106.

38. See note 8 of Ch.1.

39. William L. Laurence, *Dawn over Zero: The Story of the Atomic Bomb* (Museum Press, 1947), p.10.

40. Feynman, 'Los Alamos from Below', p.131. On Joseph Rotblat, see Norman Moss, *Men Who Play God: The Story of the H-Bomb* (Penguin, 1970), pp.97, 233 and Saburo Kugai, 'The Nuclear Umbrella in East Asia' in Edward Thompson et al. *Exterminism and Cold War* (Verso and New Left Review, 1982), p.188.

41. *In the Matter of J. Robert Oppenheimer*, pp.173, 651. For an account and interpretation of the life and work of John von Neumann, see Steve J. Heims, *John von Neumann and Norbert Wiener: From Mathematics to the Technologies of Life and Death* (Cambridge, Mass: MIT Press, 1980).

42. Churchill, *The Second World War*, Vol.6, 'Triumph and Tragedy' (Cassell, 1954), p.495.

43. D. Irving, *The Virus House* (note 36 of Ch.2), p.250; see also Groves

(note 8), pp.230-1.

44. James F. Byrnes, *Speaking Frankly* (Heinemann, 1947), p.257; Truman is quoted by Robert L. Messer, *The End of an Alliance: James F. Byrnes, Roosevelt, Truman, and the Origins of the Cold War* (University of North Carolina Press, 1982), pp.84, 86; *Leo Szilard: His Version of the Facts* (note 2), p.184.

45. See Giovannitti and Freed, pp.77-95. The first fire bombing of Tokyo on 9-10 March 1945, destroyed a quarter of the city and killed over 80,000 people; see The Pacific War Research Society, *The Day Man Lost: Hiroshima, 6 August 1945* (1972; New York: Kodansha, 1981), pp.100-3.

46. Giovannitti and Freed, p.96.

47. For a discussion of the different theses that historians have proposed to explain the dropping of atomic bombs on Japan, see Barton J. Bernstein, *The Atomic Bomb: The Critical Issues* (Boston, Mass.: Little, Brown, 1976).

48. See B.J. Bernstein, 'Shatterer of Worlds, Hiroshima and Nagasaki', *Bulletin of the Atomic Scientists* (December 1975), p.17.

49. Quoted by Sherwin, *A World Destroyed* (note 21), pp.204-5. Sherwin also writes: 'There is no suggestion in the memorandum [prepared by Stimson and Groves and two aides], or in the questions the Secretary placed before the assembled group, that his [Stimson's] memory was serving him well when he wrote in his autobiography: "The first and greatest problem [for the Interim Committee] was the decision on the use of the bomb — should it be used against the Japanese, and if so, in what manner?" The fact is that a discussion of this question was placed on the agenda only after it was raised casually in the course of conversation during lunch.'

50. Hewlett and Anderson, *The New World* (note 36), p.357.

51. Sherwin, *A World Destroyed* (note 21), p.306.

52. Hewlett and Anderson, p.360.

53. K.T. Bainbridge, 'A foul and awesome display' (note 31), p.143.

54. Sherwin, p.222.

55. Churchill, *The Second World War* (note 42), p.551.

56. Mee, *Meeting at Potsdam* (note 37), pp.155, 164.

57. Churchill, *The Second World War*, p.553.

58. Arthur Bryant, *Triumph in the West 1943-6, Based on the Diaries and Autobiographical Notes of Field Marshall The Viscount Alanbrooke* (Collins, 1959), p.478.

59. Sherwin, p.227.

60. Harry S. Truman, *Memoirs. Vol.1: Years of Decision* (New York: Garden City, 1955), p.421, quoted by Sherwin, p.221.

61. See B.J. Bernstein, *The Atomic Bomb* (note 47), p.131.
62. Mee, *Meeting at Potsdam* (note 37), pp.20, 307, xiv, 289. For a scathing review of Mee's book, see B.J. Bernstein, *Political Science Quarterly* 90 (1975) pp.553-5. Together with many other impassioned criticisms of the author, Bernstein accuses Mee of 'facile' and 'promiscuous psychologizing' with respect to Truman, Churchill, and Stalin. For my part I would rather be explicitly presented with such 'facile psychologizing' than given to understand, quite implicitly, that the three leaders, and particularly Truman and Churchill, were in the main unneurotic, uncomplicated men, whose principal purpose was to achieve the overall good of their 'nation' and of humanity in general. For Bernstein's own authoritative appraisal of Potsdam and the reasons behind Hiroshima and Nagasaki, see Bernstein, *The Atomic Bomb* (note 47). S.J. Heims, however, in *John von Neumann and Norbert Wiener* apparently accepts Mee's verdict, see especially pp.230-1. But see also the hostile review of Heims's book by the distinguished ex-Los Alamos physicist, Sir Rudolf Peierls, in *New York Review of Books*, 'Odd Couple', Vol.29 (18 Feb. 1982), pp.16-18. One might note the conclusion of Lloyd S. Etheredge that 'the personality makeup of presidents and foreign policy elites contains those ingredients — and in significant measure — that make war more likely'; see Etheredge, *A World of Men: The Private Sources of American Foreign Policy* (Cambridge, Mass.: MIT Press, 1978), p. xiv.
63. Stimson's memorandum to the President is printed in full in Gar Alperovitz, *Atomic Diplomacy: Hiroshima and Potsdam. The Use of the Atomic Bomb and the American Confrontation with Soviet Power* (Secker & Warburg, 1966), pp.277-9.
64. Lawrence is quoted by Herbert Childs, *An American Genius* (note 24), p.340.
65. Robert R. Wilson, 'A Recruit for Los Alamos', *Bulletin of the Atomic Scientists* (March 1975), p.43. Feynman in 'Los Alamos from Below' (note 3), p.132, recalls: 'After the [Trinity test], there was a tremendous excitement at Los Alamos. Everybody had parties, we all ran around. I sat on the end of a jeep and beat drums and so on. But one man I remember, Bob Wilson, was just sitting there moping.'
66. See Sherwin, *A World Destroyed* (note 21), pp.109-10, 284. Leakage to the Russians did occur. Klaus Fuchs, a German-born physicist working in the British team of scientists at Los Alamos, was convicted in 1950 of supplying information to the war-time allies of Britain and America.
67. *Leo Szilard: His Version of the Facts* (note 2), pp.183-5, 206.
68. The Franck Report is reprinted in Jungk (note 26), pp.311-20.

69. Sherwin (note 21), pp.212-3.

70. Sherwin, pp.304-5.

71. *Leo Szilard: His Version of the Facts* (note 2), p.211. On Szilard's petition and Arthur Compton's poll of scientific opinion at the Chicago Laboratory, see Alice K. Smith, *A Peril and a Hope: The Scientists' Movement in America 1945-47* (U. of Chicago Press, 1965), pp.48-59.

72. Sherwin, p.218; *Szilard: His Version of the Facts*, p.163. Sherwin notes that although 'Teller has written (and on numerous occasions stated in public) that he originally favored Szilard's petition, but had been talked out of it by Oppenheimer', the evidence suggests 'that Teller's views were never in conflict with Oppenheimer's on this matter': see Sherwin, pp.218-19 footnote.

73. Sherwin, p.217. On Bernard Feld, see Ian Low, 'Science for Peace' (note 4). Alice K. Smith (note 71) does, however, write of 'a welling up of individual anxieties [at Los Alamos] which might have added up to significant protest had any one person been ready to organize them' (p.62). Hans Bethe also writes: 'I had been absorbed in the work but as soon as the test was successful at Alamogordo I joined the discussions that were then being held by many people at the laboratory about what to do with the bomb and atomic energy in general...': see Jeremy Bernstein, *Hans Bethe, Prophet of Energy* (note 15), p.87. For Bernard Feld's struggle against the nuclear arms race, see B.T. Feld, *A Voice Crying in the Wilderness: Essays on the Problems of Science and World Affairs* (Pergamon, 1979).

74. *Leo Szilard: His Version of the Facts* (note 2), pp.187-8.

75. See Jungk (note 26), p.203.

76. Alice K. Smith (note 71), pp.80-1. The account that gave rise to the feelings of guilt was John Hersey, *Hiroshima* (Penguin, 1946).

77. E. Teller with Allen Brown, *The Legacy of Hiroshima* (Macmillan, 1962), pp.6-7.

78. Quoted by P. Goodchild, *J. Robert Oppenheimer* (BBC, 1980), p.167. See also Lansing Lamont, *Day of Trinity* (Hutchinson, 1966), p.265, and Philip M. Stern with the collaboration of H.P. Green, *The Oppenheimer Case: Security on Trial* (St Albans, Herts: Rupert Hart-Davis, 1971), p.82.

79. Frisch, *What Little I Remember* (note 29) pp.176-7.

80. Feynman, 'The Pleasure of Finding Things Out' (note 3), p.635.

81. Quoted by Jungk (note 26), p.202. See also Bernard T. Feld, 'Nuclear Proliferation — Thirty Years after Hiroshima', *Physics Today* (July 1975), p.29: 'This inexcusable, militarily irrelevant destruction of a city and its population, when the Japanese were already suing for peace, was for no military purpose other than the testing of a new type of

weapon and the demonstration of its effectiveness'. In his interview with Ian Low (note 4) Feld states that everyone at Los Alamos thought the destruction of Hiroshima 'was great' but news of the destruction of Nagasaki struck him 'like a cold shower'.

82. W.L. Laurence, *Dawn over Zero* (note 39), p.188.

83. *Ibid.*, pp.198-9.

84. Simone de Beauvoir, *The Second Sex* (note 37 of Ch.2), p.95.

85. According to Daniel J. Kevles, *The Physicists: The History of a Scientific Community in Modern America* (New York: Knopf, 1978), p.334: 'From the days of John Wesley Powell to those of Robert Millikan, American scientists had scarcely been concealed from public notice. But unlike any of its predecessors, this generation was dominated by physicists who seemed to wear the "tunic of Supermen", in the phrase of a *Life* reporter, and stood in the spotlight of a thousand suns.'

Samuel K. Allison, 'The State of Physics, or the Perils of Being Important', *Bulletin of the Atomic Scientists*, (January 1950), p.3, writes: 'Suddenly physicists were exhibited as lions at Washington tea parties, were invited to conventions of social scientists, where their opinions on society were respectfully listened to by lifelong experts in the field, attended conventions of religious orders and discoursed on theology, were asked to endorse plans for world government, and to give simplified lectures on the nucleus to Congressional committees.'

86. Laura Fermi, *Atoms in the Family: My Life with Enrico Fermi: Designer of the First Atomic Pile* (Allen & Unwin, 1955), p.257.

87. S. de Beauvoir, *The Second Sex* (note 37 of Ch.2), p.691; B. Brode, 'Tales of Los Alamos' (note 27), p.159.

88. Laura Fermi, 'The Fermis' Path to Los Alamos' in Badash et al. (note 3), p.95.

89. See Jungk (note 26), p.282. L. Kowarski refers to Oppenheimer as '*the* father of the atomic bomb' in 'New Forms of Organization in Physical Research after 1945' in C. Wiener (ed.), *The History of Twentieth-Century Physics* (New York: Academic Press, 1977), p.391.

90. E. Teller, 'The Work of Many People', *Science* 121 (1955), p.270.

91. See David Holloway, 'Entering the Nuclear Arms Race: The Soviet Decision to Build the Atomic Bomb', *Social Studies of Science* 11 (1981) pp.159-97.

4. The Creation of the Hydrogen Bomb: 'One of the most fantastic adventures that a scientist can have'

1. See my *Liberation and the Aims of Science*, Ch.11, and especially Alice K. Smith, *A Peril and a Hope* (note 71 of Ch.3). On the postwar military funding of basic science, see Daniel S. Greenberg, *The*

Politics of Pure Science: An Inquiry into the Relationship between Science and Government in the United States (New York: New American Library, 1967), especially Ch.7. High-energy physics certainly got off to a good start. In early 1947 Oppenheimer gave a lecture at the New York meeting of the American Physical Society on the first results obtained with the world's then most powerful accelerator, built at Berkeley under the direction of Ernest Lawrence who had been provided at the end of the war with funds amounting to $170,000 by General Groves. 'There are rich days ahead for physics,' declared Oppenheimer, 'we may hope to be living in one of the heroic ages of physical science.' The continuing Cold War has helped to ensure government and military funding of 'pure' science both in the United States and elsewhere. According, for example, to Greenberg (p.221n), 'while American scientists became quite skilled at obtaining funds by sounding claims about Soviet progress, there is evidence that Soviet scientists were not at all laggard in exploiting the Cold War to obtain funds from their government'.

2. B.J. Bernstein, *The Atomic Bomb* (note 47 of Ch.3), p.132.

3. A.K. Smith and C. Wiener, *Robert Oppenheimer* (note 16 of Ch.3), p.320.

4. Arthur Bryant, *Triumph in the West* (note 58 of Ch.3), pp.508-10.

5. See my *Liberation and the Aims of Science*, pp.244-45.

6. D.A. Rosenberg, 'American Atomic Strategy and the Hydrogen Bomb Decision', *Journal of American History* 66 (1979), pp.67-8, 71; see also D.A. Rosenberg, pp.25-30. 'US Nuclear Stockpile, 1945 to 1950', *Bulletin of the Atomic Scientists* (May 1982), pp.25-30.

7. Quoted by S.J. Heims (note 41 of Ch.3), p.247.

8. Russell, *Saturday Review of Literature* 37 (16 October 1954), p.25.

9. Otto Nathan and Heinz Norden (eds), *Einstein on Peace* (New York: Schocken, 1968), pp.465, 497, 487.

10. *Ibid.*, pp.538, 553, 554, 570, 557. See also my *Liberation and the Aims of Science*, Appendix, 'Einstein's Political Struggle', reprinted in Maurice Goldsmith, Alan Mackay and James Woudhuysen (eds), *Einstein: The First Hundred Years* (Oxford: Pergamon, 1980), and Bernard T. Feld, 'Einstein and the Politics of Nuclear Weapons' in Gerald Holton and Yehuda Elkana (eds), *Albert Einstein: Historical and Cultural Perspectives* (Princeton UP, 1982).

11. Einstein, *Ideas and Opinions* (New York: Dell, 1973), p.38. Alexander Moszkowski, *Conversations with Einstein*, tr. Henry L. Brose (Sidgwick & Jackson, 1972), pp.240-1. (Moszkowski was a well-known Berlin journalist and music critic who, at the age of nearly 70, met and talked with Einstein in the years 1919 and 1920). Einstein's

son is quoted by Ronald Clark, *Einstein: The Life and Times* (New York: Avon, 1972), p.50. But note the following comment by Einstein about himself in *Ideas and Opinions*, pp.20-1: 'My passionate sense of social justice and social responsibility have always contrasted oddly with my pronounced lack of need for direct contact with other human beings and human communities. I am truly a "lone traveller" and have never belonged to my country, my friends, or even my immediate family with my whole heart; in the face of all these ties, I have never lost a sense of distance and a need for solitude — feelings which increase with the years.'

12. See the references given by Rosenberg (note 6), p.63, notes 3 and 4, Gregg Herken, ' "A Most Deadly Illusion": The Atomic Secret and American Nuclear Weapons Policy', *Pacific Historical Review* (Spring, 1980), pp.51-76, and especially the overview by McGeorge Bundy, 'The Missed Chance to Stop the H-Bomb', *The New York Review of Books* (13 May 1982). My account is in *Liberation and the Aims of Science*, Chs.7 and 11.

13. H. York, *The Advisors: Oppenheimer, Teller and the Superbomb* (San Francisco: W.H. Freeman, 1976), pp.2, 157, 158-9; E. Fermi's testimony *In the Matter of J. Robert Oppenheimer* (note 6 of Ch.3), p.395.

14. York, *The Advisors*, p.62.

15. E. Teller, *Energy from Heaven and Earth* (San Francisco: W.H. Freeman, 1979), p.149.

16. J. Bernstein, *Hans Bethe: Prophet of Energy* (New York: Basic Books, 1980), p.73. Bethe also writes (p.73): 'My wife knew vaguely what we were talking about, and on a walk in Yosemite National Park she asked me to consider carefully whether I really wanted to continue work on this. Finally, I decided to do it.'

17. H. Bethe, 'J. Robert Oppenheimer' (note 24 of Ch.3), p.398.

18. E. Teller, 'The Work of Many People', *Science* 121 (1955), p.269.

19. Bernstein (note 16), p.81.

20. Bethe's testimony *In the Matter of J. Robert Oppenheimer* (note 6 of Ch.3), p.325. Teller, however, describes the situation very differently. In *The Legacy of Hiroshima* (note 77 of Ch.3), p.40, Teller writes: 'Despite the urgency of the situation, Oppenheimer during these years of struggle with atomic questions did not lose sight of the more distant possibilities. He urged me to continue exploring the thermonuclear field, even though it was beyond the immediate aim of the laboratory. This was not easy advice for him to give or for me to take. It is hard to work apart from others in a scientific community, especially when most people are working towards a goal of the highest interest and urgency.

21. Jungk (note 26 of Ch.3), p.242; Teller (note 18), p.270.

22. Quoted by P.M. Stern, *The Oppenheimer Case* (note 78 of Ch.3), pp.76-7.

23. S. Ulam, *Adventures of a Mathematician* (New York: Scribner, 1976), p.210.

24. E. Teller, *The Legacy of Hiroshima* (note 77 of Ch.3), p.45.

25. N.P. Davis, *Lawrence and Oppenheimer* (Cape, 1969), p.298.

26. Bernstein, *Hans Bethe* (note 16), pp.92-3. Bethe writes (p.92-4): 'During the discussion with Teller, my wife came into the room and said to both of us very earnestly, "You don't want to do this." She felt that the atomic bomb was bad enough, and that increasing its power a thousand times was simply irresponsible. I was still undecided about what to do... In my decision not to return to Los Alamos, I was persuaded not by Oppenheimer but by my wife and by Weisskopf and Placzek... I have explained this to Teller many times, but he and others still blamed Oppenheimer for my not returning to Los Alamos.'

27. *Ibid.*, pp.93-4.

28. Ulam (note 23), pp.216-17.

29. Teller, *The Legacy of Hiroshima* (note 77 of Ch.3), pp.51-3. For a rather different account of the meeting between Teller and Dean, see R.G. Hewlett and F. Duncan, *A History of the United States Atomic Energy Commission* (Washington: USAEC, 1972), Vol.2: *Atomic Shield*, p.541.

30. Bernstein, *Hans Bethe* (note 16), p.95.

31. *In the Matter of J. Robert Oppenheimer* (note 6 of Ch.3), pp.251, 229, 81.

32. Ulam (note 23). pp.223-4.

33. Teller, 'The Work of Many People' (note 18), p.274; *The Legacy of Hiroshima*, p.22; *Energy from Heaven and Earth* (note 15), p.151, see also Norman Moss, *Men Who Play God* (Penguin, 1970), p.78. The giving of male names to the first fission and fusion bombs exploded, namely 'Little Boy' and 'Fat Man', 'George' and 'Mike', perhaps reflects the male sexist desire for the first-born to be a son, after which daughters become more acceptable. Since the destructive, all-devouring female witch-figure is pervasive in Western (male sexist) culture, from this point of view it would be acceptable for nuclear weapons to be given either female or male names. Presumably, however, no sane male would ever willingly make such female companions for his male monsters (recall how Frankenstein had told himself, as he laboured over the female monster he was to tear to pieces before she was finally assembled: 'she might become ten thousand times more malignant than her mate, and delight, for its own

sake, in murder and wretchedness'). Moreover, the destructive power of nuclear weapons is supposed to be under, and to remain under, male control. Nevertheless, I would expect that nuclear weapons have also been given female as well as male names. There might, after all, be a desire to pretend that these monsters are just lovable, cuddly, badly misunderstood little creatures.

34. Andrei Sakharov, the 'father' of the Soviet H-bomb, writes in his article, 'How I came to dissent', *New York Review of Books* (21 March 1974), p.11: 'A few months after defending my dissertation in the spring of 1948, I was included in a research group working on the problem of a thermonuclear weapon. I had no doubts about the vital importance of creating a Soviet superweapon — for our country and for the balance of power throughout the world. *Carried away by the immensity of the task*, I worked very strenuously and became the author or co-author of several key ideas. In the Western press I have often been called "the father of the hydrogen bomb". This description reflects very inaccurately the real (and complex) situation of collective invention — something I shall not discuss in detail (emphasis added). No discussion is given at all to the notion of 'fathering' an H-bomb.

35. V. Bush, *In the Matter of J. Robert Oppenheimer* (note 6 of Ch.3), p.562.

36. Bernstein, *Hans Bethe* (note 15 of Ch.3), p.94.

37. BBC television programme, *Horizon*, 9 February, 1981. For details of the film, produced by Brian Kaufman, See Dietrich Schroeer, *Bulletin of the Atomic Scientists* (May 1980), pp.55-6.

38. H. York, *The Advisors* (note 13), pp.133-36. When news of the Livermore superfizzle reached Ulam and von Neumann, Ulam recalls that von Neumann laughed to him: 'There will be dancing in the streets of Los Alamos tonight': *Adventures of a Mathematician* (note 23), p.222.

39. E. Teller in *The Legacy of Hiroshima* (note 77 of Ch.3) writes: 'Our early failures and their continued successes produced an unavoidable and expected result: We were subjected to a heavy dose of ribbing from our colleagues at the original weapons laboratory. These gibes had an effect that was to endure and was for the best. The young scientists of Livermore developed an ambition for excellence, an appetite that was hard to satisfy, an overwhelming desire for progress that was to keep us going.'

40. H. York, *Race to Oblivion* (New York: Simon & Schuster, 1970), p.93.

41. York, *The Advisors* (note 13), pp.136-7. See especially the article by the Livermore weapons physicist Hugh E. Dewitt, 'Nuclear Weapons', *Science and Public Policy* (April 1982), pp.58-63. Dewitt writes: 'We now have two very large permanent laboratories still competing with each other. In 1982 this competition is more for funding

of large projects, scrambling for the contract to weaponize a nuclear design for deployment in the American stockpile, and persuading the branches of the US Armed Services to accept a variety of proposed new designs for different military purposes.'

42. For an account and interpretation of Oppenheimer's 'trial', see especially P.M. Stern (note 78 of Ch.3). Note that four years earlier, because of his opposition to the making of atomic weapons, compounded by membership of the French Communist Party, Frédéric Joliot-Curie was dismissed from his position as High Commissioner for Atomic Energy by the French Prime Minister, Georges Bidault.

43. Teller's testimony, *In the Matter of J. Robert Oppenheimer* (note 6 of Ch.3), p.726.

44. E. Teller, 'The Work of Many People' (note 18), pp.275, 267, 273.

45. *Ibid.*, p.274.

46. *Ibid.*, pp.267, 275.

47. Quoted by Cecil H. Uyehara, 'Scientific Advice and the Nuclear Test Ban Treaty', in Sanford A. Lakoff, *Knowledge and Power* (New York: Free Press, 1966), p.158; E. Teller and Albert L. Latter, 'The Compelling Need for Nuclear Tests', in L.B. Young and W.J. Trainor (eds), *Science and Public Policy* (New York: Oceana Pubs, 1971), pp.371, 372, 377.

48. Teller, *Energy from Heaven and Earth* (note 15), p.155.

49. York, *Race to Oblivion* (note 40), pp.238; *The Advisors* (note 13), p.ix.

50. York, *The Advisors*, pp.126, 130.

51. *Ibid.*, pp.105, 11; *Race to Oblivion*, p.235.

52. *Ibid*, p.235.

53. Ulam, *Adventures of a Mathematician* (note 23), p.256. P. Abbs, 'Ethical Imagination or The Nuclear Holocaust: Reflections on Education, War and Peace', *Teachers College Record* (Autumn, 1982). I am indebted to John Krige for sending me a copy of this paper.

54. M. Smith, 'Delight grips US as shuttle blasts off', *Guardian* (13 April 1981) p.1.

55. E. Teller, 'Role of Physicists in the 1980s', *Physics Today* (February 1981), p.136. See also the (frightening) article by William J. Perry and Cynthia A. Roberts, 'Winning Through [Technological] Sophistication: How to Meet the Soviet Military Challenge', *Technology Review* (July 1982), pp.27-5.

56. M. Smith (note 54), p.1.

57. The *Guardian* (2 April 1981), p.1.

58. Sheila Durie and Rob Edwards, *Fuelling the Nuclear Arms Race: The Links Between Nuclear Power and Nuclear Weapons* (Pluto, 1982).

59. F. Bacon, 'The Masculine Birth of Time' in B. Farrington (ed.), *The*

Philosophy of Francis Bacon (Liverpool UP, 1970), p.62.

60. Andreas Huyssen 'The Vamp and the Machine: Technology and Sexuality in Fritz Lang's Metropolis', *New German Critique*, No 24-5 (Fall/Winter 1982), p.227.

61. E. Teller, *Energy from Heaven and Earth* (note 15), pp.187-8. For a critique of patriarchy and nuclear power, see Susan Koen and Nina Swain, *Handbook for Women on the Nuclear Mentality* (WAND, Box 421, Norwich, England, 1980). I am indebted to Lesley Burr for recommending this book to me. The illustration on p.27 is especially relevant to Teller's comments.

62. Laura Nader, 'Barriers to thinking new about energy', *Physics Today* (February 1981), pp.10, 100, 104. I am indebted to Tony Leggett for telling me about this article.

63. Michael Frenchman, 'Science and Technology in India', advertisement in *Scientific American* (August 1982), p.113.

64. N. Bradbury, 'Los Alamos — The First Twenty-Five Years', in L. Badash et al. (note 3 of Ch.3), pp.171-72.

65. Sir Solly Zuckerman, *Science Advisors, Scientific Advisors and Nuclear Weapons* (Menard Press, 1981), pp.13, 10, 11, and *Nuclear Illusion and Reality* (Collins, 1982), p.131. Dewitt writes (note 41) p.60: 'From my 25 years as a Livermore Lab staff member and thus as an observer from inside of the American nuclear weapons establishment, I believe that Zuckerman's eloquent assessment is absolutely correct. The nuclear weapons labs are indeed the well springs of the nuclear arms race and as such they represent an extraordinary influence on human affairs... It is my impression that the American public, even its most literate and sophisticated fraction, does not appreciate the power and influence that this network of nuclear weapons experts exercises in national affairs.'

66. See especially Lloyd S. Etheredge, *A World of Men: The Private Sources of American Foreign Policy* (Cambridge, Mass.: MIT Press, 1978), two quotations from which are given in the front of this book. In his speech in May 1981 accepting the Albert Einstein Peace Prize the once Cold War warrior George F. Kennan declared (see the special supplement of *Disarmament Times*, Vol.4, June 1981): 'We must remember that it has been we Americans who, at almost every step of the road, have taken the lead in the development of this sort of weaponry. It was we who first produced and tested such a device; we who were the first to raise its destructiveness to a new level with the hydrogen bomb, we who introduced the multiple warhead; we who have declined every proposal for the renunciation of the principle of "first use"; and we alone, so help us God, who have used the

weapon in anger against others, and against tens of thousands of helpless non-combatants at that...

What is it then, if not our own will, and if not the supposed wickedness of our opponents, that has brought us to this pass?

The answer, I think, is clear. It is primarily the inner momentum, the independent momentum, of the weapons race itself... I see this same phenomenon playing its fateful part in the relations among the great European powers as much as a century ago. I see this competitive buildup of armaments conceived initially as a means to an end but soon becoming the end itself. I see it taking possession of men's imagination and behaviour, becoming a force in its own right, detaching itself from the political differences that initially inspired it, and then leading both parties, invariably and inexorably, to the war they no longer know how to avoid.'

In his article, 'Do the physicians have the power to cure the nuclear warmongers?', Anthony Tucker writes in *The Guardian* (1 April 1982), p.19: 'One focus of IPPNW [International Physicians for the Prevention of Nuclear War] will be crucially different. The medics, the psychiatrists, the medical physicists, may well be the only groups whose combined understanding can unmask the seemingly psychotic drive toward war, and systematic public conditioning for war, which now grips some Western Governments. This is the sickness which we must cure.'

5. When the Ice Breaks: 'Some questions have to remain unanswered. At some point we have to stop'.

1. Max Horkheimer, the 'Frankfurt School' philosopher, writes: 'The disease of reason is that reason was born from man's urge to dominate nature, and the 'recovery' depends on insight into the nature of the original disease, not a cure of the latest symptoms... The subjugation of nature will revert to subjugation of man, and vice versa, as long as man does not understand his own reason and the basic process by which he has created and is maintaining the antagonism that is about to destroy him.' See Horkheimer, *Eclipse of Reason* (1947; New York: Seabury Press, 1974), p.176.

2. *Leo Szilard: His Version of the Facts* (Cambridge, Mass.: MIT Press, 1980), pp.16-17. Ulam, *Adventures of a Mathematician* (New York: Scribner, 1976), p.5.

3. H.G. Wells, *The World Set Free* (Macmillan, 1914), pp.268-73. For a discussion of Wells, see Roslynn D. Haynes, *H.G. Wells: Discoverer of the Future, The Influence of Science on his Thought* (Macmillan, 1980).

4. *The World Set Free*, pp.274, 280-1.

5. *Ibid.*, p.284.

6. J.D. Bernal, *The World, the Flesh and the Devil* (1929; Cape, 1970), pp.18-9, 30.

7. *Ibid.*, pp.36, 38, 45.

8. *Ibid.*, pp.52, 54, 56.

9. *Ibid.*, pp.61, 64. Bernal certainly seemed to enjoy risk-taking and the experience of danger. C.P. Snow in 'J.D. Bernal, A Personal Portrait' printed in M. Goldsmith and A. Mackay (eds), *The Science of Science* (Penguin, 1960), writes, pp.28-9: '[In the second world war Bernal] was at the top of his form, in a fashion more Bernalesque than one could have thought possible... He made his activities more adventurous than any of us liked: his physical courage, as much as his moral courage, is absolute, and throughout the war he took risks that we should have prevented if we could have found a way. It wasn't sensible for him to rush off to St Pancras Station in 1940 to deal with an unexploded bomb... None of that was adventurous enough for him: before long, through ingenious steps he made his way via active bombing to Combined Operations, where he became scientific adviser to Lord Mountbatten. Here he was in his various elements: happy, resourceful, untiring, pushing through his own bright ideas and others'... He went all over the world, Burma, India, twice across Africa... On D-day he did go — he ought to have been stopped — just to make sure that his researches had given the right answer. There he stood on the beach, dressed, somewhat improbably, in the uniform of an Instructor-Lieutenant R.N.'

10. *The World, the Flesh and the Devil* (note 6), p.73.

11. *Ibid.*, p.66.

12. In *World Without War* (1958; Routledge, 2nd edn., 1961), Bernal writes, pp.270-1, 278: 'The objective to be reached at the end of the process of the scientific Industrial Revolution is not any kind of steady state, not one of a Utopia where mankind has achieved its objectives and can sit down to enjoy the fruits of the labours of past generations. The state of the future as of the past will be one of transition, but we may hope that difficulties which will have to be faced will be to a far less extent than they are now those created by man's stupidities... We may look forward, as thousands of young people are today doing, first to the conquest and then to the exploitation of outer space... Once freed from the old limitations, men will rush forward until they come up against new ones.'

   For further discussion of J.D. Bernal, see my *Liberation and the Aims of Science*, pp.325-7 and *Science and Sexual Oppression*, pp.19-21. Maurice Goldsmith has written a biography of Bernal, *Sage, A Life of*

J.D. Bernal (Hutchinson, 1980), which is reviewed by R.M. Young, 'The Relevance of Bernal's Questions', in *Radical Science Journal*, No.10 (1980). See also the invited paper by J.R. Ravetz, 'Bernal's Marxist Vision of History' and R.S. Westfall's response in *Isis* 72 (1981), pp.393-405.

13. Freeman J. Dyson, *Disturbing the Universe* (New York: Harper, 1979) Chs.3 and 4. The quotation is from Dyson, 'Reflections: The Sell-Out', *The New Yorker* (21 Feb. 1970), p.59 and is also given in Kenneth Brower, *The Starship and the Canoe* (Whizzard Press in association with A. Deutsch, 1980), p.19. I am grateful to Tony Leggett for drawing my attention to Brower's moving account of the very different lives of Freeman Dyson and his son George.

14. Dyson, *Disturbing the Universe*, pp.51, 53.

15. *Ibid.*, p.96.

16. *Ibid.*, pp.111, 127.

17. *Ibid.*, p.128. Dyson's article, 'The Future Development of Nuclear Weapons', is printed in *Foreign Affairs* (April 1960), pp.457-64.

18. *Disturbing the Universe*, p.130.

19. *Ibid.*, pp.129, 113. See also F.J. Dyson, 'Death of a Project', *Science* 149 (1965), pp.141-4.

20. *Disturbing the Universe*, p.134.

21. *Ibid.*, pp.114-15.

22. *Ibid.*, p.91.

23. F.J. Dyson, 'Human Consequences of the Exploration of Space', *Bulletin of the Atomic Scientists* (September 1969), p.13.

24. *Disturbing the Universe*, p.237. See also F.J. Dyson, *The World, the Flesh and the Devil, The third J.D. Bernal memorial lecture, delivered at Birkbeck College, 1972* (Birkbeck, 1972). Quoting Freeman Dyson, Louis J. Halle, author of *The Cold War as History*, argues passionately in his article 'A Hopeful Future for Mankind', *Foreign Affairs* (Summer, 1980), that mankind should commit itself in the near future to the colonisation of outer space — so that the human species will survive, according to Halle, a nuclear catastrophe on earth. He concludes pessimistically, p.1136: 'However, the natural conservatism of our human societies, associating security with the womb of Mother Earth, appears to rule out the chance that our kind will realize this possibility of salvation with the dispatch that might otherwise be expected.'

25. Quoted by Robert Olby, *The Path to the Double Helix* (Macmillan, 1974), p.237. For a discussion of the contribution made by physicists to the attack on 'the secret of life', see Donald Fleming, 'Emigré Physicists and the Biological Revolution', in D. Fleming and Bernard Bailyn (eds.), *The Intellectual Migration: Europe and America,*

1930-1960 (Harvard UP, 1969).

26. George Wald, 'The Case against Genetic Engineering', *The Sciences* 16 (September 1976), reprinted in James D. Watson and John Tooze (eds.), *The DNA Story: A Documentary History of Gene Cloning* (San Francisco: W.H. Freeman, 1981), p.112. In similar vein to Wald, the Chairman of the Division of Biology at the California Institute of Technology, Robert Sinsheimer, writes: 'I can state my objective very simply: the atomic age began with Hiroshima. After that no one needed to be convinced that we had a problem. We are now entering the Genetic Age; I hope we do not need a similar demonstration.' See his article, 'An Evolutionary Perspective for Genetic Engineering', *New Scientist* 73 (20 January 1977), reprinted in *The DNA Story*, p.220. Interestingly the Nobel laureate biologist Walter Gilbert of Harvard University declares that molecular biologists have only themselves to blame for the scare surrounding recombinant DNA research and application. 'The recombinant DNA technology in biology', he writes, 'was seen as akin to the nuclear physics of the nuclear energy programme and the nuclear bomb. In some ways this was encouraged by the biologists; there's a curious form in which those who began the recombinant DNA work almost said: "Stop us, we're doing something important, and you can tell it's important because it's dangerous". And there's a macho impulse to say: "Here, you can see I'm really doing an important experiment because if those bacteria got out of the test-tube they would really cause trouble". It was entirely imaginary.'

See Walter Gilbert, 'Imagined Worlds: Serpent in the Garden of Eden', *The Listener* (11 March 1982), p.11. For a thought provoking discussion of 'molecular biology' see Edward Yoxen, 'Life as a Productive Force: Capitalising the Science and Technology of Molecular Biology' in Les Levidow and Bob Young (eds.), *Science, Technology and the Labour Process: Marxist Studies*, Vol.1 (CSE Books, 1981).

27. See Henry T. Nash, 'The Bureaucratization of Homicide', *Bulletin of the Atomic Scientists* (April 1980), reprinted in E.P. Thompson and Dan Smith (eds.), *Protest and Survive* (Penguin, 1980), p.68.

28. For an analysis of the economic basis of American militarism, see my *Liberation and the Aims of Science*, Ch.7.

29. For an account of the first-strike policy adopted by the American government, see Robert C. Aldridge, *The Counterforce Syndrome: A Guide to the United States Nuclear Weapons and Strategic Doctrine* (1977: Institute for Policy Studies, 1901 Q Street, N.W., Washington, DC 20009 — also The Transnational Institute, Paulus Potterstraat 20, 1071 DA, Amsterdam; 2nd edn, 1979). Robert Aldridge was a

Lockheed engineer for 16 years designing submarine-launched ballistic missiles until the change in American policy and what was required from him brought about his courageous resignation and the writing of *The Counterforce Syndrome*. For analyses of the arms race, see especially: A. Wolfe, *The Rise and Fall of the Soviet Threat* (Washington: Institute for Policy Studies, 1979); John Krige, 'The Politics of Truth. Experts and Lay people in the Nuclear Debate' in N. Blake and K. Pole (eds), *Philosophers Against the Bomb* (Routledge, forthcoming, 1983); Michael Pentz, *Towards the Final Abyss* (J.D. Bernal Peace Library, 58 Dorothy Gardens, Thundersley, Benfleet, Essex SS7 3AE, 1980); Robert Nield, *How to Make up your Mind About the Bomb* (Andre Deutsch, 1981); Martin H. Ryle, *The Politics of Nuclear Disarmament* (Pluto, 1981); Sir Martin Ryle, FRS, *Towards the Nuclear Holocaust* (Menard Press, 1981); Mary Kaldor, *The Baroque Arsenal* (New York: Hill & Wang, 1981); E.P. Thompson, *Beyond the Cold War* (Merlin Press jointly with European Nuclear Disarmament, 1982); CIS Report, *War Lords: The UK Arms Industry* (Counter Information Services, 9 Poland Street, London, W.1., 1982).

30. John W. Gofman, *An Irreverent, Illustrated View of Nuclear Power* (San Francisco: Committee for Nuclear Responsibility, 1979), p.187.

31. Frank Barnaby, 'Military Scientists', *Bulletin of the Atomic Scientists* (June-July 1981), p.11.

32. A.J. Lane, Letter to the *Guardian* (15 August 1980), p.10.

33. Paul Hoch, *White Hero, Black Beast: Racism, Sexism and the Mask of Masculinity* (Pluto, 1979), p.41.

34. W.F. Libby, 'Man's Place in the Physical Universe', in John R. Platt (ed.), *New Views of the Nature of Man* (University of Chicago Press, 1965), pp.14-5.

35. A.S. Eve (note 18 of Ch.2); Professor Huxley's address is printed in full in *The Times Higher Educational Supplement* (2 September 1977), p.4.

36. R. Feynman, 'The Pleasure of Finding Things Out', *The Listener* (26 November 1981), p.636. The quoted words 'Nature's there and she's going to come out the way she is' are from the television interview itself. In *The Listener*'s edited version the remark is given as 'Nature is going to come out the way it is'!

37. J. Bronowski, 'Science in the New Humanism', *The Science Teacher* (May, 1968), p.14; W.F. Libby, 'Creativity in Science' in J.D. Roslanski (ed.), *Creativity: A Discussion at the Nobel Conference* (Amsterdam: North Holland, 1970'), p.36; Bronowski, pp.16, 72.

38. R.C. Lewontin, 'Honest Jim Watson's Big Thriller about DNA'

(1968), reprinted in J.D. Watson, *The Double Helix: A New Critical Edition*, ed. by G.S. Stent (Weidenfeld & Nicolson, 1981), p.186.

39. One might note the words of Sir Lawrence Bragg in his foreword to Watson's *The Double Helix* (Penguin, 1970): 'The latter chapters, in which the birth of the new idea is described so vividly, are drama of the highest order; the tension mounts and mounts towards the final climax.' Once again, the metaphor of the 'pregnant phallus' springs to mind.

40. See, for example, Warren O. Hagstrom, *The Scientific Community* (New York: Basic Books, 1965), pp.167-76, 'The Hierarchy of the Sciences'; Norman W. Storer, 'The Hard Sciences and the Soft: Some Sociological Observations', *Bulletin of the Medical Library Association* 55 (1967), pp.75-84.

41. G. Kistiakowsky, quoted in P. Goodchild, *J. Robert Oppenheimer* (BBC, 1980), p.134.

42. F. Crick, *Of Molecules and Men* (Washington paperback edn, 1967), p.10; J.D. Watson, *The Molecular Biology of the Gene* (Elmsford, New York: Benjamin, 1965), p.67. For a critique of reductionism in science, see my *Liberation and the Aims of Science*, Ch.10.

43. L.M. Lederman, 'A Great Collaboration', *Science* 164 (11 April 1969), p.169, states that 'high energy physics is the most exciting, vital and crucial frontier science. Its intellectual level is the ultimate that has been reached in human history', quoted by Jerry Gaston, 'Competition for Priority of Discovery in Physics', *Minerva* 9 (1971), p.480; see, for example, Barry Commoner, *The Closing Circle: Confronting the Environmental Crisis* (Cape, 1972), pp.189-93.

44. See Goudsmit's comment in *Proceedings of the Tenth International Congress of the History of Science* (Paris: Hermann, 1964), p.132.

45. Hagstrom, *The Scientific Community* (note 40) ascribes mathematics a high prestige within the sciences, see his discussion, p.189.

46. C.S. Sherrington, 'Science and Medicine in the Modern University', *British Medical Journal* 2 (1903), p.1193, quoted by Judy Sadler, 'Ideologies of "Art" and "Science" in Medicine: The Transition from Medical Care to the Application of Technique in the British Medical Profession', in W. Krohn, E.T. Layton, Jr., P. Weingart (eds), *The Dynamics of Science and Technology, Social Values, Technical Norms and Scientific Criteria in the Development of Knowledge* (Reidel, 1978), p.214.

47. I. Lakatos, 'Criticism and the Methodology of Scientific Research Programmes', *Proceedings of the Aristotelian Society* 69 (1968), p.151 note; Lakatos, 'Falsification and the Methodology of Scientific Research Programmes' in I. Lakatos and A. Musgrave, *Criticism and*

the Growth of Knowledge (Cambridge UP, 1970), p.117; Kuhn, 'Notes on Lakatos' in *ibid.*, pp.235, 264. For an account of the Popper-Kuhn-Lakatos debate in the philosophy of science, see my *Liberation and the Aims of Science*, Ch.1.

48. S.G. Brush, *Annals of Science* 39 (1982), pp.79-80.

49. Reported by William J. Broad, 'History of Science Losing its Science', *Science* 207 (25 January 1980), p.389. See also pp.934-5.

50. Nathan Reingold, 'Science, Scientists, and Historians of Science', *History of Science* 19 (1981), p.282.

51. Paul Feyerabend, *Against Method* (New Left Books, 1975), p.295. See especially Nicholas Maxwell, 'Science, Reason, Knowledge, and Wisdom: A Critique of Specialism', *Inquiry* 23 (1980), pp. 19-81.

52. See, for example, Rosemary R. Ruether, *New Woman, New Earth: Sexist Ideologies and Human Liberation* (New York: Seabury Press, 1975), Chs. 3 and 4. See also Christina Larner, 'Was Witch-Hunting Woman-Hunting?', *New Society* (10 October 1981), pp.11-2.

53. John Donne, 'The Anatomy of the World', quoted by Carolyn Merchant (note 16 of Ch.1), p.133.

54. L. Jordanova (note 39 of Ch.1), p.61.

55. See my *Science and Sexual Oppression*, Ch.5.

56. J.W. Prescott, 'Body Pleasure and the Origins of Violence', *Bulletin of the Atomic Scientists* (November 1975), p.19.

57. Lars Ullerstam, *The Erotic Minorities: A Swedish View*, tr. Anselm Hollo (1964; Calder & Bryars, 1967). He writes, for example, of the desirability of 'mobile brothels' to provide for hospitals, mental hospitals, and institutions, paralysed, housebound patients, and old people... In the controversial spirit of Charles Fourier, he continues, p.131: 'All these would be grateful for the most straightforward manipulations, such as masturbation or a striptease performance. The employees of these mobile brothels might be called *erotic Samaritans* and should be held in great esteem. One would wish that cheerful, generous, talented, and morally advanced persons with a knowledge of the joys of giving would feel attracted to this humanitarian profession.'

58. Ron Lacey, 'Teachers at the School for Lovers', *The Guardian* (1 July 1979).

59. Prescott (note 56), p.18.

60. See especially Dorothy Dinnerstein, *The Rocking of the Cradle and the Ruling of the World* (Souvenir Press, 1976).

61. Bettelheim (note 14 of Ch.1), p.265.

62. This point of view is argued in some detail in my *Science and Sexual Oppression*, Chs.2 and 8. For a courageous defence of sado-masochistic practices between 'consenting adults' by a woman who

has been involved in the lesbian-feminist movement for 10 years, see Pat Califia, 'Feminism and Sado-masochism', *Heresies*, No. 12, *Sex Issue*. She herself, she writes, is 'basically a sadist'. For a controversial opinion on pornography, see Paula Webster's article on 'Pornography and Pleasure' in the same issue of *Heresies*. For feminist critiques of pornography, see Andrea Dworkin, *Pornography: Men Possessing Women* (The Women's Press, 1981), Susan Griffin, *Pornography and Silence: Culture's Revenge against Nature* (The Women's Press, 1981) and Chris Stretch, 'Men's Images of Men: Gay Porn. Is it any Different?', *The Leveller* (30 October—12 November 1981), pp.12-14. See also Maria Marcus, *A Taste for Pain: On Masochism and Female Sexuality*, tr. Joan Tate (1978; Souvenir Press, 1981), and *Feminist Review*, No 11 (Summer, 1982), *Sexuality*. See also Susan Weisskopf Contratto, 'Maternal Sexuality and Asexual Motherhood', *Signs* 5 (1980) pp.766-82.

63. A. Lovens and L. Hunter Lovens, *Energy/War: Breaking the Nuclear Link* (New York: Harper Colophon, 1981), p.157. Their book is dedicated 'to the memory of Lew Kowarski (1909-1979) and to the other nuclear pioneers who changed their minds'.

64. J. von Neumann, quoted by Eugene Wigner in *Symmetries and Reflections* (Bloomington: Indiana UP, 1967), p.261.

65. In a critical review of S.J. Heims's book, *John von Neumann and Norbert Wiener* (note 41 of Ch.3), Freeman J. Dyson, 'History without Hindsight', *Technology Review* (February/March, 1981), pp.17-19, explains von Neumann's advocacy of preventive war in the following way: '[T]here is the fact that von Neumann in the late 1940s and early 1950s advocated a preventive war against the Soviet Union. The phrase "preventive war" conveys today an impression of militarism gone mad. But to the generation that lived and suffered through the 1930s, the phrase had quite another meaning. It was widely held, especially by liberal intellectuals, that the French and British governments had behaved in a cowardly and immoral fashion when they failed to march into Germany in 1936 to stop Hitler from remilitarizing the Rhineland. A preventive war at that time, when Germany was still effectively disarmed and incapable of serious resistance against invading forces, might have overturned Hitler's regime in a few days and saved 50 million human beings who were to die in World War II.

'I am not arguing that a preventive war would have been either feasible or effective. But the idea of preventive war as a morally acceptable option was widely accepted by von Neumann's generation, who looked back to 1936 as a tragically missed opportunity. To them, the idea of forestalling a terrible catastrophe by *bold preventive action* was not inherently insane nor inherently criminal. Von Neumann argued in 1950 that America was facing the same choice that France and Britain faced in 1936, when the Soviet Union was just beginning to acquire nuclear weapons...' (emphasis added).

To me, however, von Neumann's idea of subjecting the Soviet Union to a nuclear blitz on the grounds that such a blitz would serve to prevent a possible full-scale nuclear war between the Soviet Union and the United States at some later date is one that comes very close to meriting the description of inherently insane and/or criminal. It is certainly difficult to see how the nuclear destruction of a country and the decimation of its population can ever be legitimately spoken of as 'bold preventive action'. It is surely masculinity gone mad.

66. *Anticipation*, No. 28, 'Energy for my Neighbour' (December 1980), p.78.

67. For an instructive analysis of capitalist science and technology, see especially David Albury and Joseph Schwartz, *Partial Progress: The Politics of Science and Technology* (Pluto, 1982), and Mike Hales, *Science or Society* (Pan, 1982).

68. For discussion of the masculinity of science and the status of women in science, see, for example, Dorothy Griffiths and Esther Saraga, 'Sex differences and cognitive abilities: a sterile field of enquiry?' and Helen Weinreich-Haste, 'What sex is science?', in Oonagh Hartnet, Gill Boden and Mary Fuller (eds), *Sex-Role Stereotyping* (Tavistock, 1979); Lynda Birke, Wendy Faulkner, Sandy Best, Deirdre Janson-Smith, Kathy Overfield (eds), *Alice through the Microscope: The Power of Science over Women's Lives* (Virago Press, 1980); Barbara F. Reskin, 'Sex Differentiation and the Social Organization of Science', in Jerry Gaston (ed.), *Sociology of Science* (San Francisco: Jossey-Bass, 1978); Jonathan Cole, *Fair Science: Women in the Scientific Community* (New York: Free Press, 1979); Kate Hinton, *Women and Science* (Department of Liberal Studies in Science, Manchester: SISCON Project, 1976); Alison Kelly (ed.), *The Missing Half: Girls and Science Education* (Manchester University Press, 1981); Evelyn Fox Keller, 'The Anomaly of a Woman in Physics', in S. Ruddick and P. Daniels (eds.), *Working it Out* (New York: Pantheon, 1977) and 'Feminism and Science', *Signs* 7 (1982), pp.589-602; Jacqueline Feldman, 'People, Knowledge and Science', in Torgny Segerstedt (ed.) and Elisabeth Wood (technical editor), *Ethics for Science Policy, Proceedings of a Nobel Symposium* (Oxford': Pergamon Press, 1979).

69. Barry Commoner 'Is Biology a Molecular Science?', in M. Grene (ed.), *Anatomy of Knowledge* (Routledge, 1969), p.99.

70. F. Barnaby, 'Ethical Dilemmas in Weapons Development', in Segerstedt (note 6, last reference) p.123. But see Michael Pentz, 'The Threat of Nuclear War and the Responsibility of Scientists', in Michael Clarke and Marjorie Mowlam (eds), *Debate on Disarmament* (Routledge & Kegan Paul, 1982); also Egbert Boeker, 'Science and the Nuclear Arms Race', in C.F. Barnaby and G.P. Thomas (eds), *The Nuclear Arms Race: Control or Catastrophe* (Frances Pinter, 1982).

71. See, for example, Joseph Rotblat (ed.), *Scientists, The Arms Race and Disarmament: A Unesco/Pugwash Symposium* (Taylor & Francis, 1982). Information on the independent organisation of scientists, Scientists Against Nuclear Arms (SANA) can be obtained from 11 Chapel Street, Woburn Sands, Milton Keynes MK17 8PG. See also the journals *Science for People*, *Radical Science Journal*, and *Science for the People*.

72. E. Mendelsohn, 'A Human Reconstruction of Science', *Boston University Journal* (Spring, 1973), pp.45-52, quoted by Wolf Schäfer, 'Finalization in Perspective: Toward a Revolution in the Social Paradigm of Science', *Social Science Information* 18 (1979), pp.929-30.

73. As Rosemary Ruether writes in *New Woman, New Earth* (note 52), p.83: 'The liberation of all human relations from the false polarities of masculinity and femininity must also shape a new relationship of humanity to nature.' See also Charles Birch and John B. Cobb, Jr.,*The Liberation of Life: From the Cell to the Community* (Cambridge UP, 1981).

74. Mary Shelley, *The Last Man* (1826; Lincoln, U. of Nebraska Press, 1965), p.168.

75. See *Bulletin of the Atomic Scientists* (December 1981), p.37; also Ruth Adams and Susan Cullen (eds), *The Final Epidemic* (Chicago: Educational Foundation for Nuclear Science, 1982).

76. *The Last Man* (note 74), p.23.

77. *Ibid.*, p.179.

78. Mary Wollstonecraft, *Vindication of the Rights of Woman* (1792; Harmondsworth: Penguin, 1975), p.155.

Afterword

1. Ann Paul, 'Birth Reborn', *The Listener* (11 March 1982), pp.5-6. See also the very positive response by Hugh Jolly, physician in charge of the Department of Paediatrics at Charing Cross Hospital, London, 'The Odent way of birth — can it happen in Britain?', *The Listener* (18 March 1982), pp.7-8, and the letters on p.13. Also Sheila Kitzinger, 'Changes in Childbirth', *The Listener* (18 November 1982), pp.6-8.

We were already working with tritium in Los Alamos as far back as 1945. I remember the time when Dr Oppenheimer... went to a large safe and brought out a small vial of a clear liquid that looked like water. It was the first highly diluted minute sample of superheavy water, composed of tritium and oxygen, ever to exist in the world, or anywhere in the universe, for that matter. We both looked at it in silent, rapt admiration. Though we did not speak, each of us knew what the other was thinking. Here was something, our thoughts ran, that existed on earth in gaseous form some two billion years ago, long before there were any waters or any forms of life. Here was something with the power to return the earth to its lifeless state of two billion years ago.

William L. Laurence, *The Hell Bomb*, 1951

Within the next ten thousand years we can expect many complex systems to be worked out in fair detail. Above all, we are likely to see an enormous flowering of engineering projects, applying the fundamental knowledge then known to systems of ever-increasing power, subtlety and complexity. Provided mankind neither blows itself up nor completely fouls up the environment and is not overrun by rabid antiscientific fanatics, we can expect to see major efforts to improve the nature of man himself. What forms these may take, how successful they will be and how much time will be needed to change human nature radically we can hardly surmise...

Francis Crick, *Life Itself: Its Origin and Nature*, 1981

Name Index